THE
NEEDLEPOINT
BOOK

Jo Ippolito Christensen

is the author of **Trapunto** and co-author,
with Sonie Ashner, of **Needlepoint Simplified,
Bargello Stitchery, Cross Stitchery,** and
Appliqué and Reverse Appliqué.
She has taught many courses in needlepoint,
among them classes in Creative Stitchery
at the University of Alaska,
and judges stitchery at shows and exhibitions.

NEEDLE

Drawings by Lynn Lucas Jones

Photographs by James T. Long

THE
POINT
BOOK

303 STITCHES,
WITH PATTERNS
AND PROJECTS

Jo Ippolito Christensen

Prentice Hall Press • New York

Library of Congress Cataloging-in-Publication Data

CHRISTENSEN, JO IPPOLITO.
  The needlepoint book.

  Bibliography: p.
  Includes index.
  1. Canvas embroidery. I. Title.
TT778.C3C478   746.4'4   76-182
ISBN 0–13–610980–2
ISBN 0–13–610972–1 pbk.

Published in 1986 by Prentice Hall Press
A Division of Simon & Schuster, Inc.
Gulf + Western Building
One Gulf + Western Plaza
New York, NY 10023

Originally published by Prentice-Hall, Inc.

PRENTICE HALL PRESS is a trademark of Simon & Schuster, Inc.

Manufactured in the United States of America

10 9 8 7 6 5 4 3 2

This book is dedicated to Juanita Matthews
of Raleigh, North Carolina,
whom I have fondly called Ne-Ne since I was a child.
Thank you, Ne-Ne,
for rekindling my interest in needlepoint!

Contents

Foreword

Yolanda Christensen is a person with a deep sense of aesthetics and an interest in the welfare of others. These attributes have been enriched by her wide travels as the daughter of an Army officer and the wife of a young Air Force officer. During her college years she earned a degree in textiles and clothing. As a faculty member, it was during those years that I had the opportunity to work closely with her, and as a friend I have continued to observe her progress.

In her early career, Jo taught young people and adults to create attractive clothing for themselves and others. Through these activities she developed a rich understanding of fabric and design. This understanding, combined with her interest in beautifying the surroundings of herself and others, led her to explore a number of areas of creative stitchery, and it is here that her career has blossomed. Although she is skilled in a number of forms of stitchery, needlepoint has captured the greater part of her attention.

Jo has taught needlepoint for a number of years. She is also an accomplished writer on the topic and has co-authored a number of books, including the popular **Needlepoint Simplified, Bargello Stitchery,** and **Cross Stitchery.** This extensive experience as a teacher and writer is evident in **The Needlepoint Book.** It is a comprehensive reference book for aspiring, as well as accomplished needlepoint enthusiasts. Many will find it useful as a basic instruction book dealing with the selection of canvas and other necessary supplies for beginning projects. Others will find it an invaluable resource for identifying and learning to do specific needlepoint stitches by following the step-by-step instructions. Those who desire to create original pieces will be inspired by the three hundred or so stitches, with illustrated and written instructions for doing each. With the help of this reference book, one can progress from the simplest of projects to the most intricate pattern in which a variety of stitches are combined.

Needlepoint designs and supplies for creating your own designs are available in many needlecraft shops and department stores. Regardless of the route you choose to take, venture forth with confidence. **The Needlepoint Book** will provide the knowledge and spark the imagination to create lovely needlepoint pieces that will enrich your surroundings and add a new dimension to your life.

ELEANOR YOUNG

Textile and Clothing Specialist
University of Maryland

Preface

This book is directed to *you,* the student of needle-point—both in the classroom and out. Nearly a thousand illustrations are included to help you over the rough spots. Procedures that are considered difficult—or at best hazy—are clarified in this book. Techniques like blocking, framing, and appliqué are explained in many steps. **Nothing** is left to your imagination.

The three hundred or so stitches are explained with both photographs and drawings. If the stitch is worked in steps, they are clearly indicated on the drawings. Numbers tell you just where to begin and where to go next. Often there are two, three, or four different drawings of one stitch to make it crystal clear. Some suggestions on how and where to use the stitches are included.

Common errors in working the basic stitches are pointed out in the text. Hints on how to avoid or overcome these errors are given. Suggestions are sometimes given for more than one approach to working a stitch.

The equipment needed for needlepoint is neither complicated nor horribly costly. However, the choice of a wrong marker, for example, can ruin your work. Having the **right** equipment is all-important. A thorough discussion of all the things you will need is given in Chapter 1. Your options in selection of equipment are listed; even though I have told you what I think, the choice is still yours.

The different **kinds** of needlepoint are discussed. Again, you make the choice on what appeals to you.

If you really feel that designing your own work is what you want to do, Chapter 2 is for you. Often, getting an idea is the hardest part for some people. Others think that actually drawing the design is hardest. Still others have trouble with the color choice. The basic art principles will help you in making your own design. Both right and wrong choices are well illustrated in drawings. A discussion of the color wheel aids you in color choice. Helpful hints are given on adapting designs from other sources. Try your hand at your own design—you might surprise yourself.

Nothing is more important than proper finishing. Mediocre stitching can be overlooked if the finishing is perfect. And even flawless stitches won't be noticed if one is preoccupied with poor finishing. But **nothing** can beat the winning combination of error-free stitching and exquisite finishing. This book can help you achieve both.

Your needlepoint can be both useful and decorative. A long list gives you ideas on what to do with needlepoint—besides the obvious pictures, pillows, and footstools.

Jump in with both feet. Try making an heirloom. Let the many color photographs inspire you to make beautiful and admired works of art. I hope you will come to love needlepoint as I do.

A Few Words of Thanks

M any people have contributed to the making of this book—yes, making, not writing. The writing is only a small part of putting a book like this together.

My parents, Lt. Col. and Mrs. Luciano Ippolito, deserve a vote of thanks for the education, encouragement, and support they have given me. They even did research in the Library of Congress when I couldn't get there, and hunted copies of elusive books. Thanks, folks!

My husband, Maj. John J. Christensen, helped the most during the actual preparation of this book. He alphabetized lists, put together the bibliography, looked up words in the dictionary, numbered pages, and proofread the manuscript. And he willingly changed diapers, did the laundry, babysat our son, Peter John, put up with meetings and photography sessions in our living room, and ate lots of soup and sandwich suppers!

Others who proofread include Nyla Christensen, Jack Kern, Vicki Kern, Dody Maki, Cindy Pendleton, and Liz Rockwell. I often heard, "This sentence doesn't make sense."

Jackie Beaty, Nyla Christensen, Pat Dalthorp, Ruth Deary, Charlotte Lahti, Dody Maki, and Liz Rockwell graciously allowed me to photograph some of their projects for use in this book.

Lynn Jones, illustrator, and Jim Long, photographer, worked **very** hard to achieve the perfection that is so necessary in a book like this. They also put up with me when it seemed at times as if I would never make up my mind. They persevered, nevertheless.

Cindy Pendleton, artist, and Tom Novak, photographer, both pitched in when extra help was needed. Their excellent work appears in many illustrations throughout the book.

Terry Parks is a professional framer who did it **my** way! I am grateful to him for putting up with my insistence on perfection. He often heard, "Terry, it is lovely, but it is off 1/16"!" His work is in Figs. 1-37, 2-18, page 127, Plates 11, 27, 32, 34, 36 and 38.

Two friends, Jackie Beaty and Vicki Kern, took long hours of dictation to produce the many letters that it was necessary to send in the writing of this book. And it was Vicki Kern who turned my hen-scratching into a legible, typed manuscript. Finally, Liz Rockwell put in many hours helping me mark where to crop **hundreds** of photos.

Without these good people there would be no book. It took many kinds of talents to "make" this book. We often saw Alaska's summer sunrise. We hope that you will enjoy reading and working from this book—the product of our combined efforts.

A word of thanks goes also to the following people, who graciously gave me permission to reprint:

1. Chottie Alderson—detached canvas technique.
2. Doris Drake—reproduction of material, stitched in needlepoint, from her two books: **Doris Drake Needlework Designs** and **Doris Drake Needlework Designs II.**
3. Elsa Williams—French Knot.
4. Erica Wilson—the Rose Leaf Stitch from **Erica Wilson's Embroidery Book** (New York: Scribner's).
5. Jane D. Zimmerman—Arrowhead Fly, Crossed Mosaic, Dotted Stitch, Horizontal Old Florentine, Irregular Byzantine, Irregular Continental, Irregular Jacquard, Long-Arm Smyrna, Padded Brick, and Raised Cross, from the **Encyclopedia of 375 Needlepoint Stitch Variations.**

Thanks to Bea Lampert of the Needlepoint—ique, Anchorage, Alaska, for allowing me to use her shop as a photography studio.

1 GENERAL METHODS

ONE:

Basic
Procedures

Needlepoint can be compared to creating a painting—only you do it with yarn instead of paint. It is fun and relaxing to do, once you learn how. You can express your personality and create attractive accessories for your home, family, and friends. There are several ways you can get into needlepoint.

CHOOSING YOUR PROJECT

Ready-Center Pieces

Many people enjoy filling in the background of a ready-center piece. This is a piece that has the center, or design, already stitched by a skilled craftsman. This kind of needlepoint can be very relaxing and satisfying.

But if you feel the craftsmen have already done the best part in ready-center pieces, perhaps you should consider other types of needlepoint. You may buy a stamped design or a hand-painted design. As we will see, there are differences and similarities between these types of needlework; it is up to you to decide which you prefer.

Stamped Designs

A stamped design is pressed onto a piece of blank canvas by machine. Sometimes such patterns are stamped on crooked so that straight lines do not follow the threads—or the mesh of the canvas. Colors sometimes overlap or leave blank spaces. All these things mean that you must compensate for the errors. But once you have had some experience in needlepoint these things may not bother you.

Hand-Painted Designs

The hand-painted designs cost much more, as you might imagine. But the design is painted by someone who does needlepoint, so each mesh is painted exactly the way it should be stitched. There are no decisions for you to make. This is an easier project for the beginner to tackle than a stamped design.

Some hand-painted designs are just painted on the canvas by an artist who does not follow the mesh. These are usually more expensive than stamped designs, but not quite as expensive as the more carefully hand-painted designs.

If the stamped design is accurate enough so that you can figure out what you need to do, then you are doing basically the same kind of needlepoint involved in a hand-painted design. There is, then, only the cost difference between them.

Designs on Charts

If you are good at counting, you may wish to try a design on a chart. This chart is graph paper on which the design has been x-ed. (See Plate 16(A), Plate 20(A) or Figure 2,17(A) in the Appendix.) To work this type of design, you count the x's a few at a time and then work those stitches on your canvas—count and stitch, count and stitch, etc. This is the best way to achieve accuracy and detail.

Prefinished Articles

Now available is the prefinished article. For those of you whose weakness is finishing or for those who are not in an area in which professional finishing is available, this is quite a boon. Professional finishing is also very expensive.

Among the many prefinished items are pillows, purses, wallets, cigarette cases, tennis racket covers, golf club covers, and tote bags. Some of these have zippers that allow removal of the canvas for working.

The big drawback is that you must be very careful in your choice of stitches. Blocking is difficult at best. When you work with prefinished pieces, be sure to choose a stitch that does not distort the canvas. (See pages 70-71.)

Kits

All of the above types of needlepoint come in kits. Some kits are more complete than others. For example, a pillow kit may contain the canvas, yarn, and instructions only. Or it might come with the pillow backing, the cording and zipper, as well as the canvas, yarn, and instructions. Read the fine print so that you will know what you are buying.

Quality varies. Avoid kits with acrylic yarn. (See page 10.) Check to see that the finishing aids are of good quality. You do not want to put a cheap-looking frame on the exquisite needlepoint picture that you have just created. And a flimsy fabric for a pillow backing will lower the value of your work—and it will soon wear out.

Often kits come with just enough yarn to do the Half-Cross Stitch. (See page 184.) Unless you follow their directions to the letter, you will run out of yarn. Many kits are available (at a higher cost than the ones mentioned above) that provide sufficient yarn to work Basketweave or Continental Stitches. (See pages 180 and 183.) With these you will have enough yarn to work **almost** any stitch you choose.

Should you run out of yarn, all you need to do is write the company, sending a snip of the color you need. You will usually receive a prompt reply.

Kits can save you money—or cost you money. If you have a large cache of scrap yarn, you may be able to create the project with a painted or stamped canvas for less money. However, if you have to buy all your yarn, it might be cheaper to buy a kit.

Your Own Designs

Of course, you can always create your own designs. (We will talk more about this in Chapter 2.) Blank canvas and yarn may be purchased and you can apply your own or an adapted design. This book is written to help you do this, as well as the other types of needlepoint.

Whichever form of needlepoint you choose, I hope

you will enjoy doing it as much as I do. Perhaps I can entice you to try more than one type.

After you have had fun making your needlepoint, it will serve many purposes. The following list suggests some uses:

address book cover
barrette
bean bag
bed headboard
bell-pull
belt
bicycle seat cover
blender cover
bookends
book mark
box top
brick doorstop
bridge score-pad cover
bridge tallies
button covers
can cover
card table cover
chair cover
checkbook cover
child's grow-chart
Christmas cards
Christmas stocking
Christmas tree
    ornaments
Christmas tree skirt
cigarette case
coasters
coat hanger covers
collar and cuffs
compass case
cornice boards
cosmetic case
credit card case

cummerbund
desk set
dice
director's chair cover
dog or cat collar
dog snow boots
dog sweater
dolls
drapery tiebacks
eyeglass case
fireplace screen
flask case
flowerpot cover
flyswatter cover
footstool
game board (chess,
    backgammon)
golf club covers
guitar straps
gun case
hat
hatband
headband
ice bucket
jacket
jewelry-box cover
key chain
lamp base
letterbox
lighter case
light switchplate
luggage rack
luggage tag

meeting nametag
musical instrument case
 cover
nameplate
nametag
napkin rings
necklace
needlebook
notebook cover
notecards
paperweight
party invitations
passport folder
patch pocket
pen or pencil case
phonebook cover
piano bench cushion
picture
picture or mirror frame
pillow
pincushion
portfolio
purse
rainhat case
rug
sandals
scissors case
scrapbook cover
screen divider

shoe buckles
shoe-trees
shutters
slippers
suspenders
swinging door plate
 (under glass)
table-top wastebasket
teapot cosy
tennis racket cover
tie
tissue box cover
toaster cover
tobacco pouch
toilet seat cover
tote bag
toys
traveling jewelry case
traveling sewing kit
tray (under glass)
trivet
typewriter cover
upholstered furniture
vest
wallet
wastebasket cover
watch band
yardstick cover
yoke of garment

And the list is not complete—believe it or not! Come up with your own ideas. Cover **anything!**

EQUIPMENT

Canvas

The canvas made especially for needlepoint is loosely woven, with holes in it for the yarn to go through. It is made quite stiff with sizing.

Buy only the best quality canvas; for if the very foundation of your needlepoint is weak, the heirloom work you have done will not last. Reject any piece of canvas with flaws. These will weaken the canvas. Any reputable shop owner will gladly cut another piece of canvas for you.

There are basically two different kinds of canvas: Penelope and Mono.

PENELOPE CANVAS

Penelope is woven with pairs of threads. Each pair of threads is called one **mesh**. (See Figure 1-1.) You must learn to see each pair as one. You might be a bit dizzy at first, but it becomes much easier after a while. Note that one pair of threads is woven more closely

Fig. 1-1   *Penelope canvas (junction of mesh circled)*

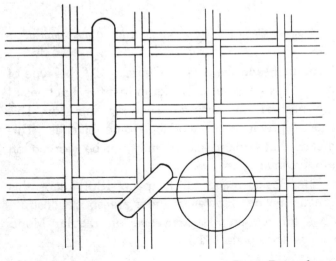

together than the pair running perpendicular to it. It is this closely woven pair that is always parallel to the selvages. It must always be held vertically.

Penelope canvas is quite strong. It should always be used for items that will receive heavy wear, such as rugs, chairs, footstools, and upholstered furniture. However, it may be used for other things as well.

MONO CANVAS

Mono canvas is so called because it is woven so that one thread equals one mesh. There are two types of mono canvas: regular and interlock.

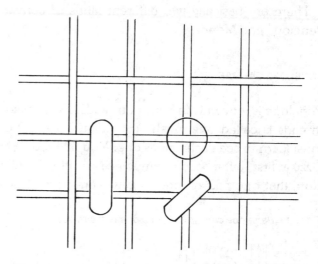

Fig. 1-2   *Regular Mono canvas (junction of mesh circled)*

Regular Mono Canvas.   (Figure 1-2). This type of canvas is somewhat unstable, in that the junctions of the mesh are not secured. They slip and slide. This causes problems in working some stitches. This means that certain stitches may not be worked on Mono canvas.

The Basketweave Stitch (page 180) keeps this canvas in line. However, there are special instructions for working Basketweave on regular Mono canvas. (See page 181.)

Interlock Mono Canvas. (Figure 1-3). This canvas secures the junction of mesh with the addition of a tiny thread, wrapped around the mesh. This thread allows us to lift the restrictions on certain stitches for Mono canvas.

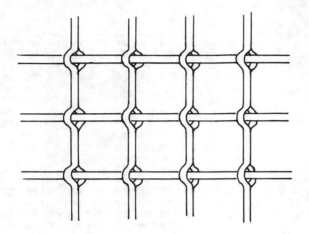

Fig. 1-3. *Interlock Mono canvas*

I personally prefer the Interlock canvas, even though the world seems to be thrilled with Regular Mono canvas. I cannot see what is so great about it— unless you do Basketweave exclusively. Maybe I'm the one out of step or maybe the world does more Basketweave than I do. I've been told that the mesh on Interlock Mono canvas break easily, but my students and I have never had this experience. It is a chore to work with sliding mesh. But try both and decide for yourself.

CANVAS MESH COUNT AND STITCH SIZE

Following either Penelope or Mono on the canvas label is a number. This number tells how many mesh there are per linear inch. (It is not accurate over a large area. See page 68.)

Penelope is usually available in sizes 3½ through 12. (Figure 1-4 a-c.) This varies with the manufacturers. Penelope 10 (Figure 1-4c) is the most widely

Fig. 1-4a *Penelope 4 canvas worked with rug yarn*

Fig. 1-4b *Penelope 7 canvas worked with rug yarn*

Fig. 1-4c *Penelope 10 canvas worked with Persian yarn*

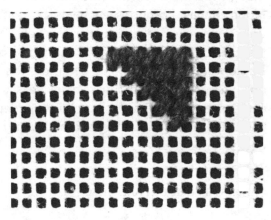

Fig 1-4d *Interlock Mono 10 canvas worked with Persian yarn*

Fig. 1-4e *Interlock Mono 14 canvas worked with Persian yarn*

Fig. 1-4f *Regular Mono 18 canvas worked with Persian yarn*

Fig. 1-4g *Silk gauze 40 worked with embroidery floss*

used Penelope canvas. It is very versatile. Many, many stitches can be worked on it with a minimum of thickening and thinning of yarn.

Penelope 7 or 8 is best for working Cross-Stitches (Figure 1-4b, page 12).

Mono comes in sizes 10 through 40 (Figure 1-4d-g). Mono 14 (Figure 1-4e) gives the best yarn coverage for working Bargello and Straight Stitches.

The sizes of needlepoint stitches have been defined by three terms: Petit Point, Gros Point, and Quick-point. **Petit Point** is worked on Mono canvas sizes 16 through 40 or on Penelope 10/20. (See pages 9-10.) **Gros Point** refers to those stitches worked on 8-14 mesh per inch. **Quickpoint** is needlepoint worked on rug canvas, sized 3½ to 7 mesh per inch. The smaller the stitch, the more detail is achieved.

Canvas is sold in widths varying from 26″ to 60″ wide. The common sizes (Penelope 8, 10, 12; Mono 10, 12, 14, 16, 18) come in 26″, 36″, and 40″ widths. Quickpoint canvases are 54″ and 60″. These measurements are approximate and vary according to manufacturers.

You may purchase canvas by the yard or in fractions of yards (⅛, ¼, ⅓, ⅜, ½, etc.). Many shops will sell it by the inch.

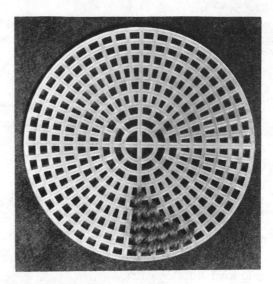

Fig. 1-5a *3″ plastic square (7 mesh/inch) worked with Persian yarn*

Fig. 1-5b *3″-diameter plastic circle worked with Persian yarn*

Fig. 1-5c *12⅜″ diameter plastic circle worked with Persian yarn*

PLASTIC CANVAS

Plastic canvas comes in rectangular sheets, large circles, and small (3") squares, circles, and triangles. (Figure 1-5a-c.) It is a bit awkward to work on, but it is nice because it has no raw edges to conceal. It makes fine Christmas tree ornaments (Plates 4 and 8, Figure 2-22 and 2-23), key chains (Plates 14, 15, and 16), dice (Figure 2-16), pictures (Plates 24 and 25), and scissors cases (Plates 22 and 23). It can be cut to any size you need. Plastic canvas usually comes 5 or 7 mesh per inch; therefore, a lot of detail is not possible.

FANCY WOVEN CANVAS

Fancy woven canvases are available in a variety of designs (Figure 1-6a,b). These designs are woven right into the canvas with two colors of thread. Many threads make up one mesh. They are mainly simple patterns or geometric designs. Worked in Continental Stitch (page 183) or in Basketweave (page 180), they are very attractive in well-planned

Fig. 1-6 *Fancy woven canvases*

a   b

color schemes. These pieces make good pillows and upholstered items.

Beware of breakaway canvas (Figure 1-7). It is designed for stitching Cross-Stitches onto fabric. When it is wet it **dissolves.** To block needlepoint, the finished product is dampened. If you have worked your needlepoint on breakaway canvas, it will disintegrate! It is very tempting to buy the breakaway canvas. It is half the price of good needlepoint canvas. At first glance it looks like needlepoint canvas, but it is actually much lighter in weight. **Do not buy breakaway (waste) canvas for needlepoint!**

Fig. 1-7 *Breakaway canvas: Penelope 13 worked with Persian yarn*

Needles

A special needle is used for needlepoint. It is a blunt-end tapestry needle. Choose the correct needle for the size canvas you use. A needle should not distort the canvas; it should drop through the hole easily.

I allow a beginner to use an 18 needle with Penelope 10 canvas, but I expect her—or him—to switch to a 20 as soon as the task of threading the needle has been conquered. The chart below should serve as a rough guideline in choosing the proper size needle:

Fig. 1-8 *Blunt-end tapestry needles: sizes 22, 20, 18, 18, 20, 22, and 13 (from left to right)*

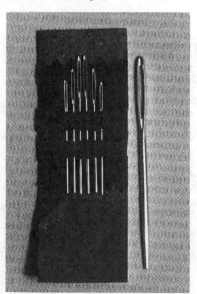

canvas size	needle size
3-5	13
7-8	14-16
10	18 or 20
12-14	20
16-20	22
22-24	24

(See Figure 1-8.) Buy needles in packages of six or singly.

THREADING THE NEEDLE

Threading the needle is regarded by many of my students as the most difficult part of learning needlepoint! It really doesn't matter how you get it threaded so long as you do not wet the yarn or in any way damage or fray it.

The paper method in Figure 1–9 is quite a reliable technique. However, if you, like me, cannot keep up with the little piece of paper, perfect another method.

My favorite method is shown in Figure 1-10. Give the yarn tip an extra twist, making it more tightly twisted. If you are right-handed place this tip of yarn between the thumbnail and index finger of your left hand. Let only a tiny bit of yarn stick up. Holding the needle in your right hand, push the needle between your fingers. And presto! Most of the time it works.

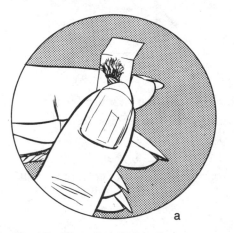 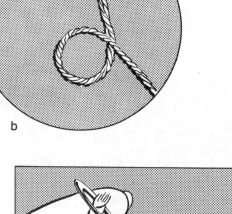

a   b

Fig. 1-9 *Threading the needle—the paper way*

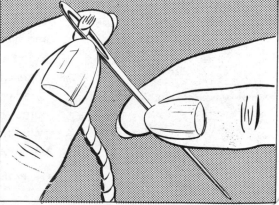

Fig. 1-10 *Threading the needle—my way*

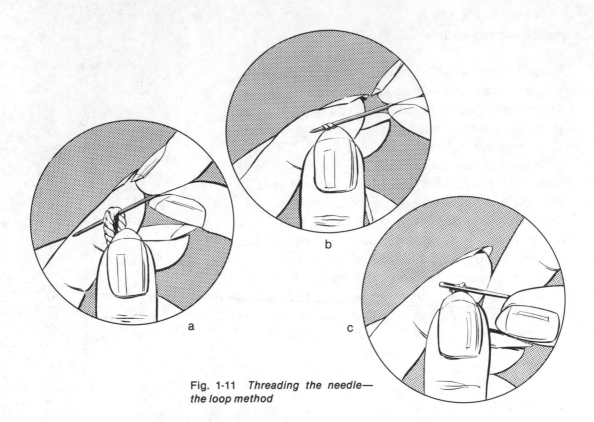

Fig. 1-11 *Threading the needle—the loop method*

Figure 1-11 shows yet another method for threading the needle. It works too—most of the time.

If all else fails, try one of those new metal needle-threaders for yarn. Let's face it; if you cannot thread the needle, you certainly cannot continue with needlepoint!

Yarn

The yarn used for needlepoint must meet certain specifications. The manufacturers of needlepoint yarn today make their yarn strong. It is wool and has long fibers which give protection against the rough canvas. Needlepoint yarn is also moth-proofed. Some brands come in matched dye lots and others do not. (Whether or not they do, you should still buy all the yarn you will need for your project.)

Tapestry Yarn. This is a smooth, tightly twisted 4-ply strand (Figure 1-12a). It is sold in 40-yard skeins, usually in matched dye lots. There is some variety in colors, but not as much as in Persian yarn, except for D.M.C. D.M.C. Tapestry wool comes in an 8.8-yard skein with some 350 colors—tremendous variety and shadings that are very good for Bargello. Because tapestry yarn is a smooth strand, it makes a smooth stitch; I like the looks of a piece stitched with it. However, tapestry yarn does not separate readily. When thickening and thinning yarn (page 32), this becomes a nuisance. When the feat is finally accomplished, the smooth quality is lost and you might just as well have used Persian yarn. The difference between tapestry yarn and Persian yarn is that tapestry yarn can be used on 10-12 mesh, whereas Persian yarn can be split and used on very fine mesh.

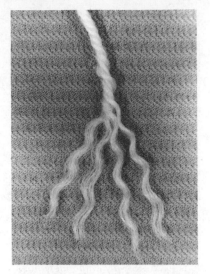

Fig. 1-12a *Four-ply tapestry yarn*

Persian Yarn. This is a loosely twisted, 3-ply yarn (Figure 1-12b). It is not smooth in appearance and it does not work up smoothly. But when you have to thicken or thin, it is a blessing. The colors are magnificent! They do not come in matched dye lots. Persian yarn is sold in 40-yard skeins and by the strand, ounce, or pound. Quality varies tremendously.

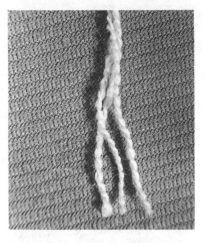

Fig. 1-12b *Three-ply Persian yarn*

Wool Rug Yarn. (Figure 1-12c.) This yarn is used for Quickpoint stitches. You may combine several strands of Persian yarn to cover the canvas if you would rather. Be sure to keep the strands smooth; do not allow them to twist.

Fig. 1-12c *Three-ply rug yarn*

Novelty Yarns. Unusual, or novelty yarns may be used in needlepoint—but only with **caution.** Never use them on pieces that will receive any wear; usually only pictures fit this category. This is because the novelty yarns are not strong enough and can create problems.

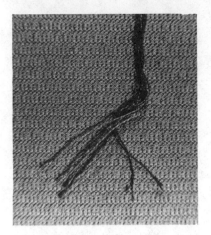

Fig. 1-12d   *Six-ply embroidery floss*

Fig. 1-12e   *Metallic yarn*

Do not use **acrylic yarns** for needlepoint, although some kits have them. They "pill" and become ugly soon and do not block well.

Knitting worsted, wool, and **synthetics** are too springy and elastic to achieve even stitches. They too "pill" and do not block well. Synthetic yarns have "memory." After being wet they go back to their original position. This is what makes them machine-washable and machine-dryable. This also means that any needlepoint worked with them would always be out of shape because the blocking would not hold without rabbit-skin glue (page 88).

Embroidery flosses (Figure 1-12d); **silk,** and **pearl cotton** make nice accents for Petit Point. They are also easier to get in and out of the small canvas holes.

Metallic Yarn (Figure 1-12e) is a novelty yarn that gives a spark where needed. It can be used to stitch an evening purse or Christmas tree ornaments (Plates 5 and 6, Figure 2-22).

Angora can give a special spot extra fluff.

Accent your needlepoint with unusual yarns. You are limited only by your imagination.

HOW MUCH TO BUY

How much yarn do I need? This question baffles beginners. It's not really such a mystery. Ideally, you should work a square inch of the stitch you want to use, on the canvas you choose, with the same brand and color of yarn you will use. Keep track of the amount of yarn used. Then figure out how many square inches there are in your design. Multiply the amount of yarn used by the number of square inches. This gives you the amount of yarn you will need.

This method is not always convenient. A competent shop owner can usually estimate quite accurately. Many have a gadget that figures it for a few selected stitches. Most—but not all—the stitches in this book can be worked with the same amount of yarn needed for the Continental or Basketweave stitches.

Choose your colors in daylight, if at all possible.

Other Items

Not much equipment is needed to do needlepoint. Besides the yarn, canvas, and needles, you will need those items shown in Figure 1-13.

Two pairs of **scissors** are good to have. One pair should have fine points; embroidery or nail scissors do nicely. A large pair of scissors is needed to cut yarn (see page 26) and canvas. Keep one old pair of scissors just to cut canvas, because it dulls them quickly. Next make a needlepoint scissors case for your embroidery scissors and they will be portable!

Besides scissors you will need a pair of **tweezers** for ripping. (See page 37.) A **ruler,** a **waterproof marker** and masking or freezer **tape** are needed to ready your canvas for stitching. (See pages 24-25.)

In looking for a marker, shop wisely. Choose only a marker whose manufacturer guarantees that it is **waterproof**—not water-resistant. Read the fine print! Some manufacturers state in the fine print that their

Fig. 1-13 *Equipment needed for needlepoint*

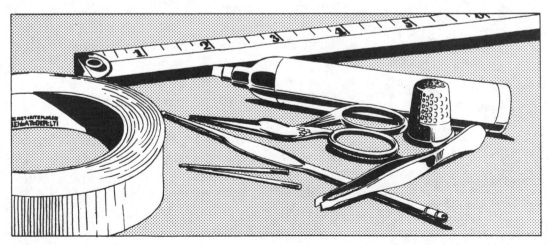

marker is not permanent on fabrics that are highly sized. In essence, that is what needlepoint canvas is.

After you have a marker that is guaranteed, **test it yourself.** Do not trust it. Even those advertised as waterproof may still run on canvas. To test a marker, write on a piece of the canvas that you will use. Run it under cold water. Blot with a tissue or a paper towel. If the color runs, you cannot use that marker on that piece of canvas. You may be able to use it on another brand of canvas, so keep it and try again.

I think the best color marker to choose is a light or medium grey. Most brands of yarns, including pastels and whites, will cover the grey line. Do not use black.

And then there is the Great Frame Debate. There are many staunch advocates of **frame** use. There are many who think they are more trouble than they are worth.

A frame is a gadget, usually wooden, that is made to hold your canvas taut across two or four bars. These bars are adjustable to any size canvas. Some styles roll up the excess canvas on two opposite sides, leaving a relatively small area that is still large enough for you to work. Some stand on the floor; some you sit on; and others you hold.

The main advantage in using a frame is that your finished canvas is not badly out of shape. (Some stitches distort the canvas and others do not.) I feel that all needlepoint should be blocked (see page 81), whether or not it is out of shape. It resets the starch. Badly misshapen pieces can be sized without a lot of trouble.

As I see it there are two main disadvantages to using a frame. First, you are forced to poke, rather than stitch with continuous motion. (See page 29.) Continuous motion, in my opinion, creates a smooth, even tension in your stitches. Rhythm develops as you stitch and you pick up speed. All this is lost in poking.

Second, your needlepoint ceases to be portable. As this family's chief errand-runner, I spend a lot of idle 15- or 20-minute periods here and there. My needlepoint bag is always ready to go. You would be surprised at what I—and **you**, too—can create while waiting for doctors, dentists, kids at baseball games, music lessons, and swim practice, etc. The name plate (Figure 2-24) was made entirely while waiting for the dentist—on several occasions. I do try to save background, Bargello, or a large area to fill in with one stitch to do at this time. This allows less chance for mistakes due to lack of concentration.

A frame would hamper my style; but you might like it—many of my friends and students do. Go to your local shop and ask to see the frames. They might even have a display model set up so that you can try it out.

Now that you have gathered all these things together, you need to have a needlepoint bag to put them in. You may want to knot your yarn for storage,

Fig. 1-14 *Knotting yarn for storage*

a   b

 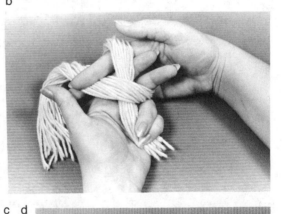

c d

 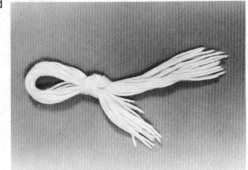

as shown in Figure 1-14. This keeps it tangle-free, yet is easy to untie when you want a strand of yarn. Loop the colors for your current project around the plastic holder from a six-pack of sodas or beer (Figure 1-15a). If your range of colors is very close, this will help to keep them sorted. One strand is easy to get (Figure 1-15b).

A needle book (Plates 9, 39, 40, and 41) will keep your needles sharp and handy.

Now your needlepoint bag is ready to go too.

Fig. 1-15a *Yarn for current project looped on plastic holder for soda or beer*

Fig. 1-15b *Remove one strand for use*

GENERAL TECHNIQUES

Preparing the Canvas

There are several simple steps you must take before you begin to stitch. First measure carefully. (For complete information on measuring, see Chapter 3, Finishing.)

Next, cut the canvas between the mesh and in a straight line.

Mark your margin with a waterproof marker. How

wide your margin is depends on what kind of a project you are working on.

Canvas ravels quite easily. Bind the edges with masking or freezer tape. (See Figure 1-16). At first you may think that because the canvas is so stiff it cannot possibly ravel. But the canvas soon loses its stiffness and then the damage begins. Take my word for it and bind those edges now. (I give an F to any student in my classes who does not do so. Do you want an F?)

With such a large, stiff piece of canvas, you may wonder how you are going to get to the center to stitch. **Do not crumple the canvas.** Roll up one side as shown in Figure 1-17. Pin at both ends. Then roll the opposite side, leaving a 3″ or 4″ strip down the middle. Pin it in place. Large safety pins, or those left-over diaper pins that you have always wondered what to do with, are good for this.

Fig. 1-16 *Bind canvas with masking tape*

Fig. 1-17 *Roll canvas for easy access to working area; pin with large safety pins*

Handling the Yarn

Needlepoint canvas is quite rough. It is hard on yarn. For this reason, needlepoint is worked with a strand of yarn 18″ long. Novelty yarns should be even shorter.

To help you resist temptation, you should cut your yarn to 18″ right after you buy it. Because yarn comes several ways, there are just as many techniques to cut it to size.

Persian yarn, which is sold by the ounce, usually comes in 60″ lengths. Cut them in thirds. Knot each third as shown in Figure 1-14.

Some Persian and tapestry yarns come in a twisted skein. Untwist the skein. Cut the circle once. Then cut the yarn into thirds. Knot each third.

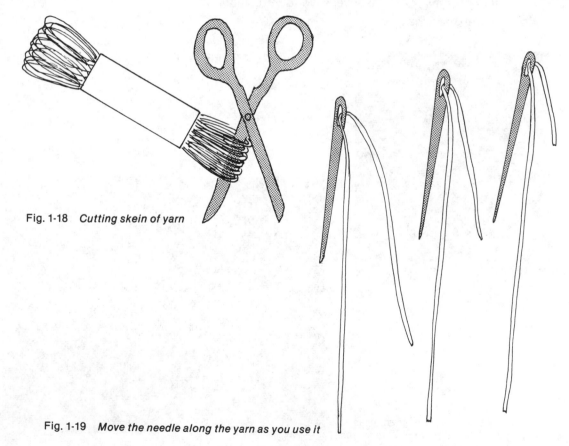

Fig. 1-18 *Cutting skein of yarn*

Fig. 1-19 *Move the needle along the yarn as you use it*

Tapestry yarn sometimes comes in a skein like the one shown in Figure 1-18. Leave the paper wrapper on and cut the loops at one end of the skein. To get one strand, pull it out from the other end.

Some tapestry yarns come in skeins that do not lend themselves to the above methods. Simply wrap the yarn around and around a box or book that is 18" all the way around. Cut in one place. Knot for storage.

Yarn has nap; some has more than others. Hold a strand of yarn up with one hand; run the other hand down the strand. Then turn the strand upside down and feel it again with the same hand. The yarn will feel smoother one way than the other. The smooth way is the way the yarn should be used in stitching. Watching the nap will produce less hairy needlepoint.

After you have threaded your needle, fold the yarn nearly in half (Figure 1-19). Slide the needle down the yarn as you stitch. This prevents wearing a thin spot at the end of the yarn where the needle was.

As you work, your yarn may tend to untwist or twist too tightly. (Figure 1-20a,b). Simply let go of the needle and let it dangle. It will spin the yarn back into place. If you do not do this often it will show up in your stitching as sloppy work.

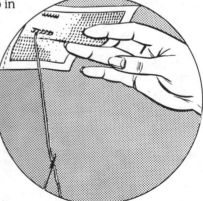

Fig. 1-20a *When yarn becomes tightly twisted during stitching, turn canvas upside down*

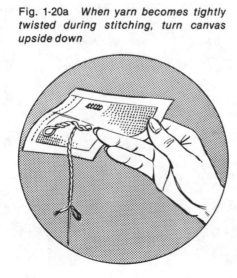

Fig. 1-20b *Let needle dangle until yarn untwists*

Beginning and Ending Threads

Never knot the yarn in needlepoint. To begin stitching, catch the tail (Figure 1-21). When taking your first stitch, leave about an inch or so of yarn on the wrong side of the canvas. Hold onto this tail so that it won't slip through. Carefully take several stitches more, making sure that you cover the tail with each successive stitch. This buries and anchors the tail securely.

Fig. 1-21 *Catch yarn tail on wrong side of canvas with needle and continue catching tail until completely buried*

To end your yarn, weave the needle in and out of the wrong side of the stitches you have just worked. Clip the yarn close to the back, leaving none sticking out (Figure 1-22). To begin the next yarn, bury the tail in these stitches you have just worked. There is one exception, which is cited below.

It is difficult to secure a tail when a stitch has no backing. Simply weave it in and out of a few mesh of blank canvas that will be covered by the stitch you are preparing to work.

Fig. 1-22 *Clip loose ends closely (after burying them) to produce neat back (long ends look messy, can get caught up in other stitches, and produce lumps on right side of canvas)*

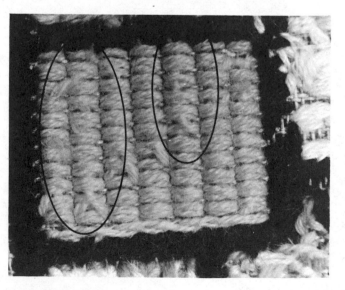

Stagger your starts and stops. If you do not, the tails will leave lumps. Never start or end in the same area. Don't begin each yarn piece at the beginning of every row if you can help it.

In working two or more areas of the same color, do not carry your yarn on the back more than 1-1/2 inches or so. When you do carry it 1-1/2 inches, weave the yarn in and out of the stitches already there.

However, you should never carry a dark yarn across a light-colored area; it will show through on the right side. For the same reason, you should not bury a dark-colored tail on the wrong side of a light-colored area.

Continuous Motion vs. Poking

Continuous motion, shown in Figure 1-23, is like sewing—putting the needle into the canvas and bringing it out, all in the same motion. **Poking** (Figures 1-24, 1-25) is putting the needle into the canvas with the dominant hand—the right hand, for example—

Fig. 1-23 *Continuous motion*

pulling it out onto the wrong side with the right hand, inserting it into the canvas from the wrong side, and pulling the needle through with the right hand on the right side of the canvas. This way your right hand is over and under and over and under the canvas. This may be done with or without a frame.

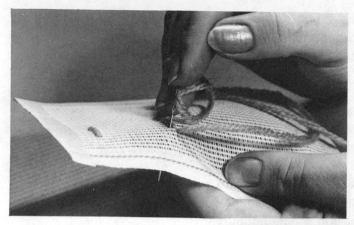

Figs. 1-24 & 1-25   *Poking*

The other method of poking is used only with a frame. The dominant hand is always held on the wrong side of the canvas and the other hand is held on the right side. The two hands now work together in stitching.

When working without a frame, I feel that continuous motion produces a stitch with the most even tension. Rhythm is developed. This method is definitely faster than poking.

If you are working with a frame, I think you should choose the method that suits you best.

Direction of Work

Try to stitch with the needle going **into** the previously worked row; try not to bring the needle **up** in these stitches. This will help eliminate snagging and splitting the yarn in rows already worked. The numbering of stitches in this book has been arranged so that this will be done wherever possible. You do not always have a choice.

Stitch Tension

The tension of your needlepoint stitches should be even, not too tight or too loose (Figure 1-26a). Each stitch should look like the rest and it should hug the canvas snugly. If your tension is too tight, the canvas will ripple (Figure 1-26b). This must not happen. Do not confuse this ripple with the distortion of a canvas that is out of shape because the stitch pulls the canvas out of square. In this case the canvas still lies relatively flat.

Fig. 1-26a   *Correct tension*

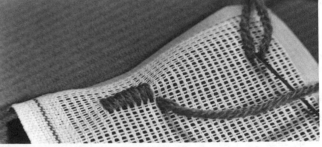

Fig. 1-26b   *Too tight tension*

You may find that long stitches require slightly more tension than shorter ones. (See Mosaic and Scotch Stitches, pages 214 and 223.)

Fig. 1-26c *Too loose tension*

A too-loose tension will look sloppy (Figure 1-26c).

Thickening and Thinning Yarns

Unfortunately, we cannot thread our needles and just stitch. One strand of yarn, whether it is 3- or 4-ply, does not always cover the canvas. The thickness of yarn varies with the type of yarn (Persian or tapestry), brand, and even color. It seems that wool does not absorb different colored dyes consistently.

Other factors that affect coverage are the size and brand of canvas, and the stitch used. With so many variables, it is impossible to tell just exactly how much yarn you need to work a given area of one particular stitch.

This problem is solved by thickening and thinning yarn. Whenever possible, I try to use Persian yarn when I have to do this. It separates easily and tapestry yarn does not. When you cut your yarn, as described on page 26, tie each bundle separately. Each strand will then be exactly the same length. This makes it easier to thicken.

To thicken, separate one strand of 3-ply Persian yarn into three separate pieces. (This is easier to do if you attack it from the middle of the strand.) Then simply add one or two of these plies to a 3-ply strand.

The addition of one ply creates a 4-ply strand; two plies, a 5-ply strand. If you need a 6-ply strand, merely put two 3-ply strands together.

To thin, just remove one or two plies.

In order to find out how thick a strand must be to work a certain stitch, you need to experiment. Work on a piece of canvas exactly like that of your project; use the same brand and **color** of yarn to work the stitch you want. Experiment until the canvas is completely covered. (Figure 1-27.)

If you get an area worked and then decide that the canvas is not well covered, don't despair. If it is a simple stitch, you can take one ply of yarn and go back over your work. This really works. However, this method is too much trouble unless the stitch is truly a simple one. It is, then, easier to rip (see page 37)and begin again.

Fig. 1-27 *Stitches on left show yarn so thin it does not cover canvas; stitches on right were worked with thickened yarn and cover properly*

Stitching a Design

When stitching a piece with a design, work the design first. Then work the background in one direction; top to bottom or upper right corner to lower left corner, or left to right, or whatever direction your background stitch follows. Don't start in one corner, stop, and then pick up in another. Your stitch pattern may not meet where the two areas come together.

After the stitching is done, and before blocking, check for errors. Do this by holding your piece up to the light. Any missed or thin stitches will immediately become obvious.

Be sure all ends are secure and clipped close to the surface. If they are not, lumps will show through on the right side.

Backing

Backing, or how the yarn covers the back of the canvas, is very important. How well a needlepoint piece wears depends on how good the backing is.

Some stitches produce an excellent backing, such as Basketweave (Figure 1-28a); some, a good backing, such as Continental (Figure 1-28b); some,

Fig. 1-28a *Excellent backing*

Fig. 1-28b *Good backing*

Fig. 1-28c *Poor backing*

like the Half Cross, make a poor backing (Figure 1-28c); and others provide almost no backing at all— for example, the Six-Trip Herringbone and the Waffle Stitch (Figure 1-28d).

Fig. 1-28d *Almost no backing*

SPECIAL TECHNIQUES

Covering the Canvas

The name of the game is "cover the canvas." So, if you have finished one of the stitches in this book and it does not quite cover—don't panic. There are lots of ways to salvage the stitch without ripping. I call it legal cheating!

Before you start your stitch you should check to be sure you have the optimum yarn thickness for that stitch, the brand and color of yarn, and size of canvas.

If you have done this and canvas still shows, then fill in areas of blank canvas with French Knots, tramé

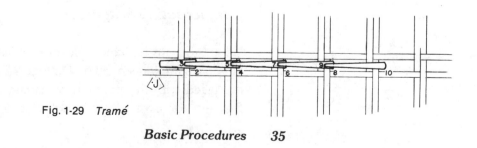

Fig. 1-29 *Tramé*

(Figure 1-29), Frame Stitch (Figure 1-30), or Back-Stitch (Figure 1-31). Sometimes you can simply go over the stitch that does not cover with one ply of yarn. It works—honest! Once in a while you can get away with sticking in an extra stitch every now and then. (For example, see the Diagonal Beaty stitch on page 193. But don't let this throw your pattern off.)

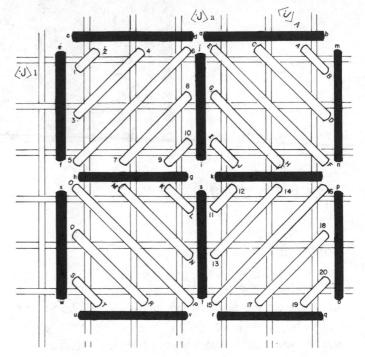

Fig. 1-30 *Frame stitch around Scotch Stitch*

Fig. 1-31 *Back Stitch*

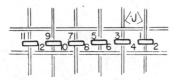

Often beads or pearls may be sewn on to help cover the canvas. (See page 295, Periwinkle Stitch.)

Remember, as long as you cover the canvas, it is **not** wrong. Just have fun and add your own touches.

Compensating Stitches

When you are working a decorative stitch anywhere but on a sampler like the one in Plates 24 and 25, you are faced with the problem of having to fill in areas that are too small for a whole motif of the stitch.

These places are filled in with what are known as **compensating stitches.**

To establish your stitch in an irregularly shaped area, work one row across the widest part. Stitch as much as you can of the motif. Then go back and fill the small areas with as much of the stitch as is possible. (See Figure 1-32.) Once you get the hang of the stitch you may be able to work the compensating stitches as you go.

Once in a great while you will come across a stitch that will not allow you to use these stitches later. (See page 172, Split Bargello.) Then the compensating stitches must be worked first.

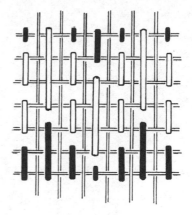

Fig. 1-32   *Hungarian Stitch*

Ripping and Mending

Sad as it may be, we all have to rip every now and then. Learning how to do this quickly and properly will help to make it less traumatic.

Never reuse yarn. The canvas is much too rough on the yarn to allow a smooth stitch the second time around.

Carefully cut the wrong stitches on the right side of the canvas with your embroidery scissors (Figure 1-33a). **Do not cut the canvas.** Turn the canvas

Fig. 1-33a   *To rip, cut stitches on right side of canvas (be careful not to cut canvas)*

Fig. 1-33b   *With tweezers, pull out incorrect stitches from wrong side of canvas*

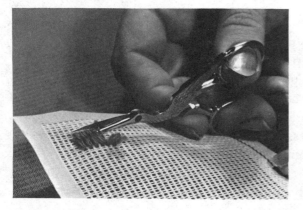

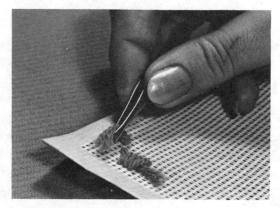

over and pull out the wrong stitches with the tweezers (Figure 1-33b). I do not recommend using a seam ripper to rip needlepoint. It is too easy to get carried away and rip more than you wanted to (canvas included).

You will have to unravel a few good stitches in order to have enough yarn to work the end in. A fine crochet hook is handy for this.

In case you do cut the canvas, it is not difficult to remedy. Cut another piece of canvas which is a little larger than your cut (Figure 1-34a). Place it underneath the cut. Match the mesh perfectly. Baste in place. Simply work your stitch through both layers of canvas, treating the two as if they were one (Figure 1-34b).

Fig. 1-34a *To mend canvas, cut patch slightly bigger than hole*

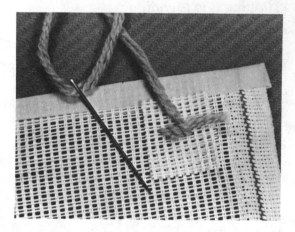

Fig. 1-34b *Work needlepoint stitches through both pieces of canvas as if they were one piece (wrong side of mended area shown)*

Piecing Canvas

Once in a while we all miscalculate and find we need more canvas to finish a certain project. The canvas can be pieced, but I do not like to do so unless absolutely necessary. Two pieces of canvas put together can never be as strong as one piece.

There are several methods for joining two pieces of canvas. However, I have found only one which I think is both invisible and sufficiently strong.

Place two pieces of canvas right sides together and stitch a seam as in making a seam in fabric. Match the mesh perfectly. On Penelope canvas, using silk thread, backstitch between the two threads of the mesh (Figure 1-35a). When you turn the canvas to the right side, there will be one thread of the mesh on one side of the seam and the other thread on the other side of the seam (Figure 1-35b). Finger-press the seam open and baste it in place. Do needlepoint through both thicknesses as if it were one (Figures 1-35b,c).

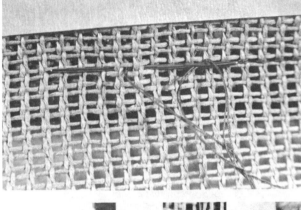

Fig. 1-35a *To piece canvas, back stitch between mesh with needle and thread*

Fig. 1-35b *There will be one thread of mesh on one side of seam and one thread of mesh on other side (see arrows on photograph; right side of canvas shown)*

Fig. 1-35c *Pull away masking tape as you stitch, not all at once or canvas will ravel (wrong side of canvas shown)*

On Mono canvas backstitch between the mesh. Follow the same procedure as described above. The only difference is that on Penelope canvas one stitch will bridge the seam and on Mono canvas there will be a stitch on either side of the seam.

Appliqué

You are not limited to one size of canvas within a design. It is possible to appliqué a larger-size canvas onto a smaller one or a smaller one onto a larger one. For example, a piece worked on Mono 10 may have one or more areas of great detail if you applique a piece of Mono 18 onto it. This way you do not have to work a whole piece in a small-sized canvas just to get one little area of detail. It also adds interest in having two or more different sizes of stitches.

The process is really not as difficult or complicated as you might think. Figures 1-36a-i and 1-37 give step-by-step instruction. (See also Plate 11.) Fabric was appliquéd onto the canvas with the Blind Stitch (page 107) to make the lady's dress.

Fig. 1-36a *To applique, first work background around spot to be appliquéd, leaving small area of blank canvas, then block (the woman's hand is being appliquéd on this piece)*

Fig. 1-36b *On another piece of canvas, stitch design to be appliquéd, leaving 3" of blank canvas all around it, then block, and ravel canvas right up to stitches*

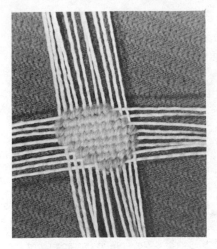

Fig. 1–36c *Ravel canvas on second, third, and fourth sides*

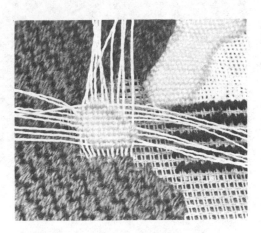

Fig. 1-36d *Lay hand in position on canvas and poke raveled canvas threads into background canvas, using needle if you like (this slows you down, however)*

Fig. 1-36e *This is how it looks on back of canvas after one side has been poked through*

Fig. 1-36f *Using needle, work loose canvas threads into stitches of background for an inch or so*

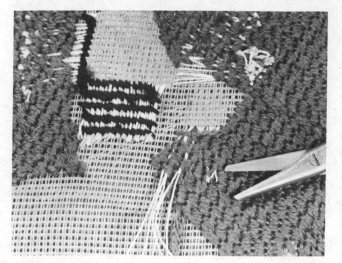

Fig. 1-36g *Cut them close. In case you have worried about the dark Continental Stitches worked every other row and about the large area of canvas—the large area is where the woman's dress (made of fabric) is to be appliquéd, the Continental Stitches are needed to give a place to work in threads from the appliquéd face and will be covered by the dress (see Plate 11)*

Fig. 1-36h *When threads on all four sides are worked in, the right side should look like this*

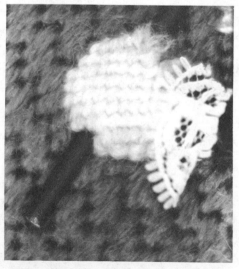

Fig. 1-36i *Work background stitches right up to appliquéd stitches, working through both pieces of canvas (check mesh on back of canvas for guidance in keeping background stitch even)*

Fig. 1-37   *Finished product*

Fig. 1-38   *Detached-canvas technique (see Appendix for stitches used)*

Detached-Canvas Technique

Clever Chottie Alderson developed this technique to add a third dimension to needlepoint. It is a fun thing to play with. Very interesting effects can be created (See Plate 46 and Figure 1-38).

You must plan in advance to do this. First draw a sketch of your final design (Figures 1-39a-c). From this drawing, make separate patterns for those components which you would like to stand out. Be sure to

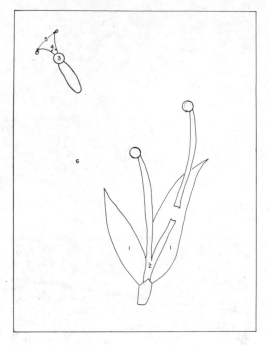

Fig. 1-39a *Detached-canvas technique: background*

Fig. 1-39b *Detached-canvas technique: attached elements*

Fig. 1-39c *Detached canvas technique: composite showing elements superimposed on background*

indicate where each piece will be attached to the main canvas. Next, make a drawing of the main canvas, minus the stand-out parts, except for where they attach. Transfer all designs to Interlock Mono canvas. Leave a margin around the stand-out parts.

Stitch the main canvas as you would any other piece—except you must leave blank those areas where the stand-out pieces go. Block. (See page 81.) While this is drying, stitch the components.

Still leaving a margin around each stand-out piece, work the needlepoint. Block. Leave the area to be attached blank. Then, **very carefully,** cut the canvas out from around the stitches. Do not cut the yarn or unravel the stitches. Handle the piece gently. Immediately coat the edges and the back side with clear nailpolish or glue made especially for needlepoint. Allow this to dry **thoroughly.**

Work the Buttonhole Stitch around the raw edges, except where the piece is to be attached to the main canvas. It should go in about two mesh. I find it easier to stitch these two mesh all the way around in Continental Stitch. This gives me a guide to follow when working the Buttonhole Stitch. When working this Buttonhole Stitch, catch a piece of light-weight wire on the wrong side. This enables you to bend and mold your pieces into pleasing curves. Refer again to Plate 46.

There are other things you can do with the free parts. Attach a tip to the main canvas, as the leaf is in Plate 46. Or apply rabbit-skin glue to the back side of the stand-out part. Mold it into the shape you want before the rabbit-skin glue dries. Or apply an iron-on interfacing to the back of each part. (See page 88.) This adds body and a lining. (However, do not do this if your needlepoint stitches are textured. Ironing will flatten them.) Or leave all components free. Or do almost anything you can think of.

Baste the stand-out pieces onto the main canvas, matching the mesh. Do needlepoint in these blank areas, treating the two pieces of canvas as if they were one.

Chottie tells us "this method is useful in making and attaching many things that you wish to have a 'Free' or dimensional look. Some other ideas are: leaves, bows, skirts, hats, feathers, wings, paws, roofs, etc."

Now you are all set to finish your project. (See Chapter 3, Finishing.)

Shading

Shading adds realism to any stitchery. Flat, unshaded colors make a design appear more modern. Use light colors for highlights and for areas that would naturally catch light. Dark colors suggest shadows, edges, and recessed areas.

The technique for shading is not difficult, but knowing where to put the different shades comes only with practice. (If you buy a painted canvas, the shaded areas are already marked for you.)

Color selection is most important in shading. Choose as many colors in your range as you can find. The closer together the colors are, the more effective your shading will be. If you cannot get the proper range of colors, **do not attempt to shade.**

For example, let us say that you have selected five colors of Persian yarn to shade a background. Letter the shades A, B, C, D, and E. It takes three areas of each color but the last (which takes only one) to advance from one shade to another. It does not sound logical, but it works for figuring out how many sections you need. Refer to the charts below for the exact composition of yarns in each of these areas. Therefore, five colors will need thirteen areas to complete this shading process.

Divide the canvas area to be shaded into thirteen equal sections. Mark them on your canvas with a waterproof marker. Start with the lightest color. Fill the first section with a 3-ply strand of Color A. In the second area, stitch with a strand composed of two plies of color A and one of color B. In the next area, use one ply of color A and two of color B. The fourth section is worked with three plies of color B. Continue this pattern until you have worked up to a 3-ply strand of the last color.

The charts on page 47 show the shading sequence for 3-ply and 4-ply yarns.

Many stitches lend themselves to shading, but none does so well as Irregular Continental. The trick is to make the line that divides each area irregular and ragged. Stagger rows and stitches. Interlocking Gobelin, Continental, and Brick make good shading stitches. The charts at the beginnings of Chapters 4 through 11 list other stitches for shading.

Once you have shaded one thing in a picture, the rest should be shaded also. Do not mix stylized designs and realistic ones.

3-Ply Yarn		4-Ply Yarn	
Area		*Area*	
1	AAA	1	AAAA
2	AAB	2	AAAB
3	ABB	3	AABB
4	BBB	4	ABBB
5	BBC	5	BBBB
6	BCC	6	BBBC
7	CCC	7	BBCC
8	CCD	8	BCCC
9	CDD	9	CCCC
10	DDD	10	CCCD
11	DDE	11	CCDD
12	DEE	12	CDDD
13	EEE	13	DDDD
		14	DDDE
		15	DDEE
		16	DEEE
		17	EEEE

Hint: Once in a while we all miscalculate and run out of yarn. If your luck runs like mine, the store is out of your dye lot. When this happens, blend the new shade into the other shade. Follow the chart AAA(A) through BBB(B).

Shadows

Shadows also contribute to realism and give a subject depth. This too should be done throughout the whole piece and not on only one or two items in your picture. Again, this is not a technique for beginners to try.

To make shadows on any given design, pick an imaginary light source first. The light must come consistently from one place, as it does in nature. The shadows fall on the opposite side of the light source.

Using tracing paper, trace the design. Then move it to the right (if the light is coming from the left) and below the design enough to make a shadow. (See Figure 1-40). The shadow's color should be a darker shade of the background's color.

Fig. 1-40 *Shadow*

MAKING A SAMPLER

Making a sampler is the very best way to learn your stitches. Use Penelope 10 canvas. It is versatile and it allows you to do the largest number of stitches with a minimum of thickening and thinning of your yarn.

There are several styles of samplers. Plates 32, 34, 36, 38, 44, and 48; Figure 2-18; and the samplers at the beginnings of Chapters 4, 6, 10, and 11 show the two basic styles that I recommend.

To get the feel of the stitch and to have enough for future reference, I recommend that you work a minimum of four square inches. Sometimes there will be stitches that will not require an area that large, and others will need an even larger area to show off the stitch's pattern.

Place these stitch areas on your canvas at random as in Plate 44 or balance their placement as in Plate

48. Figure 2-18 shows a sampler whose plan is in between these two. Both of these have a Continental background (see page 183). Or place each stitch next to the preceding one, leaving a two-mesh border, or divider, of 2 x 2 Slanted Gobelin (page 189). Simply work each stitch until you feel you have done the stitch justice. (See Plates 32, 34, 36, and 38 and the samplers at the beginnings of Chapters 4, 6, 10, and 11.)

A more advanced student may wish to turn his or her sampler into a set design; for example, a city skyline or a calico cat. This takes planning.

A sampler should be a learning experience and a reference when planning future projects.

I suggest that the following basic stitches be included in your sampler (the page number of each follows the name):

Straight Stitches
  Straight Gobelin, 136
  Brick, 138
  Hungarian, 143
  Bargello, 170–171
Diagonal Stitches
  Basketweave, 180
  Continental, 183
  Half Cross, 184
  Petit Point, 187
  Rep, 187
  Slanted Gobelin, 188
  Byzantine #1, 197
  Jacquard, 202
  Milanese, 205
  Oriental, 206
Box Stitches
  Mosaic, 214
  Diagonal Mosaic, 216
  Cashmere, 218–19
  Scotch, 223

Cross-Stitches
  Cross Stitch, 247
  Spaced Cross Tramé, 252
  Upright Cross, 264
  Binding Stitch, 269
  Herringbone, 271
  Six-Trip Herringbone, 273
  Greek, 274
  Double Straight Cross, 279
  Double Leviathan, 280
  Triple Leviathan, 281
  Medallion, 282
  Woven Band, 292
Tied Stitches
  Fly, 298
  Couching, 299
Eye Stitches
  Diamond Eyelet, 313
  Squared Daisies, 316
Leaf Stitches
  Leaf, 324

Always put your initials, or even better, your name and the date on your sampler and on every piece you make. If you care to do this, don't place your name or anything on the very edge. You must remember that the finishing of a piece—whether framing or pillow-making or any system—usually takes up a few rows on the edges.

CLEANING NEEDLEPOINT

Cleaning your needlepoint becomes necessary sooner or later. There are two acceptable methods: Wash in Woolite or use a commercial needlepoint cleaner.

Wash badly soiled pieces that have stitches that

Fig. 1-41 *How* not *to treat your needlepoint*

may snag. But wash only when absolutely necessary. The reason for this is that washing removes some of the sizing. You do not want to wash it all out, for it is this sizing that makes the canvas stiff and strong. Follow the directions on the Woolite bottle. Place the clean, wet needlepoint between two clean terry towels. Roll. Squeeze out excess water. Do not twist. Block immediately. (See page 81).

There are several commercial needlepoint cleaners that are quite good. I do not, however, recommend them for long stitches that will snag, because you must rub the needlepoint with a towel when using a commercial cleaner. A spray cleaner is good for touch-ups and spot removal.

I do not trust a dry cleaner to clean my needlepoint correctly. It cannot be steam-pressed; wool shrinks and mats when exposed to heat. If the cleaning fluid is not clean, the colors in your needlepoint may dull. (This applies to coin-operated dry-cleaning machines also.) If you are **absolutely** sure that your cleaner will change the fluid and that he will **not** press your needlepoint, then send it to the cleaners—but don't say I didn't warn you.

Never apply Scotchgard or other similar products to your needlepoint. Do not put foam rubber or other synthetic items next to your needlepoint. (See page 110.) They do not allow the wool yarn to "breathe." There have been reports of premature rotting of the yarn.

LEFT-HANDED NEEDLEPOINT

The instructions in this book are written for right-handers, but the left-handed stitcher need not despair. It will help tremendously if you turn the book upside down and work the stitches as you then see

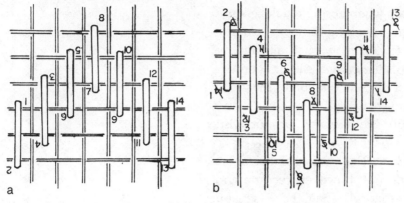

a   b

Fig. 1-42 *Take the diagram* (a) *and simply turn it upside down* (b), *following the numbers of the stitches in reverse order*

them. Reverse the words "left" and "right" and "up" and "down" in the written instructions.

I have taught many left-handed people. I have found that most of them have learned methods of their own that enable them to function in a right-handed world. There are nearly as many methods as there are people. This is particularly true of people who have done other things with their hands. If you wish to try my hint or use one of your own, it will not matter so long as the results are the same. Hold the canvas so that it is comfortable; turn it and the book so that you can attack it from the viewpoint that is most logical for you.

In this chapter I have introduced to you the basic procedures of needlepoint. You can see that it is not a difficult hobby and that with a minimum of effort and a maximum amount of pleasure, you can learn to do something with your time and your hands that will bring you joy and a feeling of accomplishment. In the next chapter we will explore design.

TWO

Design

D on't be afraid to try your own design. You don't have to pull an idea out of the clear blue sky.

The very best ideas and design sources are in children's coloring books. Other sources are afghan books (for the embroidery charts), appliqué books and other books, china, club or organization emblems, crests, fabrics, flowers, fruit, greeting cards, history, hobbies, kids' drawings, magazines, other needlework designs, paintings, pets and other animals, professions, quilt patterns, sports, travel, wallpaper, and wrapping paper.

If you absolutely cannot draw, try tracing designs that you like. Put various components together to make a design that is somewhat yours. (See Figure 2-1.) Draw each of these components on a piece of paper. Cut them out. On another piece of paper draw an outline that is the size you want your finished piece to be. Place the cut-out components in this area. Move them around until you have a pleasing design. A few basic art principles will help you to achieve this.

Fig. 2-1 *Putting components together*

BASIC ART PRINCIPLES

Unity

Unity is what holds a design together. It creates a focus of thought. It is obtained by the use of similar

54   *General Methods*

Fig. 2-2a *Unity—wrong*

Fig. 2-2b *Unity—right*

subject matter, the proper placement of your components on the page (Figure 2-2), and by judicious use of color (Plate 24).

Balance

Balance can be of two kinds: formal, or symmetrical; and informal, or asymmetrical.

Formal is the easiest type to understand. If you were to draw a line down the center of the page, the right side would be a mirror image of the left side. (Figure 2-3a.) Elements on the right side of a design may be very similar to those on the left, but need not necessarily be exactly the same. If a design is balanced formally, it will give a symmetrical, ordered appearance.

Informal balance is a little more difficult to see. Perhaps it would help if you visualized a picture in a frame hanging from a string as in Figure 2-4. One circle in the center balances. If, however, you moved

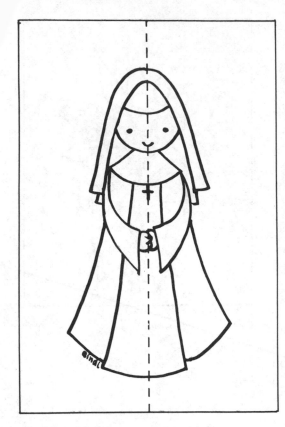

Fig. 2-3a   *Formal, or symmetrical, balance*

Fig. 2-3b   *Informal, or asymmetrical, balance*

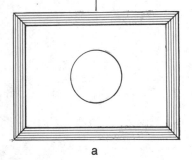

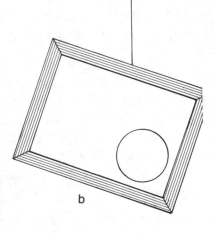

Fig. 2-4   *Balance—informal*

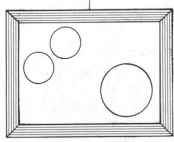

a

b

c

this circle to the lower right, the picture would tilt—in your mind's eye. The addition of two smaller circles in the upper left "straightens out" the picture and gives it balance. It is easier to make an odd number of items balance than an even number, although even numbers can work. (Figure 2-3b.) An informally balanced design satisfies the desire for unity in an asymmetrical way.

Focal Point

Every good design should have a focal point. This is something of interest that catches the eye. In Figure 2-5b it is obvious that the bee is the focal point. Figure 2-6b also has an obvious focal point in the pot of gold. Other drawings may have a more obscure center of interest. The open door of the church in Figure 2-9 are an example of this. They invite the viewer to go in. Contrast also helps to make a focal point. The dog's nose in Figure 2-10 shows this.

Placing the focal point slightly off-center usually makes a more interesting picture.

Fig. 2-5a   *Focal point—wrong*

Fig. 2-5b   *Focal point—right*

Fig. 2-6a *Proportion—wrong*　　　　Fig. 2-6b *Proportion—right*

Proportion

Proportion in basic design refers to the size of the drawing in relation to the space given. In Figure 2-6a the pot of gold is not large enough for the space given. It can be enlarged and other objects can be added to the drawing for a more interesting effect. (Figure 2–6b.)

Rhythm

Rhythm is accomplished by the proper combination of repetition and variety. Constant repetition is boring; constant variety is confusing. In both cases, unity is lost. Repetition of subject, shape, color, and texture is important, but variety of these same things is imperative, also. (Figure 2-7a,b.)

Fig. 2-7a   *Rhythm—wrong*

Fig. 2-7b   *Rhythm—right*

Texture

Texture is especially important in needlepoint. Along with rhythm and variety, texture is what makes the design interesting to the eye. Texture creates patterns of light and dark. Heavily textured areas appear darker.

If it has been made properly, you can imagine what a piece of needlepoint would feel like without touching it. Good texture may well create an overwhelming desire to touch. (Figure 2-8 and Plates, 11, 17, and 46.)

Design   **59**

Fig. 2-8   *Texture*

Lines

Lines give added qualities to a design. There are several types of lines that can be used in an artistic design to create the most visually pleasing picture.

Vertical lines are stately and suggest dignity and strength. (Figure 2-9.)

Horizontal lines can create a calm and restful mood. (Figure 2-10.)

Diagonal lines suggest dynamic movement (Figure 2-11.)

Curved lines (Figure 2-12) can be used in needlepoint to give an impression of grace and beauty.

The dominant type of line in a design should be of one kind. It isn't a good idea to try to include all types of lines.

Fig. 2-9   *Vertical lines are stately*

Fig. 2-10   *Horizontal lines are restful*

Fig. 2-11   *Diagonal lines are dynamic*

Design   61

Fig. 2-12 *Curved lines are graceful*

Color

One of the most important artistic principles in creating a design is color. It can effectively set a mood. For example, red gives a feeling of anger or passion; blue, green, and violet suggest peace or cold; and yellow and orange make the viewer think of warmth, sun, cheerfulness. The careful choice of color can be a vital element in creating your own needlepoint designs.

Choosing a color scheme need not be baffling. The color wheel should be helpful (Plate 1).

Red, yellow, and blue are the **primary colors.** Orange, green, and purple are **secondary colors. The remaining colors are called tertiary colors.**

We have all heard of **complementary colors**, but somehow searching them out on the color wheel doesn't help. These are the colors opposite each other on the color wheel—orange and blue, green and purple, etc. Many people do not think these colors are pretty together. These are the colors that were so popular in op art in the 1960s. You might like them better together in lighter shades. They make the eye dizzy when repeated in small areas.

Those color combinations which most people find pleasing are the **analogous** colors. They are any two or three colors next to each other on the color wheel, such as orange and yellow-orange.

Monochromatic colors are several tints or shades of one color. Use of these can be monotonous; adding an accent color can make your design more interesting. Bargello designs are usually worked in monochromatic color schemes.

CHOOSING YOUR COLORS

The **tips** that follow may help you in choosing your colors:

1. A light-colored background makes the other colors appear muted. Dark backgrounds give a dramatic effect to those same colors.
2. Avoid "busyness"; choose only two or three different colors for a piece. The shades or tints of these two or three colors may be used, too. (A shade of a color is produced by adding black to the color on the color wheel; this makes it darker. A tint is made by adding white to the color on the color wheel; this makes it lighter.)
3. Do not let one color overpower the others. They will seem dull by comparison.
4. Balance the bright colors and the quiet ones.
5. White makes dark colors stand out more.
6. Be sure all areas of your design will stand out against the background. For example, do not use navy blue against a black background.

Pale colors vs dark colors. Pale colors show up the stitches best. Detail is lost in dark colors; therefore, it detracts from the stitches. When your design does call for a dark color, do not waste your time on an intricate stitch.

There seem to be two schools of thought on what to do when stitching with a dark color and a light one. One school says to work all of the dark color first and the light one last. The other school says to do the opposite. Both claim their method keeps the amount of dark lint down. I can only say to try them both and see which one works best for you.

PUTTING YOUR OWN DESIGN ON CANVAS

Size of Design

Once you have a design you like, it must be made into a size suitable for needlepoint. It is best to work with broad curves and large areas. As a general rule of thumb, do not include more than two or three areas smaller than a nickel, unless you plan to use a single stitch to fill these small places.

There are several methods you can use to bring your drawing to the proper scale.

A **lithographer** will enlarge or reduce your drawing for a nominal fee. This is by far the easiest and most accurate method.

The grid method is a good way to make your design the correct size by yourself (Figure 2-13). To enlarge your drawing, draw a 1/4" grid on the original. If you do not want to draw on the original, trace it onto tissue paper. Then draw the grid over it. On another sheet of paper draw a 1" grid with the same number of squares.

This enlarges the drawing four times. Reverse the process to reduce the drawing four times. Juggle the size of the grids to change the original drawing to the size that you need. Transfer the design to the larger grid, square by square. On an intricate design, this can be tedious. However, on most designs suitable for needlepoint, it is not too bad a job.

If you have access to an **opaque projector**, it is even easier than using the grid method. However, with this method you may not be able to get your design in focus at the proper size.

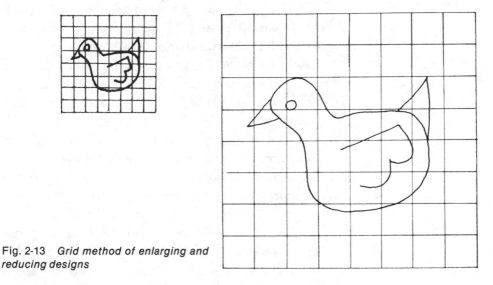

Fig. 2-13 *Grid method of enlarging and reducing designs*

Transferring the Design

Now that you have a design that is the correct size, it is a relatively easy matter to transfer it from paper to canvas.

First, trace around all the outlines on the paper design with a black felt-tip marker. If you use the broad-tipped marker and feel it is too big, then your drawing is too small for the needlepoint—unless you plan to do a lot of Petit Point.

Using masking tape, tape a large piece of white paper to a table top. Tape your design on top of the paper. Center your canvas over the drawing, leaving a 3″ margin on all sides. (Most projects need this 3″ margin, but some do not. Check Chapter 3, "Finishing," before you cut your canvas.) Tape the canvas to the table. (You'd better buy stock in masking tape before it goes up!)

Always use **waterproof** materials when working on needlepoint canvas. Use your grey marker (page 22) to draw the 3″ margin all the way around the canvas. (If you are making a picture, see page 91.) Then, trace your design onto the canvas. Easy, isn't it?

You may or may not wish to color in the design on the canvas. This can be done by painting with one of two media: **waterproof markers** or **acrylic paints**.

As I see it, there is one advantage and one disadvantage in painting your design. The disadvantage is that it is more trouble than just leaving it in simple outline form.

The advantage, however, may outweigh the disadvantage. When the canvas is painted in colors that correspond to your yarn colors, stitches that do not **quite** cover will be less noticeable. If the lack of coverage is slight, you may not have to thicken your yarn. Painting could save you time in the long run. There are some stitches that won't quite cover when worked with three-ply yarn. And when worked in four-ply, it is too thick. When it seems you can't win, paint the canvas.

Following are a few hints for working with acrylic paints. They can be thinned and lightened in color by adding water. This is important, for the paint must not clog the holes. Ideally, there should not be any paint showing on the wrong side. Use just enough to do the job.

A broad brush will be needed for the larger areas, and a finer one for the small areas. Do not get the brushes very wet. Too much water will dissolve the sizing.

If you have made a mistake, paint over it with white

or tan (to match the canvas). Then correct your mistake.

Acrylic paint is easily removed **before** it dries, so be sure to wash your brushes immediately after using— in water. Once it has dried thoroughly it is absolutely waterproof. **But test it yourself.** Run a dry patch under water and blot it with a tissue or paper towel. Just to be sure it won't run, spray the dried paint **and marker** with an acrylic spray. Allow it to dry thoroughly. Test again. (Do you get the feeling that I don't trust anyone?)

Iron-on transfers are now available, but these, too, must be tested. It would be a tragedy if your paint or marker ran during blocking and spoiled your needlepoint (see pages 21–22).

There is one other way to put a design on canvas. A graph or chart, as it is called, gives details, shading,

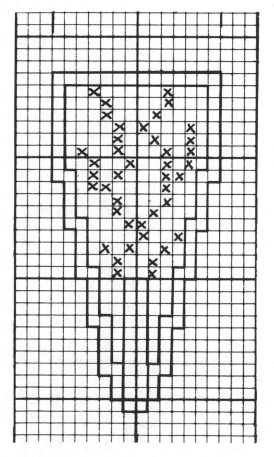

Fig. 2-14 *Chart for a scissors case*

and geometric designs the precision they need (Figure 2-14). Each color area is outlined in Continental Stitch and filled in with Basketweave.

For each x on the drawing, make one Continental or Basketweave stitch. If you can count and you have lots of patience, you have got this technique whipped!

In planning your own chart, you must be aware that the canvas is not perfectly square. If you need 50 mesh, count them; do not measure 5″ (if, for example, you are working on Penelope or Mono 10 canvas). Work on graph paper that has the same number of squares per inch as your canvas has mesh per inch. This will give a finished drawing approximately the same size that your finished needlepoint will be.

Color-key your graph as shown in Plate 20(A) or use colored pencils or markers.

Choosing the Stitches for Your Design

An important step in executing your needlepoint design successfully involves the selection of the appropriate stitches for your work. You will learn more about individual stitches in Part Two, but for now a few hints might be in order. (Also, don't forget the design hints in Chapter 1, particularly in the sections on shading and shadows [pages 45 and 47].)

First of all, let the stitches do the designing for you. Avoid realism if you plan to use decorative stitches. If you want realism, use Basketweave (page 180) wherever you can. Petit Point (page 187) adds detail. The Continental Stitch (page 183) gets you in and out of tight places. Rely on surface embroidery for very small places, such as people's faces. (page 70).

MIXING STITCHES

You should be aware also of design problems that may arise when you mix stitches. Straight stitches and diagonal stitches do not fit well together. If you **must** mix them, do the diagonal stitches first.

Many stitches have several uses related to design effectiveness. Some are better for certain things than others. For example, very large stitches need very large areas for their patterns to show up. There are many special uses for particular stitches that will make your design more striking and pleasing to look at.

Letters and Numbers. These can be best worked either in the Continental or the Cross-Stitch. Follow the chart at the end of the Appendix or one in an alphabet book, or work your own out on graph paper. Always put your initials and the date on your work. If you wish to incorporate your initials into a fancy monogram, plan it out first on graph paper (Figure 2-15). If you do not wish your initials and the date to be prominent, work them in a color that is just one shade lighter or darker than the background.

Fig. 2-15 *Planning a monogram*

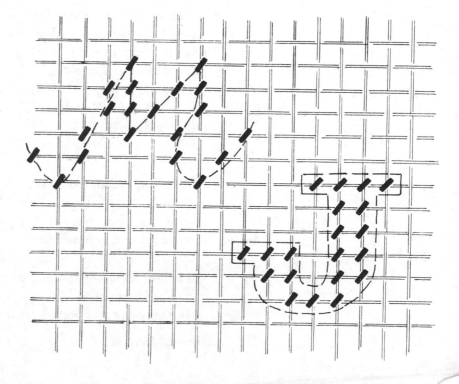

Mottos and sayings are popular additions to samplers. Consider adding one to your work. (See Plate 33 and Figure 2-17.)

Border Stitches. These stitches help to dress up any needlepoint. They make a ready-center piece or a painted canvas more your own. Some suggestions for border stitches are: Cashmere, Mosaic, Scotch (and their reversed versions), Stem, Fern, Ray, Bound Cross, Fly, Triangle, Woven Band, Six-Trip Herringbone, Two-Color Herringbone, and Woven Band. There are many more. Check the charts at the beginning of each section of stitches.

Curved lines are difficult, at best, to work effectively. Couching (page 299) and Chain Stitch (page 338) work better than any I have found. Van Dyke works, but it cannot get around tight corners and curves. Both of these may be worked on top of the background stitch or in a space left for them. How much relief you want depends on which method you use. This will vary from design to design.

Surface Embroidery. This is needlepoint that is worked on top of a background stitch. It adds high relief and makes it easier to get a background stitch around intricate Cross-Stitches.

Consider using the Spider Webs, many Cross-Stitches, Chain, Couching, Thorn Stitch, and many others in this manner.

Distortion of the Canvas

Many types of stitches will distort the canvas. This is a nuisance, but it can be compensated for in stitching. Plate 44 shows how several diagonal stitches were slanted in alternating directions so that distortion would be lessened.

The very worst offenders are the Continental Stitch,

Jacquard, Byzantine, Milanese, Oriental, Scotch, Mosaic, Cashmere, and most of their variations. Generally they are the Diagonal Stitches.

Those stitches that do not distort the canvas are Basketweave, Straight, Cross, Leaf, Eye, and Tied stitches.

Try not to distort the canvas for items other than a picture. If you do have a distorted canvas, it must be held rigid with rabbit-skin glue or a commercial substitute. (See page 88.)

The following photographs will give you an idea of the variety of projects you can design and stitch. (See the Appendix for the stitches used.)

Fig. 2-16   *Dice on plastic (author)*

Fig. 2-17   *"Justice tempered with mercy" (author)*

Fig. 2-19   *Wooden pincushion (author)*

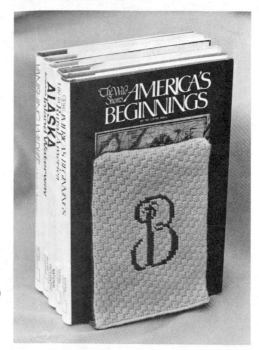

Fig. 2-20   *Wooden pincushion (author)*

Fig.   2-18   *Semi-planned sampler (Jackie Beaty)*

Fig. 2-21   *Bookends (Jackie Beaty)*

Fig. 2-22 *Christmas-tree ornament on plastic Jackie Beaty*

Fig. 2-23 *Christmas-tree ornament on plastic: candle (author)*

Fig. 2-24 *Name plate (author)*

The following drawings may be worked in various sizes. The larger the drawing, or the more space there is between lines, the easier it will be for you to stitch. Have a lithographer enlarge the drawings that appear small to you. A rule of thumb: Do not have more than two or three areas smaller than a dime in your picture if you wish to use decorative stitches. This does not apply to areas that will be filled by one decorative stitch. (Decorative stitches are those other than the Tent Stitch.) Pieces worked all in Tent Stitch may be smaller than those stitched in decorative stitches. Petit Point pieces may be smaller yet than those in Tent Stitches.

Fig. 2-25

Fig. 2-26

Fig. 2-27

Fig. 2-28

JAMES JUSTIN
APRIL 2, 1972
8 lbs. 12 oz.

Fig. 2-29

Fig. 2-30

Fig. 2-31

Fig. 2-32

Fig. 2-33

Fig. 2-34

Fig. 2-35

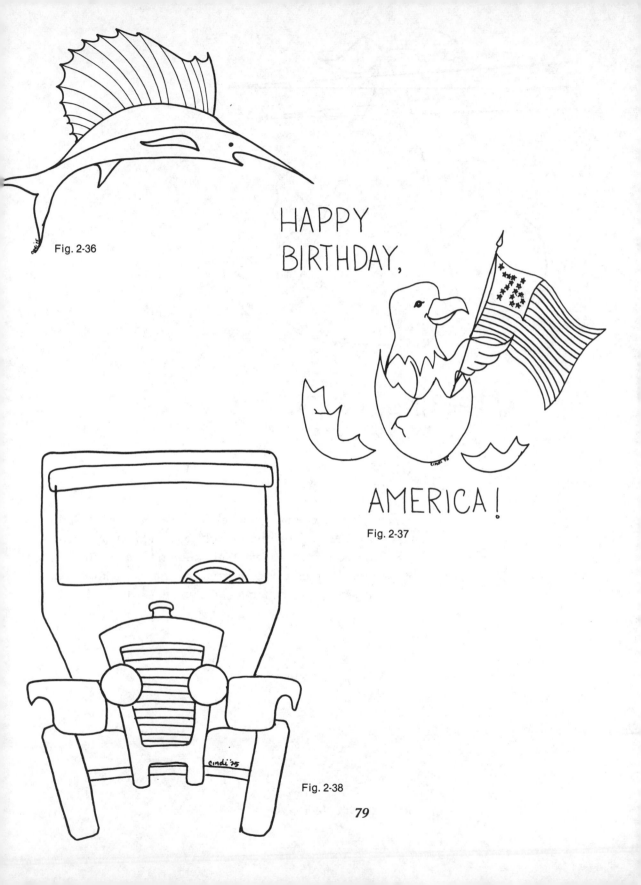

Fig. 2-36

HAPPY
BIRTHDAY,

AMERICA!

Fig. 2-37

Fig. 2-38

79

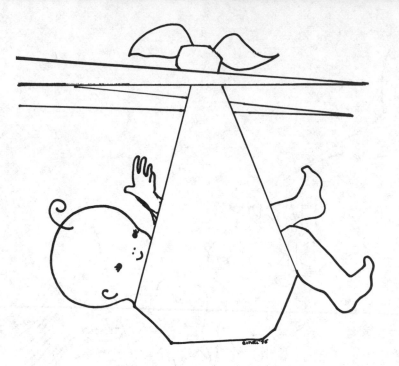

KATHERINE LOUISE
OCT. 29, 1973
7 lbs.

Fig. 2-39

In this chapter you have read about design—and you can see that the thought of designing and creating your own needlepoint shouldn't scare you. The next chapter will cover one of the most important aspects of needlepoint—how you finish it.

THREE:

Finishing

O nce the stitching is completed, many people think that their part in doing a needlepoint piece is over; it isn't. Finishing can make or break your needlepoint. Well done, it can overshadow inexpert work; poorly done, it can spoil a flawless piece of stitching.

BLOCKING

Professional blocking is costly, and it is simple enough so that **you** can learn to do it yourself.

The first step is to make a blocking board. Go to the lumberyard and ask for a scrap of insulation board or fiber board. If possible, get the man who operates the

saw to cut down a $4' \times 8'$ sheet to $2'$ square. There seem to be many names for this product. Perhaps it would help to mention that this is the material that some bulletin boards are made of. Pins and staples go into and pull out of it easily. It is porous, and needlepoint dries more quickly on it than on anything else. A piece $2'$ square should be large enough at the start.

It is absolutely necessary to cover this board. This is to protect the needlepoint from stains and snags. There are two good covers that you can use.

A piece of brown **paper** should be taped in place all the way around the board. This means both sides, for the color can rub off on your clothes. Use very wide masking tape. Next, draw a grid on the paper with a black **waterproof** marker. The lines **must** be perpendicular and parallel. One-inch squares make it easier to block your needlepoint, although they are not absolutely necessary.

When you have drawn all the lines, thoroughly saturate the paper with water. After it dries, the paper will be taut. Until it does dry it will look like such a mess that you will be certain you have done something wrong. You have not. When it dries, spray it with a spray plastic to make the paper last longer.

The other cover is **gingham** fabric. Gingham with half-inch squares works well, but so do other sizes. The gingham **must** be woven. (If it is, it will look the same on both sides of the fabric.) Ideally, 100% cotton is best. However, in this day and age of permanent press, it may be difficult to find.

Tape a brown paper bag over the board. Shrink it by wetting it. Allow the paper to dry. Then tack the gingham onto the board with **rust-proof** tacks or small nails. Put them very close together (every 1/4" to 1/2"). As you tack, make sure that the lines in the gingham remain perpendicular and parallel. Pull the fabric as tight as you can.

The cover on the board should be taut. (If it is not, a tuck could be caught under your needlepoint; this would throw the lines off and then the needlepoint would be crooked.) Pour very hot water over the fabric. Let the excess run off. 100% cotton will shrink, making the fabric cover taut. **Some** permanent press fabrics may shrink enough; most will not.

Measure the size of your canvas (where the needlepoint will be) before you even start to stitch. This will be an invaluable help in blocking. The finished piece should be this size.

Figure 3-1 shows the steps in blocking a needlepoint piece. A badly misshapen piece will take **lots** of muscle power and two or sometimes three people to block it.

Pieces that consist of all flat stitches should be blocked face down. However, most pieces have some textured stitches; these should be blocked face up. This will prevent crushing these stitches.

On those pieces that have a blank margin of canvas, use a staple gun to block. You may use a hammer and rust-proof tacks, but it is a lot of trouble. Place the staples very close together in this area of blank canvas—so close that they nearly touch. Putting the staples at an angle will make it easier to hold a misshapen piece in place.

For those pieces that do not have a margin on blank canvas, block with stainless steel (not steel plate) T-pins. The heavier-weight ones are necessary because the lighter-weight ones will bend under tension. Place the pins 1/4" apart and two or three mesh in from the edge. Carefully put the pins between the stitches. (Figures 3-1j-l.)

If there are holes when you take out the pins, they can be removed. Hold a steam iron over the holes **briefly**. Then, using a pin or needle, carefully push the yarns back together, closing the hole. **Never touch the iron to the needlepoint.**

Allow your needlepoint to dry thoroughly. This usually takes 24 to 48 hours. Sometimes it can take a week or longer. Do not remove the needlepoint from

Fig. 3-1a *Wet needlepoint with spray of water*

Fig. 3-1b *Place one corner of needlepoint at an intersection of two lines on blocking board*

Fig. 3-1c *Staple in place, using three or four staples; they will be under lots of tension later*

84

Fig. 3-1d *Measure along one side as shown in Fig. 3-5 and staple this second corner*

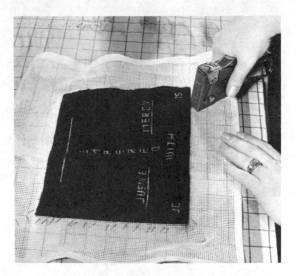

Fig. 3-1e *Position third corner, measure side between second and third corners, and staple third corner in place (if needlepoint has dried out, dampen again); then staple the two sides between the three corners in place along the lines (note position of staples—slanted to hold better; place them very close together to give needlepoint a smooth, not scalloped edge)*

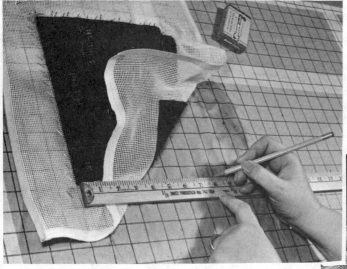

Fig. 3-1f *Measure one free side to find point for fourth corner and mark this on blocking board with pencil; then measure other free side to find point for fourth corner and mark this on blocking board*

Fig. 3-1g *Your mark should look like this*

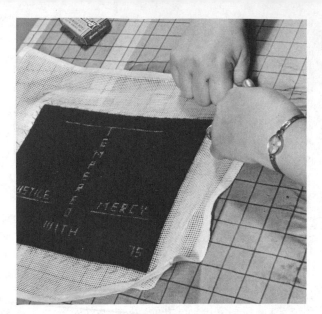

Fig. 3-1h *Pull fourth corner to meet mark (this is where muscle power comes in—if your needlepoint is badly distorted, you may need the help of one or two other people to pull the piece into place); then staple fourth corner securely, pull third side into place and staple, and staple fourth side into place (measure periodically to double-check yourself, and when you have finished, measure again—perfection is of the utmost importance; use edge of ruler or yardstick to ensure that sides are straight and, if not, remove staples and staple again)*

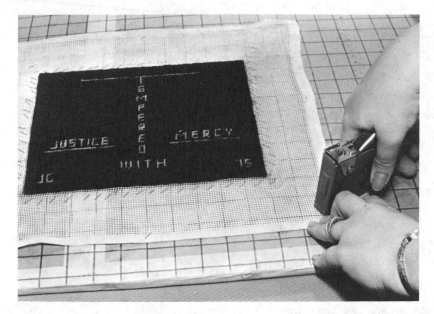

Fig. 3-1i *Staple corners down so they will dry without wrinkles and let your needlepoint dry flat*

Fig. 3-1j *To block a piece with no margin of blank canvas, use "T" pins, starting with three corners as in the other method of blocking*

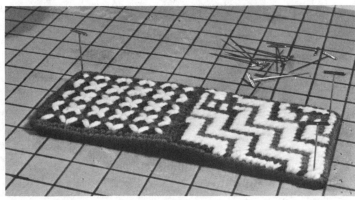

86

Fig. 3-1k *Begin in middle of one side with pins and do one small section at a time; pins should be ¼" to ½" apart*

Fig. 3-1l *If one side or section is badly out of shape, block it first, then block the rest*

the blocking board until it is **absolutely** dry or it may revert to the crooked shape it was in.

Keep your blocking board flat until your needlepoint dries. Do not tilt the board against a wall or anything else. If you do, there will be a watermark on your needlepoint after it dries. I have not found a miracle to remove a watermark. Also, if your needlepoint is not evenly dampened before blocking, a watermark may form.

Should your marker, paint, or yarn bleed color when dampened, there are some things that can be done about it. First, cry a lot. But while you are crying, do not allow your needlepoint to dry! Put it in a cold-water soak overnight. The theory here is that if the color will run, given time, maybe it will keep running—right out of the yarn. This does not always work, however.

If it fails, sponge the stain with a mixture of ammonia and water. Use one tablespoon of ammonia per cup of water. Rinse thoroughly.

If this doesn't work, the only thing left for you to do is to rip (sorry!) the stained stitches. Then, of course, you must stitch again.

Finishing **87**

The best cure is the proverbial ounce of prevention. Use only **waterproof** markers and paint that **you** have tested. (See pages 21-22.)

A **light** dose of steam will fluff textured stitches. Take care not to steam to the point of shrinking and matting the wool.

A piece of needlepoint that is somewhat limp can be revived with a dose of spray sizing on the wrong side.

There is just one other problem that might turn up. No matter how precisely you may have blocked, some pieces may pop out of shape shortly after being removed from the blocking board. Many stitches distort the canvas. You can compensate for this in stitching (see pages 70-71) or after blocking.

Pieces that are not badly out of shape can be kept in shape with iron-on interfacing. Choose a heavy-weight interfacing. It may be purchased anywhere fabrics are sold. It is usually kept under the counter, so you will have to ask for it. Do not use it on pieces that have textured stitches. They will be crushed under the iron.

Badly distorted needlepoint pieces can be straightened only with rabbit-skin glue. It can be bought in art supply stores. Rabbit-skin glue comes in powder form, which must be cooked into a gel. Complete instructions come with it. When it cools it will gel— honestly. I was so sure I had done something wrong when I made it for the first time that I started a second batch. It took the first batch about six or eight hours to gel. And three hours after that my second batch gelled, too. I had more rabbit-skin glue than I could use! After a week it smelled as if a rabbit had died in my refrigerator! Be more patient than I was.

To apply, block pieces with flat stitches face down. Allow to dry. With a knife, spread the rabbit-skin glue on **thinly**. Allow to dry.

Textured stitches need different treatment. Build a frame that is larger than the finished needlepoint area

(Figure 3-2). Staple the area of blank canvas onto it. This is easier to do if you block it first. Draw lines on the frame to help you if necessary.

If you have no margin of blank canvas, your frame must be 1/4″ smaller on all four sides (inside dimensions) than your needlepoint. For example, if your needlepoint is 8″ × 10″, the measurement on the inside of your frame should be 7-1/2″ × 9-1/2″.

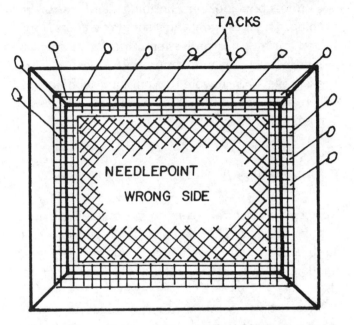

Fig. 3-2 *Frame for applying rabbit-skin glue to textured needle-point*

Unless you have super-strong thumbs, you will not be able to use T-pins for attaching your needlepoint to your frame. Use rust-proof tacks and a hammer. Block first. Tack the needlepoint in place, face down. The thickness of the frame (about 1/2″-3/4″) will be enough to keep the textured stitches from being crushed. Spread the rabbit-skin glue thinly on the wrong side of the canvas. Allow to dry.

This frame does not have to be fancy, but it should be covered, to protect your needlepoint from stains and snags.

FINISHING TECHNIQUES

I am convinced that poorly finished items take away from the quality of even the best stitching. On the other hand, if your stitching is not quite perfect it can be disguised reasonably well by exquisite finishing. Nothing, however, can beat the winning combination of professional-looking finishing and error-free stitching. This is my goal and it should be yours, too.

You can get this professional look at home with proper instructions and some effort. Because whole books have been devoted to finishing techniques, I will consider only a few of the basic types of finishing in this book.

Framing a Picture

Needlepoint pictures seem to be one of the most popular projects. They can also be the most costly to finish. If you plan your needlepoint so that it fits a standard-sized **frame**, it will cut your cost considerably.

These frames come already put together and are much more economical than custom-made frames. There are also precut strips of frame molding that come in pairs, with hardware and instructions for putting the frame together. Before you cut your canvas, visit the local art supply store and ask for the exact sizes that these two types of frames come in. There are many attractive styles. Choose a simple one that will not detract from your stitching.

No matter what kind of frame you choose, it will have to be deep enough to accommodate a stretcher frame. If you are not sure, buy the stretcher frame first and test it for fit before buying the frame. The stretcher frame should not stick out beyond the frame on the back.

If, however, you are in love with one frame in particular that is not deep enough, you can still use it. It involves a lot of work, though, so you'd better love that frame a lot!

Lace your canvas over a piece of masonite with heavy thread as shown in Figure 3-3. Do **not** use cardboard; it will bend under the tension put on it, and you will not be able to get the needlepoint taut.

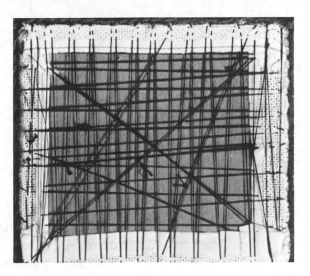

Fig. 3-3 *To wrap a piece of needlepoint around a masonite board, lace sides together with heavy thread (this is a long job)*

Canvas board (available in art supply stores) can be cut into ovals or any shape you want. The needlepoint can be stapled on, as it is onto a stretcher frame.

Never put your needlepoint under glass. It will crush your stitches and hide the texture from admirers. Wool also needs to breathe.

There is a trick in getting your needlepoint to fit the frame you choose. It is imperative that you measure carefully. Allow a 3″ margin of blank canvas on all four sides. In other words, if you wish to make a piece that will be 8″ x 10″ when you are finished, add three inches to either side of the eight inches and the ten inches. 3″ + 8″ + 3″ = 14″ and 3″ + 10″ + 3″ = 16″. So you need to cut a piece of canvas 14″ × 16″ in order to have a finished size of 8″ × 10″. (See Figure 3-4.)

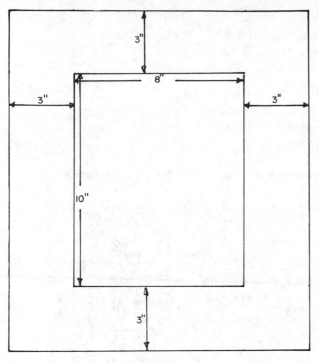

Fig. 3-4 *Margins for a picture*

At first glance this may seem to be a lot of wasted canvas. Let me assure you, it is not. When it comes time to block you will be grateful that you have something to hang on to, particularly if your needlepoint is badly out of shape. The framing process will also eat up much of this blank canvas.

Mark your margins next. See Figure 3-5. Draw a line to indicate the margins. It should be two mesh (one on either side) short of 8″ and two mesh short of 10″. In essence you have left a blank mesh all the

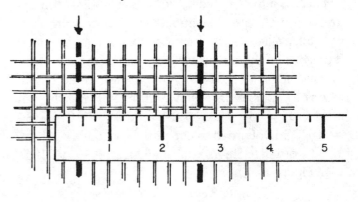

Fig. 3-5 *Measuring margins for a*
3″ picture

way around your finished work. This extra mesh is your "fudge" factor.

If you plan to have a border, remember that the lip of the frame covers 1/4″ of your needlepoint, or about two mesh. One of these two mesh is the blank mesh you have already provided for. The other should be one row of Continental Stitches (page 183). Then comes your border. If you stitch the border right to the edge, 1/4″ of it will be hidden. On a very wide border this will not matter. However, a border that is only two mesh wide can be swallowed whole by the frame (Plates 32, 34, 36, 38, for example).

Work the needlepoint and block.

You will need a **stretcher frame** to stretch your needlepoint. Art supply stores carry stretcher bars that are sold in pairs. They usually come only in whole inches and are inexpensive. They are easily assembled (Figure 3-6a). You may need a hammer to tap the stretcher bars in place. Use a square or something else with a 90° angle to be sure that the corners are exactly 90°. Put the stretcher frame into the frame to be sure that it will fit. (Figure 3-6e).

Staple or tape a piece of **cardboard** onto the front of the stretcher frame. It should be slightly smaller than the stretcher frame. Do not use corrugated cardboard; it is too thick.

Stretch the needlepoint over the stretcher frame. Start at the corners, making them just as perfect as you possibly can, and staple them in place. The extra row of mesh you left now gives you a margin of error. Under no circumstances should yarn from the worked needlepoint go over the edge of the stretcher frame. There is simply not enough room between the stretcher frame and the frame for any excess materials. Do not worry if that row of blank canvas shows. The lip of the frame will cover it.

Staple the rest of the canvas in place. Make sure the needlepoint is perfectly straight. If it is not, do it again and again and again until it is **perfect!**

Fig. 3-6a *Equipment needed for framing needlepoint*

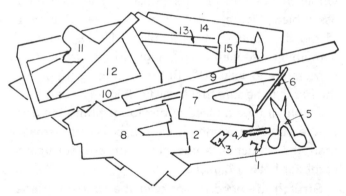

Fig. 3-6b *(1) tacks, (2) cardboard, (3) razor blade, (4) saw-tooth hanger, (5) scissors, (6) pencil, (7) staple gun, (8) stretcher frame, (9) ruler, (10) frame, (11) square, (12) needle-point, (13) hammer, (14) paper bag, (15) glue*

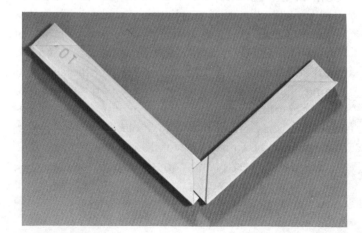

Fig. 3-6c *Stretcher-frame pieces fit together at the corners like this; they may need a tap of the hammer to get them all the way together*

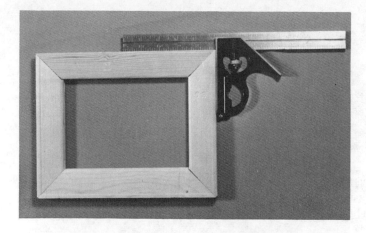

Fig. 3-6d *Use a square to be sure each corner is 90°*

Fig. 3-6e *Try stretcher frame in frame for size; note that there is very little extra room*

Fig. 3-6f *Cut piece of cardboard a little smaller than stretcher frame and staple it in place on stretcher frame; wrap needlepoint around stretcher frame so that cardboard lies next to needlepoint*

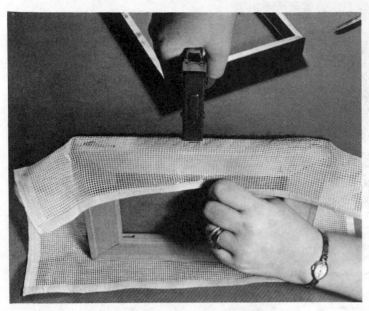

Fig. 3-6g *Staple corners first, then sides*

Fig. 3-6h *When all sides are stapled, miter corners on back; staple middle of piece brought to wrong side of stretcher frame first*

Fig. 3-6i *Next staple sides of that same piece*

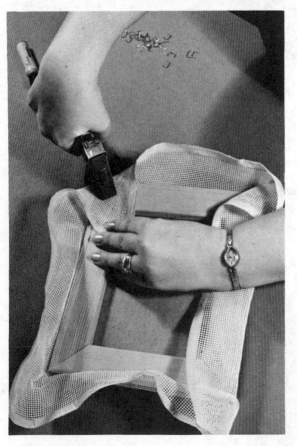

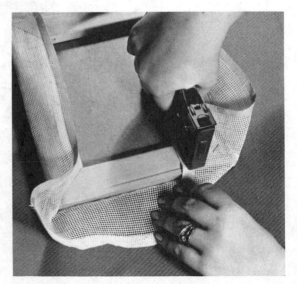

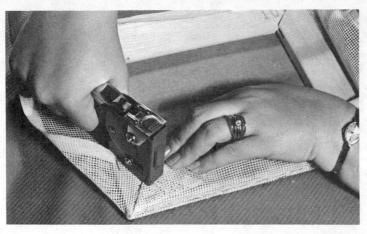

Fig. 3-6j *Fold one side of canvas to back to form one half of mitered corner, then fold other side back and staple; do other three corners then staple sides between mitered corners*

Fig. 3-6k *Put stretcher frame in frame; staple or nail stretcher frame in place*

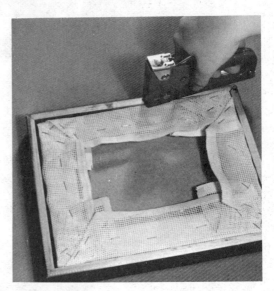

Fig. 3-6l *Wet piece of brown paper for back*

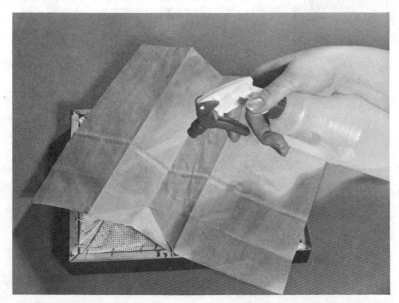

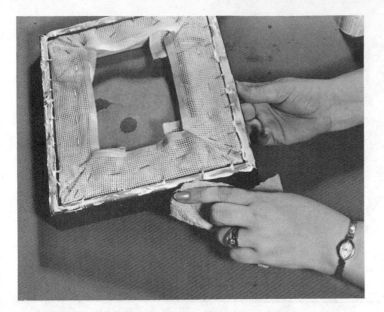

Fig. 3-6m *Apply Elmer's Glue to back of frame, and wipe away excess glue with damp paper towel*

Fig. 3-6n *Place paper over back of picture frame and trim away excess paper with single-edged razor blade; again wipe away excess glue*

Fig. 3-6o *Find center of picture and attach saw-tooth hanger; the paper will dry out, and you will have a picture that looks better than a professional could do it (see Figure 2-17)*

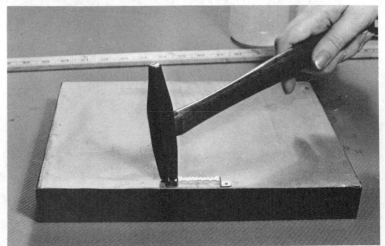

I feel strongly that the finishing technique makes or breaks a project. (See page 90.) It is at this point that **you** make or break **your** project. Be sure that your needlepoint is on the stretcher frame **perfectly**.

Next, put the stretcher frame into the picture frame. Double-check, now, to be sure it is perfectly stretched. Secure it by stapling or tacking. On a 3″ x 5″ index card, write your name, the date, and your address. Tape it to the back of the cardboard. (Surely your needlepoint will outlive you. This will help historians of the future.)

For a professional look, cover the back with brown paper. A brown paper bag will do nicely. Be sure the paper is a couple of inches larger all the way around than your frame. Run a narrow line of Elmer's glue around the outside edge of the back of the frame. Wet the paper thoroughly. Place it over the glue on the back of the frame.

On very large pictures, put the paper on dry and wet it afterwards. A large piece of paper that is wet is unwieldy. The extra paper should hang over the edge of the frame. Allow it to dry. Again, it will look so bad you will be sure you have done something wrong. But you haven't. In about an hour, you will be in for quite a surprise—that paper will magically shrink and be very taut.

Using a **sharp** single-edged razor blade, trim the excess paper away just inside the edge of the frame. **Don't** saw the paint away on the side of the frame by running the razor blade on the edge.

Attach a saw-tooth hangar and you are ready to receive compliments!

See Plates 26, 27, and 32 to 38 for good examples of framing technique. Also see Plates 11 and 46.

Pillows

The pillow is another popular, yet expensive-to-finish needlepoint item. If you sew, even just a little bit, you

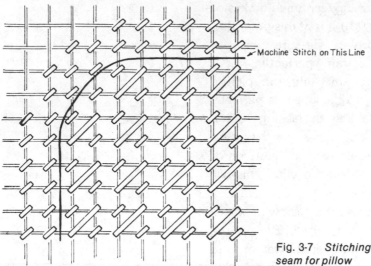
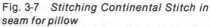
Machine Stitch on This Line

Fig. 3-7 *Stitching Continental Stitch in seam for pillow*

can make your own. You will need a sewing machine, fabric, and polyester fiber stuffing (this is more washable than cotton batting and more durable than foam rubber).

When you stitch your needlepoint, work two extra rows of Continental all the way around the finished design. Machine stitch between these two extra rows and your design. (Figure 3-7) This gives much needed strength and stability to the seam. Block.

THE INNER PILLOW

Make an inner pillow that is 1″ **larger** than your needlepoint; for example, if your needlepoint is 14″ × 14″, make the finished size of your inner pillow 15″ × 15″. Use a sturdy but not heavy machine-washable fabric for the inner pillow.

Preshrinking. Before you make it, preshrink the inner pillow fabric by washing in the washing machine with water just as hot as the fiber will allow. Dry in the dryer at the hottest setting that the fiber will allow. Leave a 5/8″ seam allowance. Stitch all four corners and three sides, leaving an opening through which you can stuff (Figure 3-8). Stuff with a polyester batting, which can be purchased at fabric shops. Make a plump pillow. Stitch the fourth side closed on the sewing machine. (This inner pillow is machine-washable and dryable as it is.)

BACKING

In selecting a fabric for a pillow backing, you must consider several points: (1) durability of the fabric, (2) elegance that will set off your needlepoint, and (3) washability.

Because needlepoint is so long-wearing, you will want to choose a backing with equal **durability**. And you certainly do not want to downgrade your needle-point, so select fabric with **elegance**.

Because the rest of your pillow is washable (either by hand or machine) you may want to make the backing fabric also **washable**. This is not absolutely necessary. However, if you do select a washable fabric, preshrink it according to the instructions given above.

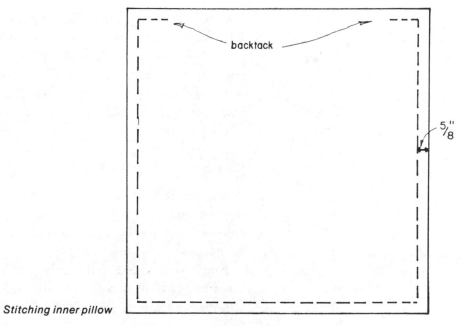

Fig. 3-8 *Stitching inner pillow*

The fabric that I recommend is **Ultra Suede**. It is a synthetic fabric that strongly resembles suede, yet it is washable and it does not waterspot! It comes in a remarkable variety of colors. Look for it at fabric shops.

No-wale corduroy gives the look and feel of velveteen, yet it, too, is washable. Cotton suede is also a good choice. Of course, nothing can imitate the elegance of velvet, but it is not washable. (Velvet is hardly the most durable fabric, but it feels s-o-o-o good!)

TRIMMING

It is at this point that you must decide how you want to trim the pillow once it is finished.

Cording. Although this is a popular choice, I cannot recommend it unless you are an experienced seamstress. As a home economist with a B.S. degree in textiles and clothing, I still find cording difficult. It is something that must be practiced. For that reason I am not including instructions for cording here.

Twisted cord. This resembles cording, yet it is quite a bit easier to make and it is prettier, I think.

It takes two people to make a twisted cord. Measure the distance around the outside of your pillow. Multiply this number times three. This is the length yarn you will need to make one twisted cord long enough to go all the way around your pillow. For example, if your pillow is $14'' \times 14''$, the circumference is $56'' \times 3'' = 168''$.

Cut six strands $168''$. (How many strands you choose determines the thickness of your cord. Six makes a nice-sized cord for a pillow.) You will need an uncut skein of yarn to do this.

Knot the strands at both ends. Put a knot through all strands in the middle. Put a pencil between the strands at each end. (See Figure 3–9.) You hold one pencil and give the other to a friend. Twist until the yarn kinks. Keeping the yarn taut, hook the center knot over a hook (or a chair back, or finger). Give your pencil to the person holding the other pencil. (He now holds both pencils.) Keep the yarn taut.

Remove the center of the yarn from the hook. Slowly release the tension. The two pieces will now twist together. If you go too fast the twist will be uneven. Tie the ends together with a strand of yarn so the twisted cord will not untwist. Hand-sew it in place along the seam, using an invisible stitch. Tuck the ends in (Plate 20).

Fig. 3-9   *Making twisted cord*

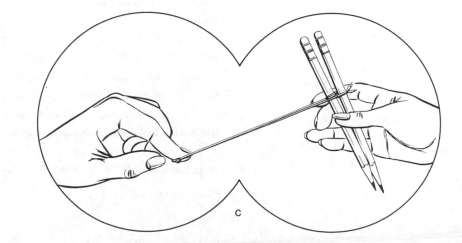

a

b

c

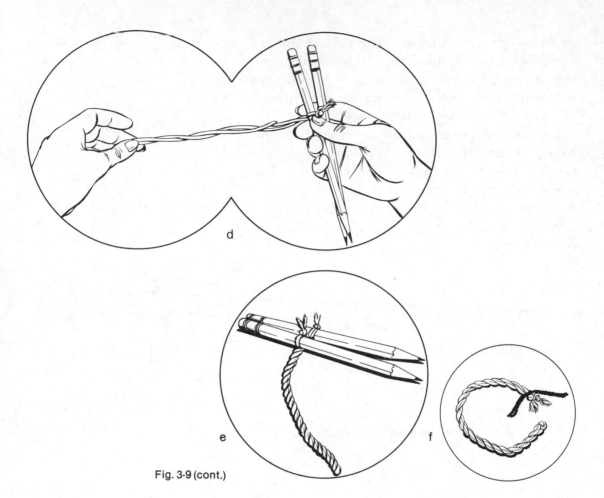

d

e

f

Fig. 3-9 (cont.)

Tassels.   These make a nice finish for a pillow (Plate 47), although they do not have as formal a look as cording.

To make tassels (Figure 3-10), wrap yarn around a piece of cardboard about 4″ long. Using a single strand of yarn, 6″-or-so long, tie the yarn together at the top of the card. Leave the strings hanging. Remove the yarn from the card. About 3/4″ to 1″ down, wrap a strand around all of it several times and tie. Let the ends of that yarn hang down. Cut through the loops at the bottom of the tassel. Trim the ends of that yarn that is hanging down even with the rest.

Once you have chosen your backing fabric, **machine-stitch** it to the needlepoint. Place right

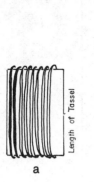

a   b   c

Fig. 3-10 *Making a tassel*

CUT

d   e

sides together. Put the tassels beween the two pieces pointing toward the center. Let the free-hanging yarns at the top fall in the seam allowance. (Figure 3-11.) Catch these when you stitch the seam.

FINAL SEWING

Now stitch between the two rows of Continental stitches and your pillow's needlepoint (Figure 3-7). **Round the corners as you stitch the backing on** (Figure 3-12). (If you can plan for this when you stitch the needlepoint, it would be better. In other words, stop your needlepoint where the corners would be rounded. If you did not plan ahead, it is not disastrous; you can make up for it now.) Be sure each corner has the **same** curve. Again, stitch all four corners and three sides. Back-tack well at the beginning and end of your machine stitching.

Trim the seam to within 5/8″ of the stitching on the rounded corners, even if you have to cut the needlepoint. (See Figure 3-12, not 3-8.) Zig-zag the raw edges together all the way around, except for the opening you have left. Zig-zag those raw edges separately. Turn.

Fig. 3-11 *Inserting tassel in seam*

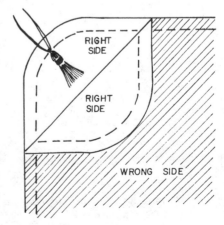

RIGHT SIDE

RIGHT SIDE

WRONG   SIDE

Finishing   **105**

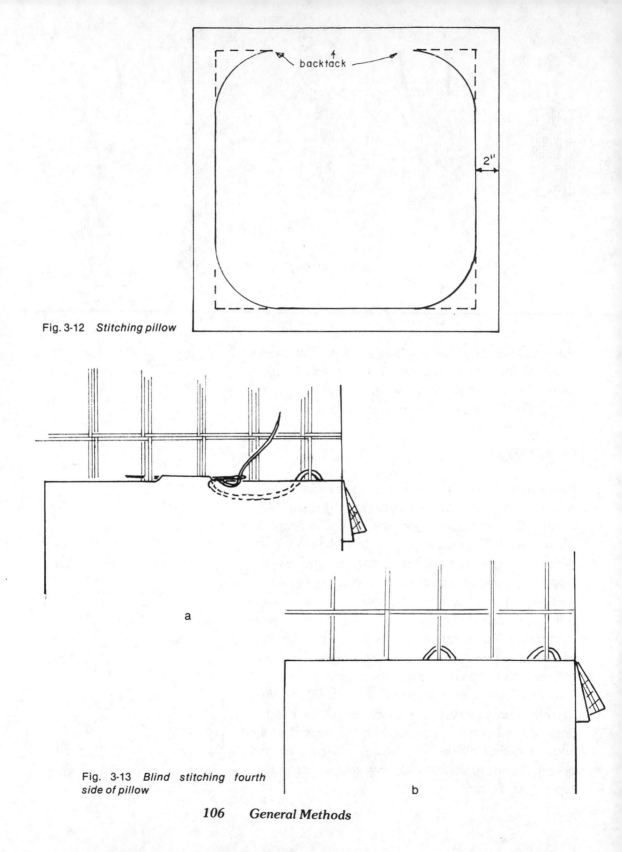

Fig. 3-12 *Stitching pillow*

Fig. 3-13 *Blind stitching fourth side of pillow*

a

b

backtack

2"

Put the inner pillow into the needlepoint cover. Remember that the inner pillow is bigger than the needlepoint cover. Be careful not to break the machine stitching at the edges of the opening. Push the inner pillow into the corners well. (Limp corners cry, "Homemade!") If necessary, take a wad of polyester batting and stuff it into the corners, between the cover and the inner pillow.

When you are satisfied with the way the pillow looks, pin the fourth side, tucking in the fabric 5/8". Sew, using the Blind Stitch shown in Figure 3-13. Run the needle in the fold of the fabric. Bring it out every 1/4" to 3/8". Pick up one mesh (on Mono canvas—one thread on Penelope) and reinsert the needle into the fabric. This makes a stitch that does not show, hence, the name Blind Stitch.

INSERTS

Another attractive method for finishing a pillow is to insert a small needlepoint piece into a larger piece of fabric. Make the corners of the needlepoint square.

This is a delicate procedure that must be done entirely by hand. Stitch your needlepoint according to the instructions given above for a regular pillow.

Next measure your needlepoint **very carefully**. Do not include the two rows of Continental Stitch that will be in the seam allowance. On the wrong side of your fabric, mark off the area that will be filled with needlepoint with tailor's chalk (Figure 3-14). This is your seam line. Measure 5/8" **in** from that line. This is your cutting line.

Double-check all your measurements. When you are sure that your lines are correct, cut on the solid line. Slash the corners **almost** all the way to the seam line.

Place the needlepoint right side up, on a flat surface. Lay the pillow top over it. It should also be right side up. Very carefully tuck the seam allowance under and pin in place. Use the Blind Stitch (Figure 3-13) to hold the needlepoint in place. Be sure the canvas and the fabric are stitched on grain.

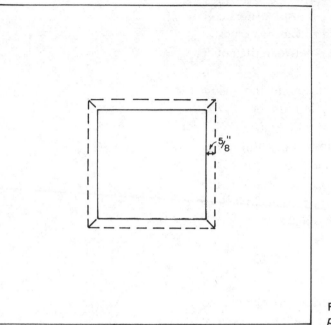
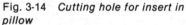

Fig. 3-14 *Cutting hole for insert in pillow*

This seam may be left as is or it may be finished in one of three ways. You may insert cording into the seam; a twisted cord may be tacked over it; or it can be finished with a row of Binding Stitches (Plate 10).

In order to put in a row of the Binding Stitch, you must use Penelope or Interlock Mono canvas. Leave a blank mesh all the way around your needlepoint (Figure 3-15). Hand stitch on the solid line (Figure 3-15a). The blank mesh will show when you are through stitching. It should be the last bit of canvas seen before the fabric begins (Figure 3-15b). Work in Binding Stitch (page 269) on this blank mesh. Turn your canvas 90° to the right at each corner.

The Binding Stitch or the twisted cord will cover your seam—and some not-so-perfect hand stitching.

Perhaps you might want to frame the insert with ribbon, decorative braid, or lace. Use your imagination. Have fun!

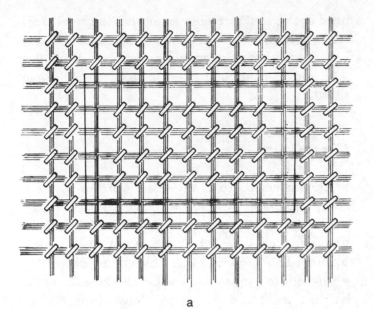

a

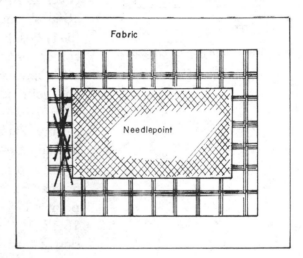

Fig. 3-15 *Measuring for Binding Stitch around insert*

b

Pincushions and Christmas Tree Ornaments

Nearly the same procedures are used in making pin-cushions (Plates 17/18 and 42) as are used in making pillows. But there are two differences. First, they are smaller. Second, they are stuffed with steel wool wrapped in polyester batting. (This is to protect your needlepoint in the remote event that the steel wool rusts.) (See page 122 for another type of pin cushion.)

Christmas tree ornaments may be made in this way, too, but no inner pillow is needed. Stuff only slightly.

Chess Board

Stitch a chess board cover (Plate 45) like a pillow cover and block. Make each square 18 mesh by 18 mesh when stitching on Penelope 10. (If you measure a real chess board, it comes out so that each square is 17 x 17 mesh.) If you plan to use decorative stitches for the squares this will make it easier to do half of a motif when necessary. Most of the stitches cover 2, 3, 4, or 6 mesh per motif and fit into an 18-mesh square more easily. Sew a backing fabric (page 101) around three sides and two square corners as in Figure 3-16a. Remember to machine stitch between the two rows of the Continental Stitch and your needlepoint design as described on page 100. Trim the corners to eliminate bulk (Figure 3-16b). Zig-zag all raw edges together, except at the opening; zig-zag those separately. Turn.

Cut a piece of masonite 3/16″ smaller than your finished needlepoint. For example, if your needlepoint is 17″ × 17″, cut the masonite 16-13/16″ × 16-13/16″. Glue a piece of 1″ foam rubber to one side of the masonite, and cover it with a piece of lightweight fabric. It should look like the one in Figure 3-24, except the corners of the foam should not be pulled down so tightly by the fabric.

Slide this masonite into the cover you have just made. The foam rubber should be next to the fabric, not the needlepoint. If you have trouble getting the foam rubber to slide in, insert a piece of waxed paper as a lubricant. Remove it when the masonite is in place.

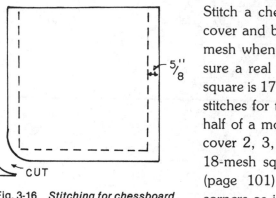

Fig. 3-16   *Stitching for chessboard*

Turn the edge of the fabric under and blind-stitch it in place as described on page 106.

Scrapbook Cover

The scrapbook cover in Plate 12 is constructed basically like the chess board shown in Plate 45. There are some differences, however.

When you cut out the backing fabric, leave a 1-1/2″ seam allowance, instead of 5/8″ (Figure 3-17a), on one end. This extra fabric will become the hinge. Sew the fabric backing and the needlepoint together as in Figure 3-16, leaving the 1-1/2″ seam allowance at the opening.

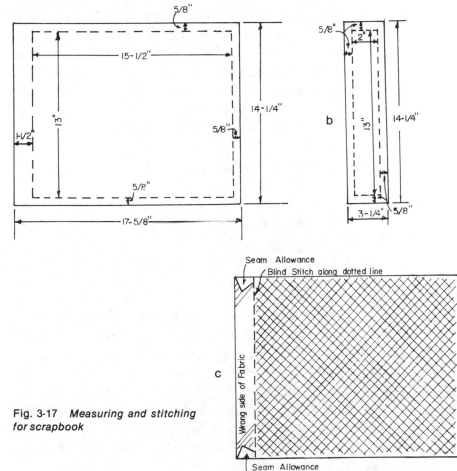

Fig. 3-17 *Measuring and stitching for scrapbook*

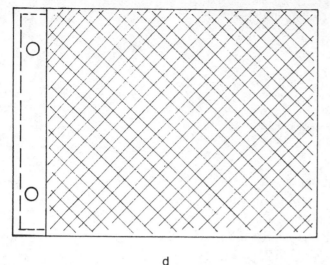

Fig. 3-17 (cont.)

d

Insert the masonite with the foam rubber side next to the needlepoint; this makes a padded cover. Use waxed paper to make it slide easier. Tuck the canvas (not the fabric, as before) in and blind-stitch it to the fabric (Figure 3-13). Leave the 1-1/2″ piece of fabric sticking out (Figure 3-17c).

Finish the 2″ x 13″ (Figure 3-17b) piece the same way as with the chess board. Tuck both raw edges in and blind-stitch. The only other difference is that it is all fabric.

Fold the seam allowance up as in Figure 3-17c. Glue them in place with Sobo glue; it is made especially for gluing fabrics.

Lay the long, skinny piece over the "hinge" (Figure 3-17d). Glue. Using a curved needle, stitch the outside edges of the "hinge" to the back of the long, skinny piece. This is for added durability. Repeat this process with the pieces for the back of the scrapbook.

Buy two screw-type binding posts from a stationery supply store (Figure 3-18). Drill two holes where these should go (Figure 3-17d)—right through the fabric, foam rubber, and masonite. Put a dab of Sobo glue around the raw edges of the fabric.

Cut pages, 12″ × 16-1/2″, from a sturdy paper.

Fig. 3-18 *Binding post*

Also cut strips, 1–1/2″ × 12″, to put between the pages where the scrapbook is bound together. These strips keep your scrapbook from bulging when it is filled.

Punch holes in the pages and the strips. Bind the scrapbook together with the binding posts.

Two-step Edge Finishing

Two-step edge finishing is a dandy method I use to finish projects that stand alone (without frames or backing). Belts (Plate 21), eyeglass cases (Plates 19, 21, and 43), needlebooks (Plates 28 and 29), brick doorstops (Plate 13), scissors cases, checkbook covers, and book covers use this method.

Two-step edge finishing leaves no raw edge of canvas with which you must contend. It also sews a seam as it finishes, if you so desire.

When planning a project, note that you only need five or six mesh all the way around beyond your design. Use five mesh for Penelope canvas and six for Regular and Interlock Mono canvas (Figures 3–19a and b).

Fig. 3-19a *Finding mesh (Penelope canvas) for Binding Stitch*

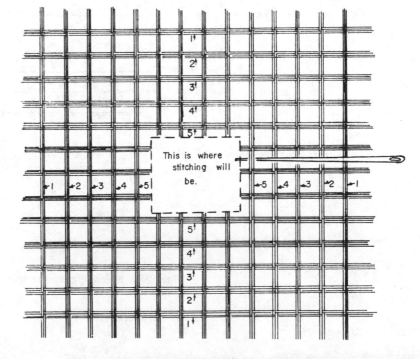

This is where stitching will be.

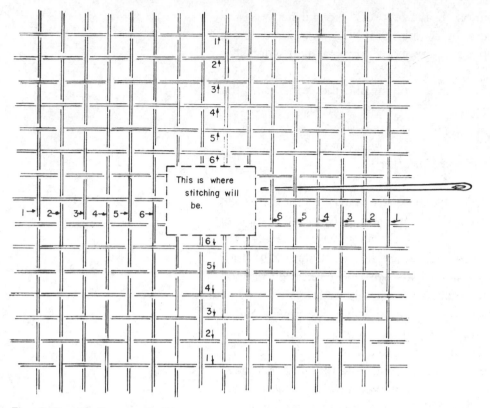

This is where stitching will be.

Fig. 3-19b *Finding mesh (Mono canvas) for Binding Stitch*

Fig. 3-19c *Folding canvas, leaving mesh for Binding Stitch at edge*

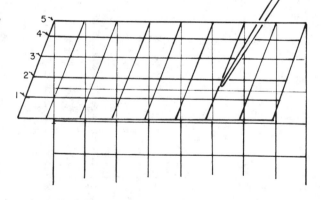

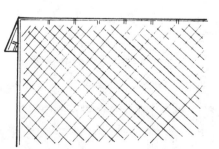

Fig. 3-19d *Stitch right up to edge*

Put your design on the canvas. Before you take even one stitch, turn four mesh under and leave the fifth (or fifth and sixth on Mono canvas) on the edge. Match the mesh up perfectly and baste in place. The common error is leaving two mesh on the edge when using Penelope canvas. This makes a Binding Stitch that is too thick.

Double-check yourself by inserting the needle under the fifth mesh (or the fifth and sixth) when the canvas is flat. Then turn the four mesh under. The needle will automatically keep the correct mesh on the edge (Figures 3-19b and c). Baste, being very careful not to let the canvas slip.

At the corners there will be four layers of canvas. Stitch through all of them as best you can. It really isn't as bad as it sounds. Do not cut the canvas. Hard wear will cause these corners to ravel if you cut them.

Work your needlepoint stitches through both thicknesses, just as if they were one. Stitch right up to that mesh (or two mesh on Mono) that is on the edge (Figure 3-19d).

Block, following the directions for blocking with no margin of blank canvas (page 83). When the needlepoint is thoroughly dry, remove it from the blocking board. Allow it to sit overnight if you have used stitches that distort the canvas. The piece will lose its shape overnight if it is going to. If it does go out of shape, apply rabbit-skin glue (page 88) at this point.

Next, stitch the Binding Stitch on the blank mesh (see page 265).

BELT

The belt in Plate 21 is made by the two-step edge finishing technique. It is fastened with very large hooks and eyes.

It is lined with double-knit, which is attached with Stitch Witchery or Polyweb (these are fabric bonding agents that fuse two fabrics together with an iron). Complete directions accompany the products, which may be bought in fabric stores. This technique cannot be used on needlepoint that has textured stitches; the iron will crush them. In this case, line the item with any suitable fabric. Attach it by turning the raw edges under 5/8" and stitching it in place with the Blind Stitch (Figure 3-13). Use this method if Stitch Witchery is not available to you.

Double-knit is good because it does not ravel, thus eliminating the need to turn under the raw edges. This eliminates some bulk.

Work the Binding Stitch around the edge (page 265). Catch the lining with the Binding Stitch. This makes for a neater finish. There is then no break between the lining and the Binding Stitch.

If you would like a buckle on your needlepoint belt, buy it first. Plan the width of your belt to fit the buckle. Allow for the bulk of the Binding Stitch. Stitch it just the same way as the one in Plate 21. Insert the ends into the buckle. Hand-stitch them securely to the back of the belt. Line.

EYEGLASS CASE

Measure the glasses that will be kept in the needle-point case (Plates 19, 21, and 43). Glasses come in too many shapes these days to guess at the size. Allow 1/2" ease. If your glasses measure 3" x 6", make the cases 3-1/2" × 6-1/2".

Leave a blank mesh (Penelope canvas) or two (Mono canvas) for the Binding Stitch. This makes a more crisp fold (Figure 3-20).

Line the same way the belt is lined—only cut the lining at the fold line of the canvas. Trim away 1/8". This keeps the fold from being bulky.

Stitch the Binding Stitch, sewing the seam as you go (page 265). Trim those edges that are not a seam with the Binding Stitch, too, for a finished look.

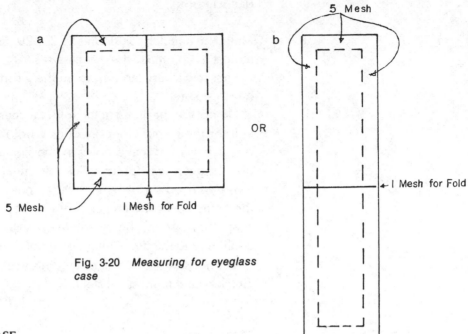

a

b

OR

5 Mesh

I Mesh for Fold

5 Mesh

I Mesh for Fold

Fig. 3-20 *Measuring for eyeglass case*

SCISSORS CASE

A scissors case is made the same way as an eyeglass case—with one exception. The canvas will have to be cut so that one or more seams are not on the straight grain. This makes the needlepoint stitching more difficult, but not impossible (see Figure 3-21).

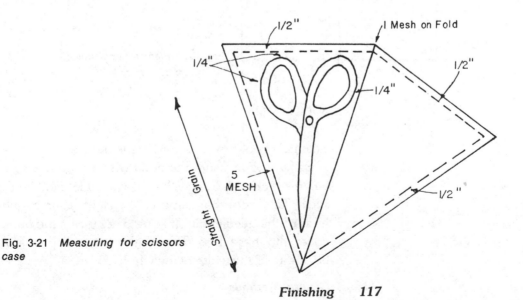

1/2"

I Mesh on Fold

1/4"

1/2"

1/4"

5 MESH

1/2"

Straight Grain

1/2"

Fig. 3-21 *Measuring for scissors case*

NEEDLEBOOK

Make the needlebook (Plates 9, 28, 29, and 39 to 41) almost as you make the eyeglass case.

First sew a very large snap on the wrong side of the needlepoint.

Do not cut the lining at the fold. Always use double-knit for the lining. Not only does it not ravel, but the needles will not leave holes in the lining when they are removed (except for quickpoint needles). Attach it as described on page 115. Next make a tiny slit in the lining, over the center of the snap. This lets the snap through so the needlebook will close. (You could not do this if the lining were not double-knit.)

Do not sew the two sides together with the Binding Stitch—bind them separately.

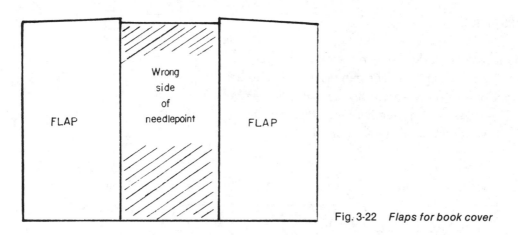

Fig. 3-22 *Flaps for book cover*

BOOK COVER

Stitch the book cover as you do the needlebook.

Be sure to measure the book with a tape measure when it is **closed**. Line with light-weight fabric. Hand-stitch flaps from that same light-weight fabric to the ends of the needlepoint (Figure 3-22). Slip the book cover into these flaps. The width of each flap should be one-third the width of the whole cover.

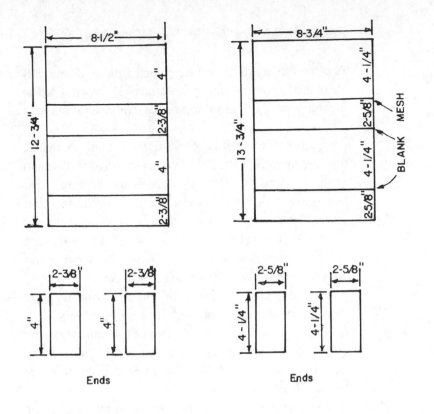

BRICK   NEEDLEPOINT

Fig. 3-23 *Measuring for brick door-stop*

BRICK DOORSTOP

Plate 13 shows an attractive brick doorstop. It, too, is worked with the two-step edge finishing technique. It is in three pieces (Figure 3-23).

It is **imperative** that you allow for the bulk of the yarn between the canvas and the brick. You **must** make the needlepoint **bigger**. If your brick measures 12-3/4" x 8-1/2" (as in Figure 3-23a), then your needlepoint must measure 13-3/4" x 8-3/4" (as in Figure 3-23b).

Leave a blank mesh on the fold lines. Work the Binding Stitch here for a sharp fold. Join all the pieces with a Binding Stitch. Insert the brick before you bind on the last end piece.

Finishing **119**

Pencil Holder or Table-Top Wastebasket

A table-top wastebasket or pencil holder (Plate 30) combines two finishing techniques: (1) two-step edge finishing and (2) overlapping of canvas to make a circle.

Use an empty coffee can (or soup can). Measure the height of the can. Add five (or six on Mono) mesh at the top and five (or six) more at the bottom. Add two more mesh; these will cover the plastic top that you will put on the bottom of the can to protect your furniture. (Do not do this for the soup can.) Measure the circumference of the can. Add 6″ to cover the bulk of the yarn and the seam allowance.

Turn four mesh under at the top and bottom; leave the fifth (or fifth and sixth on Mono canvas) (page 114) on the edge. Tape the raw edges of the canvas on the ends. Mark your canvas so that you will have 3″ of margin on either end. Work the needlepoint to these two lines. Block.

When it is dry, wrap the needlepoint around the can so that it fits snugly. Overlap the margins of blank canvas. Match the mesh. Loosen it one mesh and pin. Trim the canvas so that it overlaps 2″. Then baste, matching the mesh. Stitch through both thicknesses of canvas as if they were one. Be very careful that the ends of the canvas do not stick out between the stitches.

Work the Binding Stitch around the top and bottom of the piece.

Merely slip the needlepoint over the can. It needs no glue or anything else to hold it in place.

Bookends

Bookends (Figure 2-21) combine two techniques, also: (1) two-step edge finishing and (2) machine-stitching.

These bookend covers slip over the ugly grey metal bookends that stationery supply stores sell.

Use the two-step edge finishing along the bottom edge (page 113).

Machine-stitch a lining around the other three edges as you did for the chess board. Hem the lining at the bottom.

Insert cording, tack on a twisted cord (page 102), or leave it plain (Figure 2-21).

Simply slip the cover over the bookend.

Box Top

A box top (Plates 2 and 3) is finished by wrapping your needlepoint around a piece of masonite that has foam rubber on it (Figure 3#24). (See page 110 for more complete instructions.) Staple in place—as you did a picture on a stretcher frame.

Fig. 3-24a *To attach needlepoint box top, start with box with deep lid; cover a piece of masonite with foam rubber and lightweight fabric*

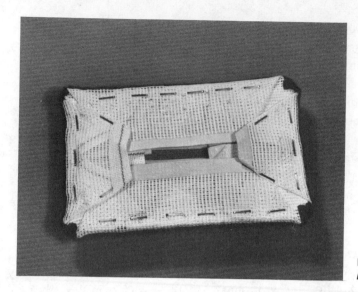

Fig. 3-24b *Place needlepoint on box lid as in Fig. 3-6n through 3-6q*

Make or purchase a wooden box with a lid that will allow the needlepoint to be inserted from inside. The masonite should be about 1/4" smaller than the lid. For example, if the lid is 4" x 6" (inside dimensions), cut the masonite 3-3/4" x 5-3/4". Insert the needlepoint into the lid from the back. Replace the back of the box top that should have come with your box.

Line the box with velvet or velveteen. Cut pieces of cardboard that are slightly smaller than the sides, bottom, and top of the box. Using Stitch Witchery, fuse your lining fabric to the cardboard and miter the corners as shown in Figure 3-25.

Fit the pieces into the box. Glue them in place.

Cut a piece of felt slightly smaller than the box and glue it to the bottom. Or cut circles of felt and glue one in each corner.

Wooden Pincushion

Wooden napkin rings make attractive pincushions (Plate 31 and Figures 2-19 and 2-20). Push the needlepoint into the hole from the back. Make a slight poof. Staple or glue into place. Insert a layer of

a

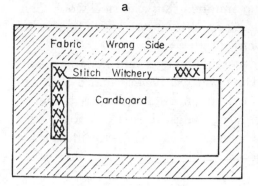

Fabric   Wrong Side

Stitch Witchery

Cardboard

b

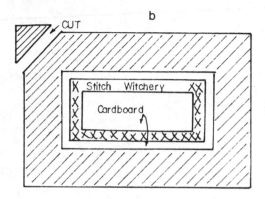

CUT

Stitch Witchery

Cardboard

c

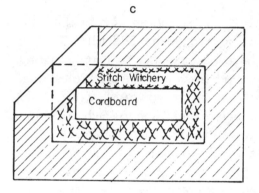

Stitch Witchery

Cardboard

d

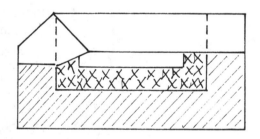

e

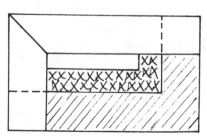

f

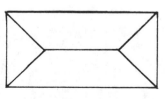

Fig. 3-25   *Lining for box*

polyester batting and then stuff with steel wool. Glue a felt backing in place. Weight down with books and allow to dry overnight.

Screw in a decorative hanger and hang in a convenient spot. Now you will have within easy reach that one pin you so often need and never bother to get out of the sewing things. (It is at this point that I used to ruin whatever I was doing—for the lack of one pin. No more!)

Upholstered Items

Upholstered items should always be worked on Penelope canvas for strength and durability.

Unless you have had experience in upholstering furniture, I would advise you to have a professional mount your needlepoint for you. Also, you should consult with him before you begin to stitch. Take the piece of furniture you wish to cover to him. Ask him to make you a **muslin** pattern—not paper. Paper does not go around curves well and precision is lost.

Trace this pattern onto your canvas. Allow a 3″ margin of blank canvas.

Take your needlepoint to the upholsterer **after** you have blocked it.

FINISHING TECHNIQUE FOR PLASTIC CANVAS

Plastic canvas simplifies finishing. There are no raw edges to ravel. It can be cut into any shape you want. There is no blocking involved, either. Simply work the Binding Stitch around the edge and you are finished.

Linings must be sewn by hand, however—unless

you would like to melt the canvas by ironing on a lining!

Plates 4, 8, 14 to 16, 22 to 25, and Figures 2-16, 2-22, and 2-23 show what an assortment of items can be made on plastic.

Key Chain

The key chain in Plates 15 and 16 is made of plastic squares bound together with the Binding Stitch. For the lining cut a long piece of light-weight fabric that is twice the length of your key chain, plus 1-1/2″ seam allowances. Fold 3/4″ down at the two narrow ends (Figure 3-26a). Press. On the side without the raw edges, stitch Velcro on the top and bottom through both thicknesses of fabric (Figure 3-26b). Leave room for a 1/2″ seam allowance. Press the Velcro together; stitch down the sides (dotted line in Figure 3-26c), leaving a 1/2″ seam allowance.

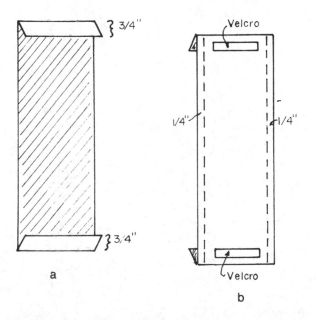

Fig. 3-26 *Making lining for key case*

Blind-stitch the lining to the tops of the key chain. Work the Binding Stitch, attaching the hardware as you go.

A key chain made in this way can be filled with change for the parking meter. When you toss your keys into your purse, they won't sink to the bottom!

The key chain in Plate 16 is made of one plastic square, cut in half; the pieces are bound together with the Binding Stitch. There is no lining.

Part One has guided you from the basic preparations through your choice of a design, to the last detail of the finishing of your needlepoint project.

Part Two will show you how to create each stitch— simply, cleanly, and effectively.

2 THE STITCHES

HOW TO READ THE DIAGRAMS

Before you even start to stitch, you will need to know the definition of the symbols used in the drawings.

⟨J⟩ shows the location of the beginning of the stitch. In stitches that are done in steps, the starts are identified by ⟨J⟩1, ⟨J⟩A, ⟨J⟩a, ⟨J⟩AA, and ⟨J⟩aa, in that order.

Arrows alone indicate a row change with no turning of the canvas. Arrows accompanied by a clock show a turning of the canvas:

T🕒 means, "Turn 90° to the right."

T🕕 means, "Turn 180°."

T🕘 means, "Turn 90° to the left."

Where it would complicate things, these arrows and clocks have been omitted. However, you can still tell where to turn the canvas. Simply turn the book so that the numbers are upright. Turn your canvas the same way and stitch.

When several stitches go into the same hole, the numbers have been omitted because there simply is not room for all of them. (See the Eye Stitches, pages 307-18.)

The numbering has been arranged so that the best backing is created. Economical yarn usually creates a poor backing. This poor backing reduces the durability of needlepoint.

A change of color is indicated by darkening the stitches, but the use of a second color is not absolutely necessary. This darkening also helps you to see the next row more clearly. Other colors (third, fourth, etc.) are indicated by different designs within each stitch. When working with two colors that cross each other, put the darker color on the bottom. Work the lighter colors last.

The canvas pictured is the canvas used for the particular stitch. Generally, all stitches can be worked on Penelope canvas; Regular Mono canvas does have some restrictions on types of stitches that can be used. These have been pictured on Penelope canvas. (These restrictions do not exist on Interlock Mono canvas.) The rest of the stitches have been drawn on Mono canvas for simplicity and clarity. See also page 175.

FOUR:

Straight Stitches

Straight Stitches are those stitches that cover the canvas vertically or horizontally. A vertical stitch covers two to six horizontal mesh and lies entirely between two vertical mesh. A horizontal stitch covers two to six vertical mesh, and lies entirely between two horizontal mesh.

A single strand of both tapestry and Persian yarn, when worked in Straight Stitches, covers Mono 14 canvas well. On Penelope or Mono 10 or 12 you will have to thicken your yarn.

Straight Stitches make beautiful patterns, and make a good background (as a rule). They work up quickly and can give a good backing if you plan on it.

Most of the Straight Stitches depend on color for their splendor. (See pages 62-64.)

Straight Stitches do not distort the canvas when you stitch. I recommend Straight Stitches for beginners.

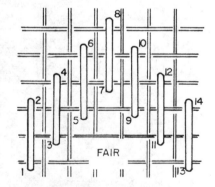

Making good backing

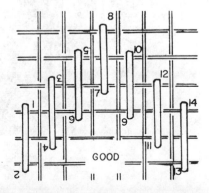

132   *The Stitches*

Key to Sampler Stitches

1. Straight Gobelin
2. Split Gobelin
3. Renaissance
4. Interlocking Gobelin
5. Brick
6. Horizontal Brick
7. Padded Brick
8. Hungarian
9. Giant Brick
10. Double Brick
11. Parisian
12. Giant Horizontal Parisian
13. Parisian Stripe
14. Double Parisian
15. Pavillion
16. Tied Pavillion
17. Horizontal Hungarian
18. Hungarian Ground
19. Double Hungarian
20. Pavillion Diamonds
21. Old Florentine
22. Horizontal Old Florentine
23. Beaty
24. Willow
25. Wicker
26. Omega
27. Horizontal Milanese
28. Vertical Milanese
29. Upright Oriental
30. Darning
31. Pattern Darning
32. Diagonal "L"
33. Roman II
34. Roman III
35. Lazy Roman II
36. Lazy Roman III
37. Gingham
38. Framed Pavillion
39. Patterned Threes
40. Pavillion Steps
41. Pavillion Boxes
42. Jacquard Palace Pattern
43. Darmstadt
44. Jo-Jo
45. Sutherland
46. Frame
47. Palace Pattern
48. Bargello Line Pattern
49. Bargello Framework
     Pattern
50. Indian Stripe
51. Split Bargello
52. Triangle Variation
53. Victorian Step
54. Princess Stitch
55. F-106
56. Woven Ribbons
57. Triangle
58. Triangle Color Variation
59. Four-Way Bargello

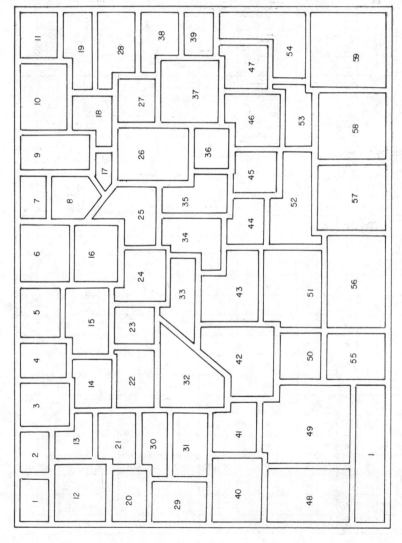

STRAIGHT STITCHES

	Border	Good Backing	Poor Backing	Background	Design	Accent	Fast	Slow	Geometric Pattern	Shading	Yarn Hog	Snags	Snag-Proof	Little Texture	Medium Texture	High Relief	Flower Stitch	Weak Pattern	Medium Pattern	Strong Pattern	Distorts Canvas
Straight Gobelin	•	•		•	•				•				•	•				•			
Renaissance		•		•	•				•				•		•			•			
Split Gobelin		•		•	•			•		•	•		•	•				•			
Inter. Str. Gobelin		•		•	•			•		•				•				•			
Brick		•		•	•				•	•			•	•				•			
Padded Brick		•		•	•				•	•				•	•			•			
Giant Brick		•		•	•		•		•	•		•		•					•		
Double Brick		•		•	•		•		•					•					•		
Horizontal Brick		•		•	•		•		•	•		•		•					•		
Parisian		•		•	•		•		•	•				•					•		
Double Parisian		•		•	•		•		•					•					•		
Giant Horiz. Par.		•		•	•		•		•	•		•		•					•		
Parisian Stripe		•		•	•				•					•				•			
Pavillion	•	•		•	•		•		•					•					•		
Hungarian	•	•		•	•	•	•		•					•					•		
Horiz. Hungarian	•	•		•	•	•	•		•					•					•		
Hungarian Ground		•		•	•		•		•					•					•		
Double Hungarian		•		•	•	•	•		•			•		•					•		
Pavillion Diamonds	•	•		•	•	•	•		•			•		•						•	
Tied Pavillion	•	•		•	•	•	•		•			•		•						•	
Old Florentine		•		•	•		•		•			•		•					•		
Horiz. Old Flor.		•		•	•		•		•			•		•					•		
Beaty	•	•		•	•		•		•			•		•					•		
Willow		•		•	•		•		•			•		•					•		
Wicker		•		•			•		•			•		•					•		
Omega		•		•					•			•		•					•		
Horizontal Milanese		•		•	•	•	•		•			•		•						•	
Vertical Milanese		•		•	•	•	•		•			•		•						•	
Upright Oriental		•		•	•		•		•			•		•						•	
Darning Stitch		•			•	•		•			•	•			•				•		
Pattern Darning		•			•	•		•				•		•				•			

STRAIGHT STITCHES (cont.)	Border	Good Backing	Poor Backing	Background	Design	Accent	Fast	Slow	Geometric Pattern	Shading	Yarn Hog	Snags	Snag-Proof	Little Texture	Medium Texture	High Relief	Flower Stitch	Weak Pattern	Medium Pattern	Strong Pattern	Distorts Canvas
Diagonal L		•		•	•		•		•			•		•						•	
Roman II		•		•	•		•		•					•					•		
Lazy Roman II		•		•	•		•		•					•					•		
Roman III		•		•	•		•		•					•					•		
Lazy Roman III		•		•	•		•		•					•					•		
Gingham		•		•	•				•					•					•		
Patterned Threes		•		•	•				•					•					•		
Framed Pavillion		•		•	•	•	•		•			•		•					•		
Pavillion Steps		•		•	•		•		•	•		•		•						•	
Pavillion Boxes		•		•	•		•		•			•		•						•	
Jacq. Palace Pat.		•		•					•			•		•						•	
Darmstadt Pattern		•		•	•	•	•		•			•		•						•	
Jo-Jo		•		•	•	•	•		•			•		•						•	
Sutherland		•		•	•	•	•		•			•		•						•	
Frame		•		•	•	•	•		•	•		•		•						•	
Palace Pattern		•		•	•				•			•		•						•	
Princess	•	•		•	•				•			•		•						•	
Indian Stripe	•	•		•	•	•	•		•			•		•						•	
Victorian Step		•		•	•				•					•					•		
Triangle	•	•		•	•	•			•			•		•						•	
Triangle Color Var.	•	•		•	•	•		•	•			•		•						•	
Triangle Variation	•	•		•	•	•			•			•		•						•	
F-106	•	•		•	•	•	•		•			•		•						•	
Woven Ribbons		•		•		•			•			•		•						•	
Bargello Line Pat.		•		•	•	•			•	•		•		•						•	
Split Bargello		•		•	•			•	•	•	•	•		•					•		
Bargello F'work Pat.		•		•	•		•		•	•		•		•						•	
Four-Way Bargello		•		•	•		•		•	•		•		•			•			•	

STRAIGHT GOBELIN

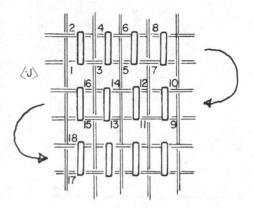

RENAISSANCE

The Renaissance Stitch is straight Gobelin over a tramé of one ply of Persian yarn or two ply of tapestry yarn. This gives subtle texture.

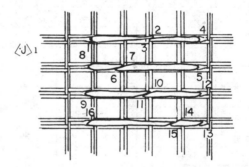

a

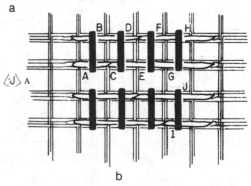

b

This stitch is based on embroidery's Split Stitch. It is particularly good for shading. Work this stitch over two to five mesh.

SPLIT GOBELIN

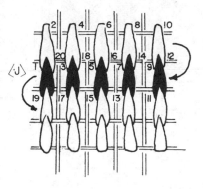

This Gobelin Stitch, too, may be worked over two to five mesh. Thicken your yarn if your stitch is over two mesh tall. It is particularly good for shading.

INTERLOCKING STRAIGHT GOBELIN

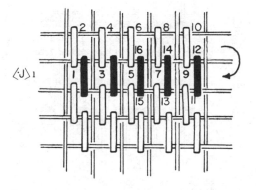

BRICK

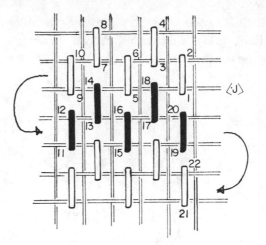

PADDED BRICK

This stitch has horizontal tramé like Renaissance which gives it a subtle texture.

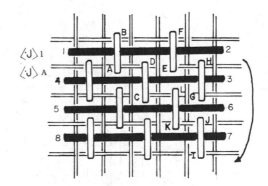

This stitch may be worked over four or six with an even step. (See page 175.)

GIANT BRICK

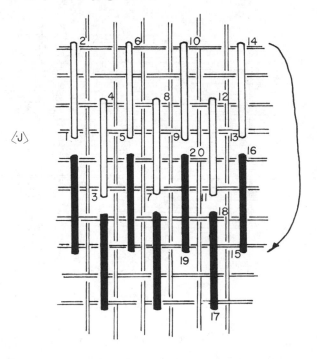

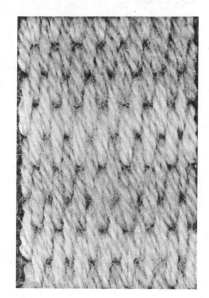

DOUBLE BRICK

HORIZONTAL BRICK

This stitch can be worked over two or four mesh.

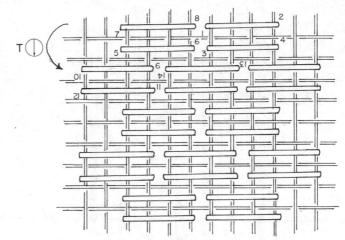

PARISIAN

Parisian is a combination of long and short stitches (over two and four mesh). The tall stitches are over the short ones.

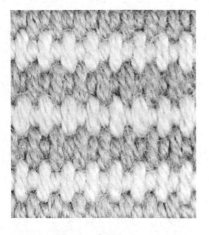

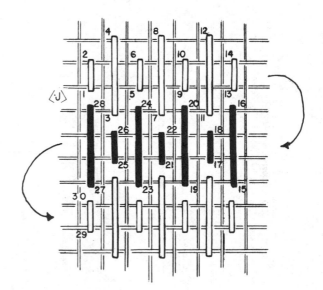

This may be worked small (2:2:4:4:2:2:4:4, etc.) as in the photograph or large (4:4:6:6:4:4:6:6, etc.).

DOUBLE PARISIAN

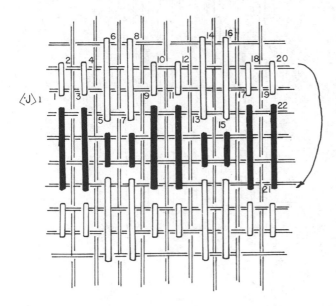

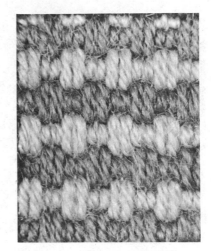

GIANT HORIZONTAL PARISIAN

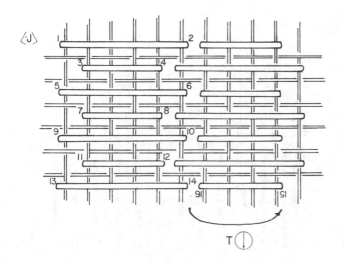

PARISIAN
STRIPE

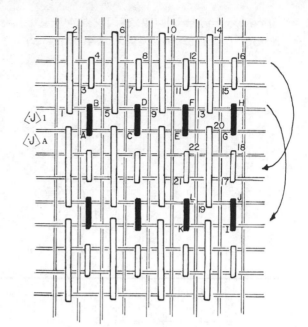

PAVILLION

The diamonds share the short stitch.

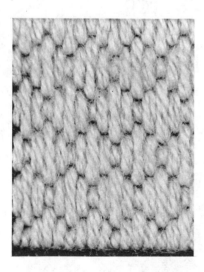

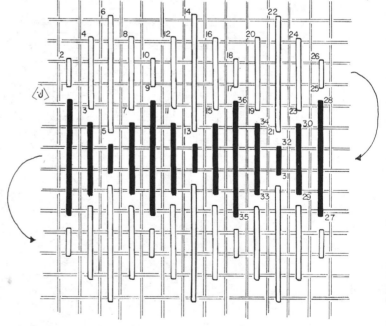

This vertical stitch establishes a diamond pattern. It is good in two colors, although it is stunning in one color. It is a set of three stitches—2:4:2. Skip a space. Repeat 2:4:2. Skip a space under the long stitch. Continue the pattern—2:4:2, then skip, then 2:4:2, etc.

HUNGARIAN

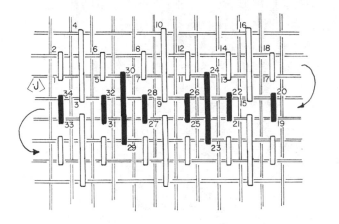

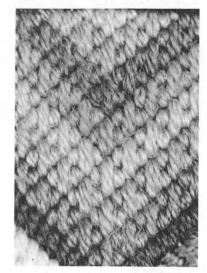

HORIZONTAL HUNGARIAN

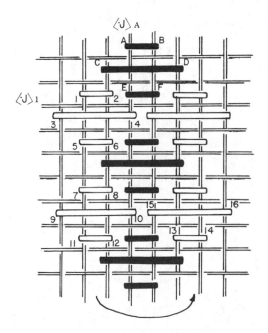

HUNGARIAN
GROUND

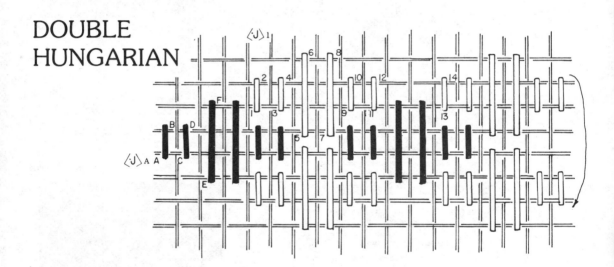

DOUBLE
HUNGARIAN

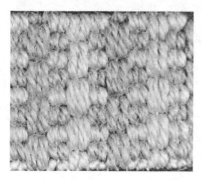

This stitch is a larger version of the Hungarian Stitch.

PAVILLION DIAMONDS

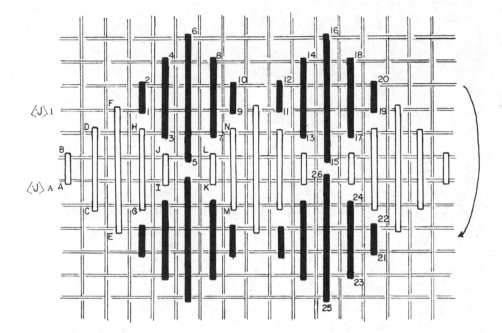

TIED PAVILLION

The long stitches need to be pulled slightly tighter than short ones. The tie is over two mesh. Back-stitch in between the diamonds to cover the canvas if necessary.

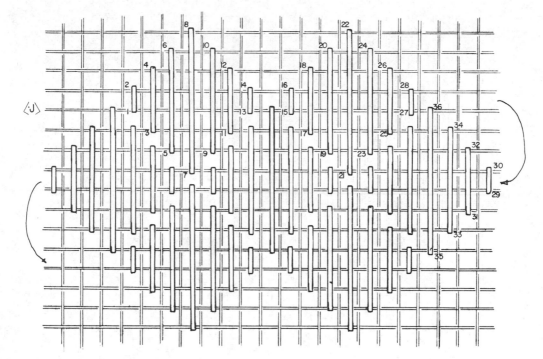

a

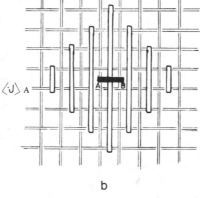

b

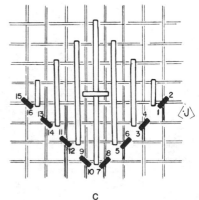

c

Short:long:short. The short stitch over the long. The smallest version is 2:6:2, the largest is 3:9:3.

OLD FLORENTINE

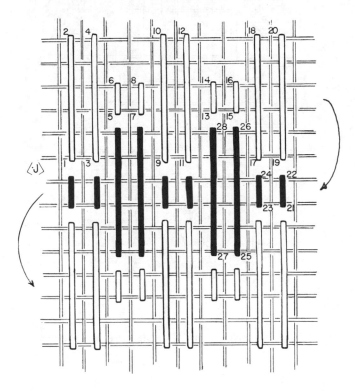

When all the short stitches are worked in a second color, the stitch resembles a woven basket.

HORIZONTAL OLD FLORENTINE

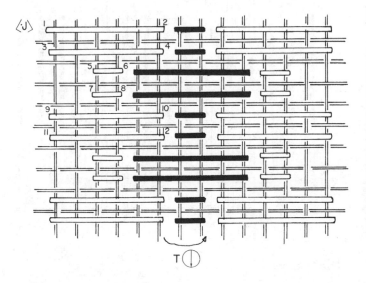

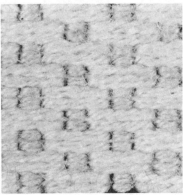

BEATY

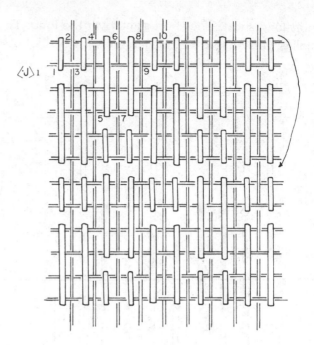

WILLOW

This is like Old Florentine except there are three sets of stitches, 2:6:2.

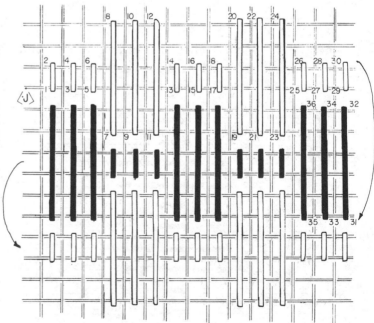

As the name suggests, this two-color stitch resembles wicker. It will look different if you use three colors. Make other color variations by stitching in diagonal stripes and horizontal stripes of color.

WICKER

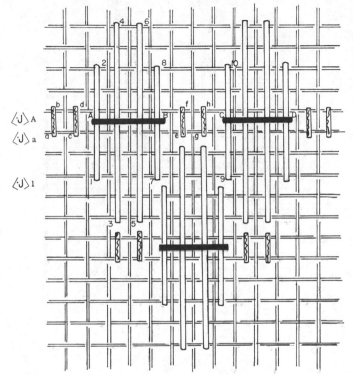

OMEGA

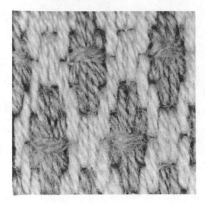

HORIZONTAL
MILANESE

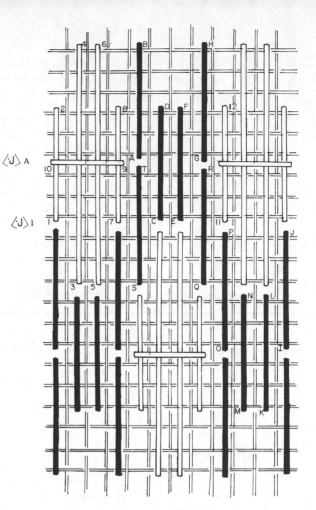

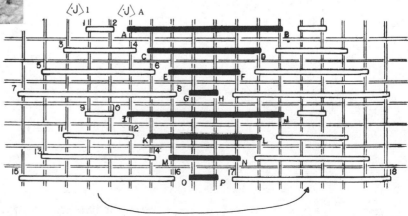

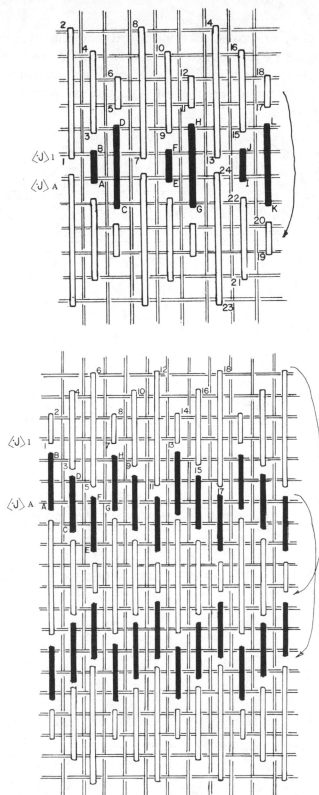

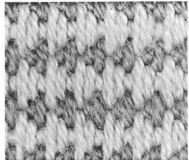

VERTICAL
MILANESE

UPRIGHT
ORIENTAL

DARNING STITCH

Make four trips across Penelope 10 and only two on Mono 14 to produce this thickly padded stitch. It makes a good sidewalk, wall, or other solid area. Vary the number of mesh that you go over and under.

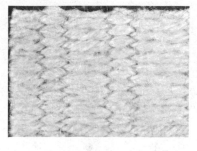

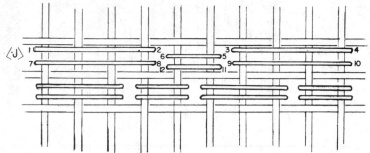

PATTERN DARNING

This fills an area that is similar to the Darning Stitch, except that it is not padded. It, too, can be worked in a varying pattern. The stitch gives a bumpy look. In shorter stitches, it could look like gravel.

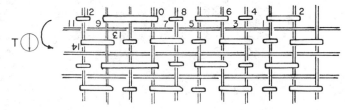

DIAGONAL "L"

ROMAN II

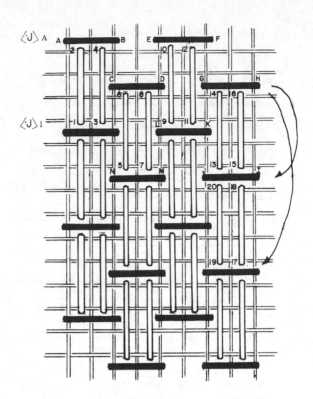

LAZY ROMAN II

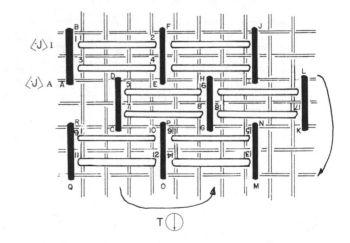

ROMAN III

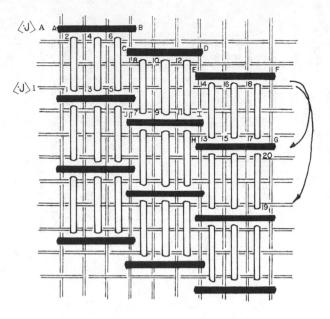

LAZY ROMAN III

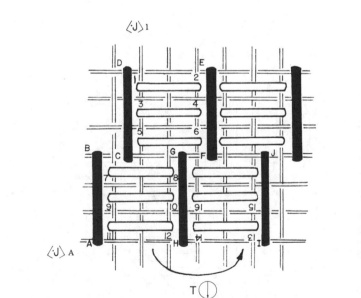

GINGHAM

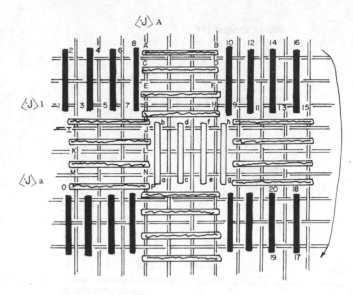

PATTERNED
THREES

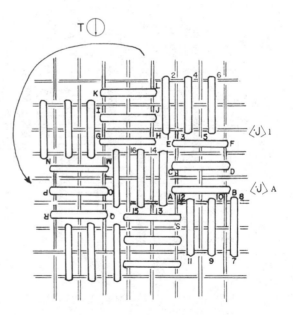

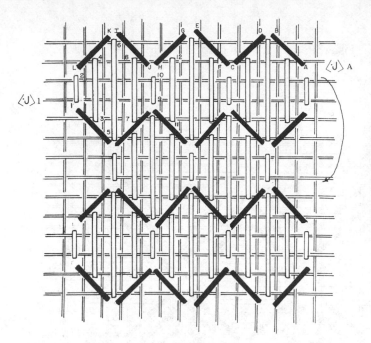

FRAMED PAVILLION

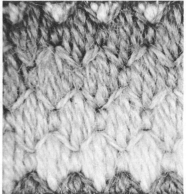

Always use three colors. This stitch resembles prisms.

PAVILLION STEPS

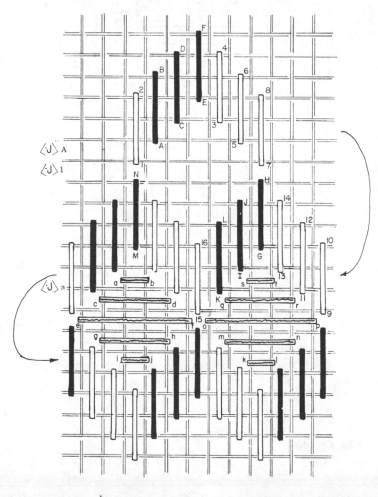

157

PAVILLION BOXES

Use thin yarn for the diagonal stripes.

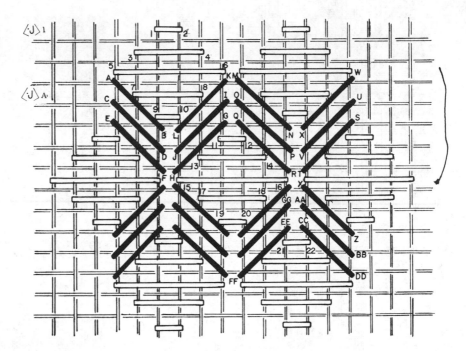

Use thin yarn for the Frame Stitch.

JACQUARD PALACE PATTERN

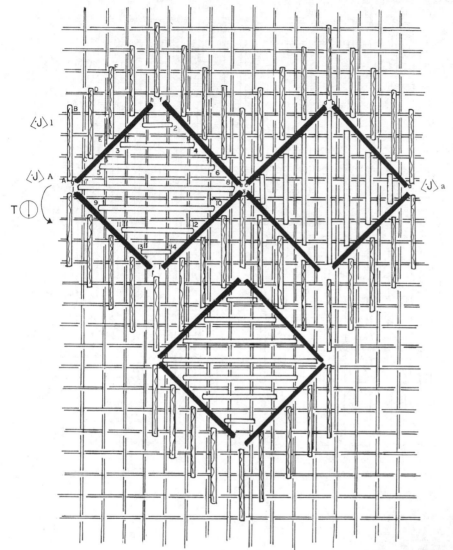

DARMSTADT PATTERN

This stitch makes good butterfly or insect wings.

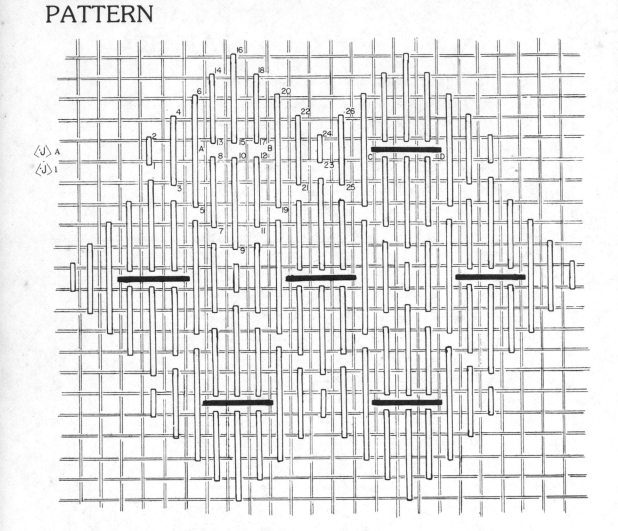

The stitches used in the following projects
are identified in the Appendix.

Plate 1. Color wheel (author)

Plate 2. Flowered box top
(Charlotte Lahti)

Plate 3. Monogrammed box top
(Ruth Deary)

Plate 4. Christmas tree ornament,
on plastic: snowman (author)

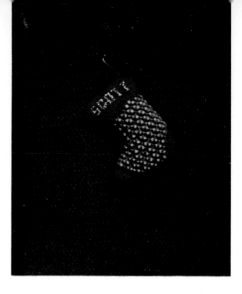

Plate 5. Christmas tree ornament:
stocking (Jackie Beaty)

Plate 6. Christmas tree ornament:
bell (author)

Plate 7. Christmas tree ornament:
Santa (author)

Plate 8. Christmas tree ornament,
on plastic: Christmas tree (author)

Plate 9. Owl needle book
(Nyla Christensen)

Plate 11. Lady in historic costume
(Dody Maki)
(Not in Appendix;
too complex to diagram)

Plate 10. Pillow insert
(Nyla Christensen)

Plate 12. Scrapbook
(author)

Plate 13. Brick door stop
(Jackie Beaty)

Plate 14. Key chain, on plastic:
front (author)

Plate 15. Key chain, on plastic:
back (author)

Plate 16. Key chain, on plastic:
flower (author)

Plates 17 & 18. Pincushion
& detail (Dody Maki)

Plate 19. Eyeglass case
(Jackie Beaty)

Plate 20. Eyeglass case
with twisted cord
(Pat Dolthorp)

Plate 21. Belt and eyeglass case
(Dody Maki)

Plate 24. Boy in bed, on plastic
(author)

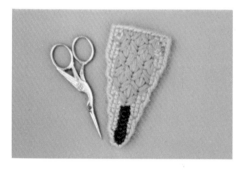

Plate 22. Scissors case,
on plastic: summer (author)

Plate 23. Scissors case,
on plastic: winter (author)

Plate 25. Girl in bed, on plastic
(Jackie Beaty)

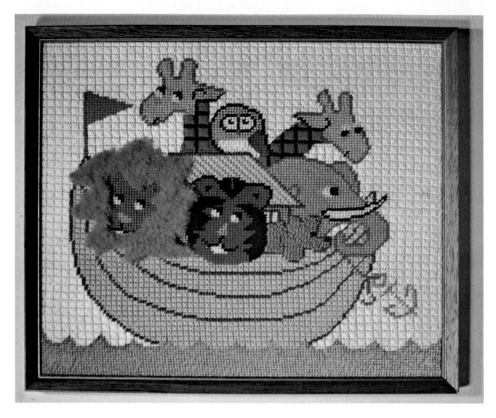

Plate 26. Noah's Ark (Pat Dolthorp)
An elaboration of a Spinnerin needlepoint kit;
used by permission of the Spinnerin Company

Plate 27. Underwater scene (Liz Rockwell)
(Not in Appendix; too complex to diagram)

Plate 28. Needle book: front (author)

Plate 29. Needle book: back (author)

Plate 30. Pencil holder
(Liz Rockwell)
(Not in Appendix;
too complex to diagram)

Plate 31. Wooden pincushion: hen (author)

Plate 32.
Diagonal-stitch
sampler (author)
(See beginning
of Chapter 5
for diagram)

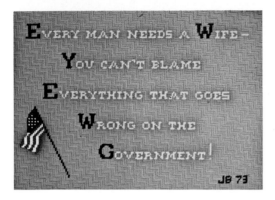

Plate 33. "Every man . . ."
(Jackie Beaty)

Plate 34. Eye-stitch sampler
(author) (See beginning of
Chapter 9 for diagram)

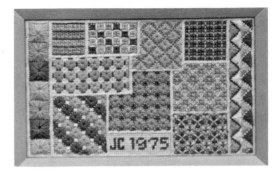

Plate 35. Stamp
(author) (Not in
Appendix; too
complex to diagram)

Plate 36. Tied-stitch sampler (author)
(See beginning of Chapter 8 for diagram)

Plate 37. Praying boy
(Jackie Beaty)

Plate 38. Cross-stitch
sampler (author)
(See beginning of
Chapter 7 for diagram)

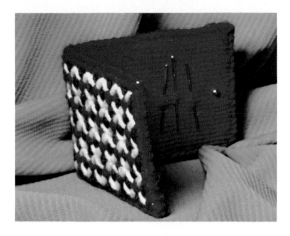

Plate 42. Bear pincushion
(Nyla Christensen)

Plate 43. Eyeglass case
(author)

Plates 39, 40, 41. Red,
white, and blue needle book,
front, back (author)

Plate 44. Free-style sampler (Liz Rockwell)
(Not in Appendix; too complex to diagram)

Plate 45. Chessboard (author)

Plate 46:
Detached-canvas
technique
(author)

Plate 47. Pillow with tassels
(Jackie Beaty)

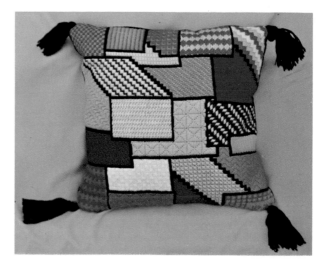

Plate 48. Planned sampler (Ruth Deary)
(Not in Appendix; too complex to diagram)

JO-JO

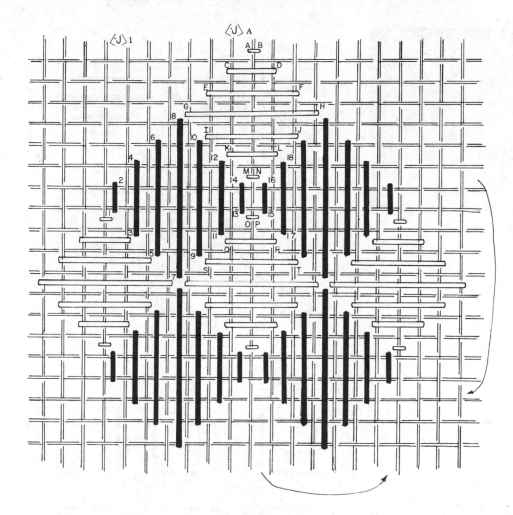

SUTHERLAND

You may want to thin your yarn. Note how color variations change the look of the stitch.

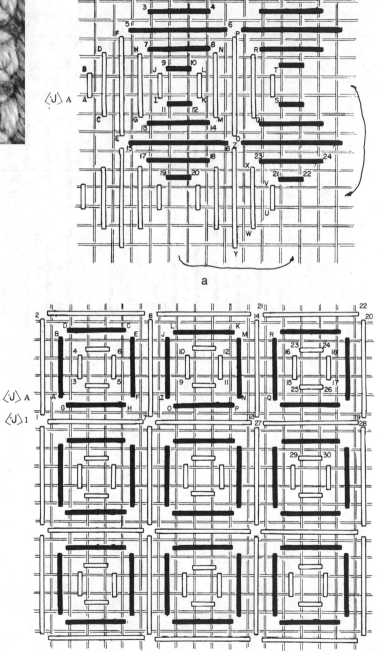

a

b

When working large stitches first, it is very easy to pull too tightly. Be careful. If, however, you wish to begin with the small stitches, watch the placement. It is not difficult to get them wrong. Work the dark shades in the center, the light on the outside.

FRAME

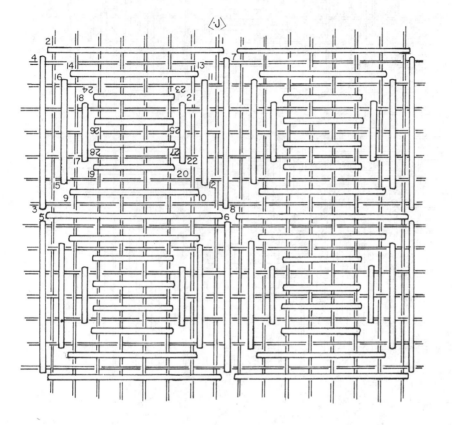

PALACE PATTERN

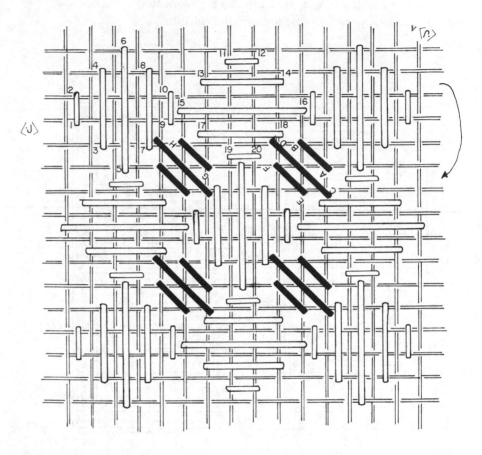

PRINCESS

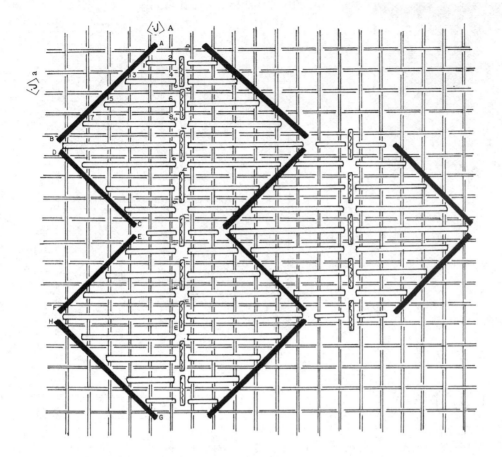

INDIAN STRIPE

This stitch is best as a single stripe; however, if you want to do a whole area in Indian Stripe Stitches, alternate the rows to make them fit.

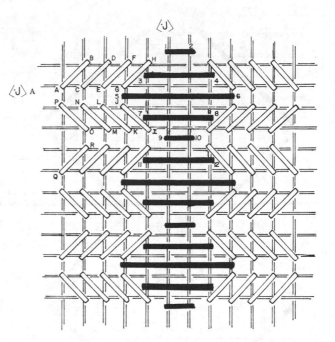

VICTORIAN STEP

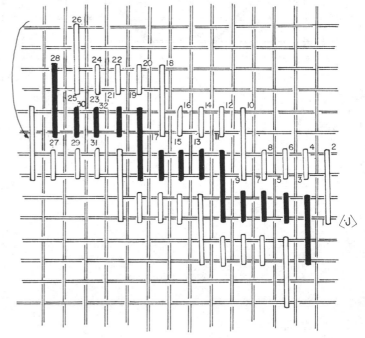

It does not matter whether you cross the right arm of a Cross-Stitch over the left, or the left over the right—as long as you are consistent. Keep this in mind when putting in the crosses.

TRIANGLE

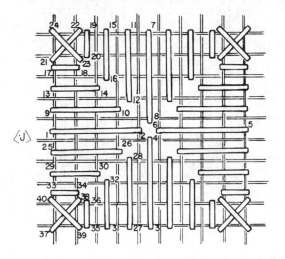

When doing two or more colors mixed up like this, the back cannot be super-neat. Avoid lumps. Always cross the Cross-Stitches consistently. (See Triangle Stitch.)

TRIANGLE COLOR VARIATION

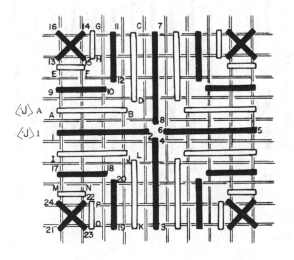

TRIANGLE VARIATION

Portions of this stitch can be used for a sail on a boat.

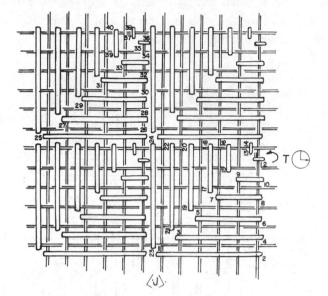

F-106

Various color combinations make this stitch look different.

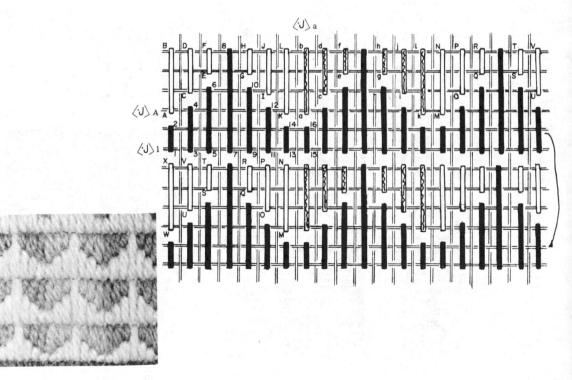

Work the compensating stitches last.

WOVEN
RIBBONS

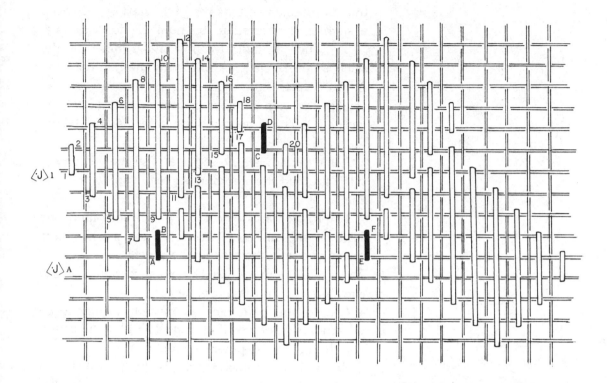

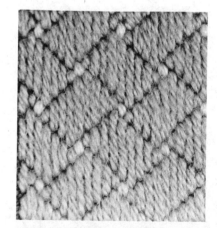

BARGELLO

Bargello is straight stitches worked in a geometric pattern. These stitches can vary in size from two mesh tall to six mesh tall. When stitches are placed next to each other in a zig-zag line, the distance between the **top** of one stitch and the **top** of the next one is called a step. It is referred to by number—for example, "4:2." The "4" indicates how many mesh tall the stitch is; the "2" tells us how many mesh in the step. A "4:2" stitch is the most common in Bargello. The smaller the step number is, the more gradual the incline (a). The larger the step number is, the steeper the incline (c).

A line pattern is a zig-zag line of stitches. Both the stitch size and the step number may vary within one line.

To produce arcs or curves, place more than one stitch on the same step (4:0). The more stitches there are on one step, the broader the curve (d).

These arcs or curves may be combined with a zig-zag line for a more interesting pattern.

A framework pattern can be made by turning a line pattern upside down. (See page 173.) Fill the center in with a secondary pattern of your choice.

Bargello has limitless variations, both in stitch and in color. There is much more to learn about Bargello. There are many other kinds of patterns. Refer to any of the many good books on Bargello that are listed in the bibliography.

Note: In working a whole piece in Bargello, start the pattern in the middle of the canvas to achieve balance.

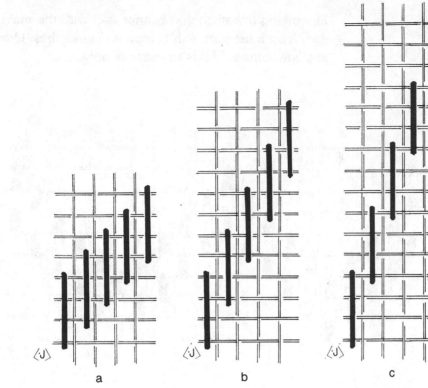

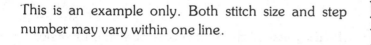

This is an example only. Both stitch size and step number may vary within one line.

BARGELLO LINE PATTERN

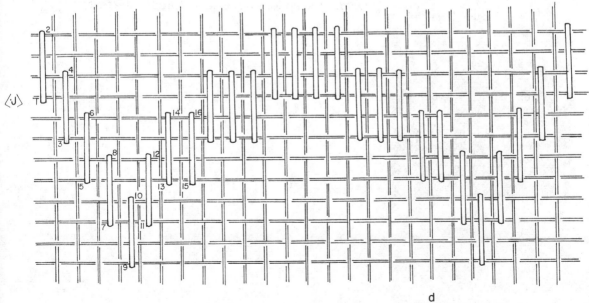

d

SPLIT
BARGELLO

In working this stitch you cannot start with the main line. You must start with compensating stitches. Use any line pattern. This is an example only.

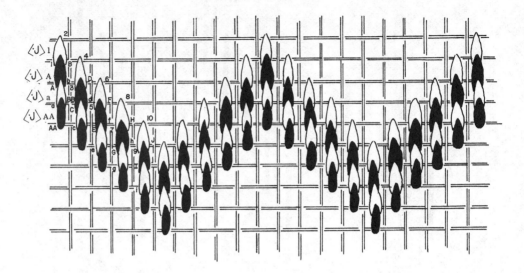

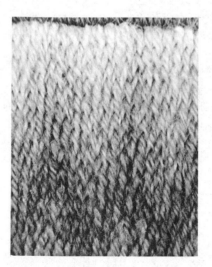

The Diagonal Stitch sampler was worked on Penelope 10 canvas. One strand of Tapestry was generally sufficient. Exceptions have been noted in the text.

Try working the framework in the darkest color and shading the center. This is an example only.

BARGELLO FRAMEWORK PATTERN

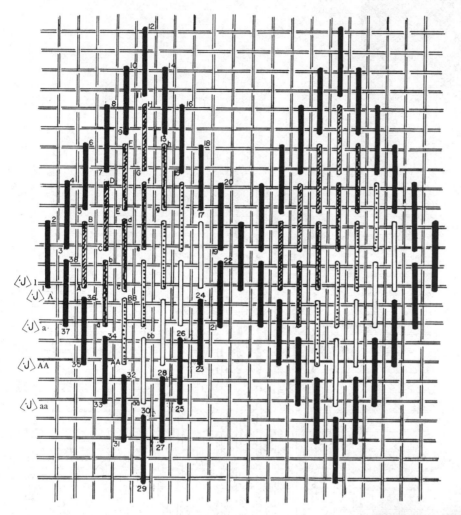

FOUR-WAY
BARGELLO

Draw lines from the center to each of the four corners. It is on these lines that you change from vertical to horizontal stitches.

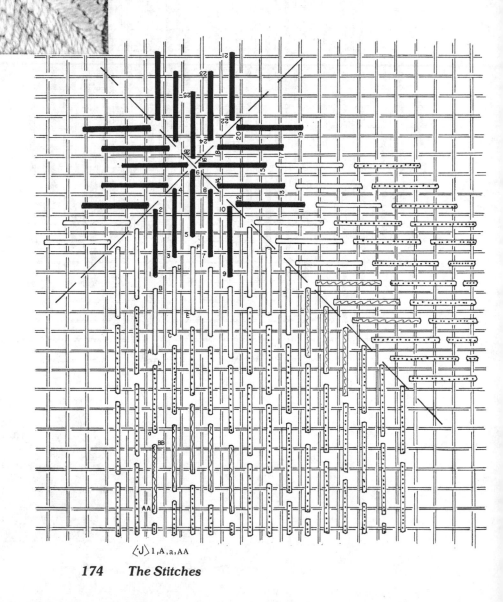

⟨J⟩1,A,a,AA

FIVE:

Diagonal Stitches

Diagonal Stitches are those which cover the canvas by crossing junctions of mesh, rather than going between them. In referring to these slanted stitches, I have designated the angle or slant they take by two numbers. The first number refers to the number of mesh that you go up or down. The second number refers to the number of mesh that you go over. For example a 1 × stitch is a Tent Stitch; a 1 × 3 stitch is shown at the right. 3 × 1 and 3 × 3 stitches are also shown at the right. For those stitches where both numbers are the same, you may count, diagonally, the junctions of mesh, instead of counting up three and over three. Whether you go up or down (for the first number) is shown in the sketch that accompanies each stitch.

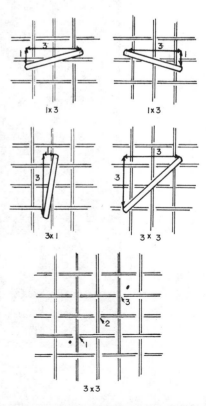

Key to Sampler Stitches

1. Half Cross
2. Continental
3. Basketweave
4. Petit Point
5. Rep
6. 2 x 1 Slanted Gobelin
7. 2 x 1 Interlocking Gobelin
8. Padded Slanted Gobelin
9. Encroaching Oblique
10. Oblique Stav
11. Byzantine #1
12. Jacquard
13. Diagonal Hungarian Ground
14. Staircase
15. Alternating Continental
16. Irregular Jacquard
17. Byzantine #3
18. Byzantine #4
19. Irregular Byzantine
20. Byzantine #5
21. Byzantine #2
22. Milanese
23. Milanese Color Variation
24. Oriental
25. Mixed Milanese
26. Knitting
27. Lazy Knitting
28. Kalem
29. Web
30. Lazy Kalem
30. Giant Knitting
32. Arrowhead
33. Byzantine Scotch
34. Stem
35. Diagonal Stem
36. Diagonal Knitting
37. Padded Alternating Continental
38. Diagonal Stripe
39. 2 × 2 Slanted Gobelin
40. Irregular Continental
41. 5 × 2 Slanted Gobelin
42. 5 × 1 Interlocking Gobelin
43. Diagonal Beaty
44. Split Slanted Gobelin
45. Interlocking Gobelin
46. 2 × 2 Slanted Gobelin

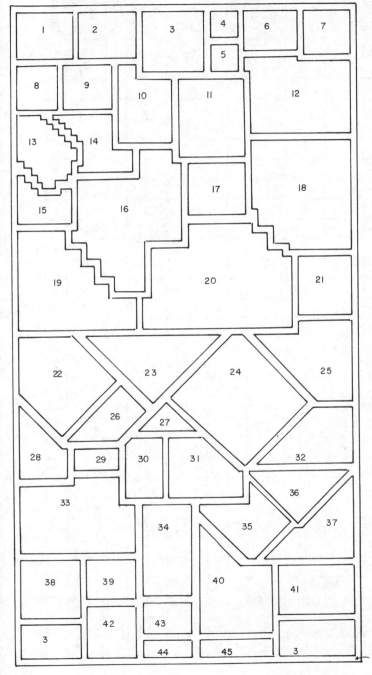

Diagonal Stitches **177**

DIAGONAL STITCHES	Border	Good Backing	Poor Backing	Background	Design	Accent	Fast	Slow	Geometric Pattern	Shading	Yarn Hog	Snags	Snag-Proof	Little Texture	Medium Texture	High Relief	Flower Stitch	Weak Pattern	Medium Pattern	Strong Pattern	Distorts Canvas
Basketweave		●		●	●								●	●				●			
Continental		●			●					●			●	●				●			●
Half-Cross			●										●	●				●			●
Irregular Cont.		●		●	●					●		●		●					●	●	
Alternating Cont.		●		●	●	●			●				●	●					●		
Padded Alt. Cont.		●		●	●	●			●				●	●							
Petit Point		●		●	●	●			●	●			●	●				●			●
Rep		●		●	●	●			●	●			●	●				●			●
Diagonal Stripe		●		●	●	●			●					●					●		●
Slanted Gobelin		●		●	●		●		●					●					●		●
2 x 2 Sl. Gobelin	●	●		●	●		●		●					●					●		●
5 × 2 Sl. Gobelin		●		●	●				●			●		●					●		●
Padded Sl. Gobelin		●		●	●			●	●					●	●				●		●
Split S. Gobelin		●		●	●				●	●			●	●				●			●
Inter. Gobelin		●		●	●				●	●				●				●			●
Gt. Inter. Gobelin				●	●		●			●		●		●				●			●
Oblique Slav			●	●	●		●			●		●		●					●		●
Encroaching Oblique				●	●					●		●		●					●		●
Diagonal Beaty				●	●		●					●		●					●		●
Knitting		●		●	●									●					●		
Lazy Knitting		●		●	●								●	●				●			
Giant Knitting				●	●		●					●		●						●	
Diagonal Knitting		●		●	●									●					●		
Kalem		●		●	●									●					●		
Lazy Kalem		●		●	●								●	●				●			
Stem	●	●		●	●									●					●		
Diagonal Stem	●	●		●	●									●					●		
Byzantine #1		●		●	●		●			●		●		●						●	●
Byzantine #2		●		●	●		●			●		●		●						●	●
Byzantine #3		●		●	●		●			●				●						●	●
Byzantine #4		●		●	●		●					●		●						●	●

DIAGONAL STITCHES (cont.)	Border	Good Backing	Poor Backing	Background	Design	Accent	Fast	Slow	Geometric Pattern	Shading	Yarn Hog	Snags	Snag-Proof	Little Texture	Medium Texture	High Relief	Flower Stitch	Weak Pattern	Medium Pattern	Strong Pattern	Distorts Canvas
Byzantine #5		•		•	•		•					•		•						•	•
Irregular Byzantine		•		•	•		•					•		•						•	•
Byzantine-Scotch		•		•	•		•					•		•						•	•
Jacquard		•		•	•									•						•	•
Irregular Jacquard		•		•	•		•					•		•						•	•
Diag. Hungarian Gr.		•		•	•		•							•						•	•
Staircase		•		•	•									•						•	•
Milanese		•		•	•	•						•			•					•	•
Milanese Color Var.		•		•	•	•						•			•					•	•
Oriental		•		•	•	•						•		•						•	•
Mixed Milanese		•		•	•	•			•		•	•			•					•	•
Arrowhead		•		•	•	•			•					•					•		•

BASKETWEAVE

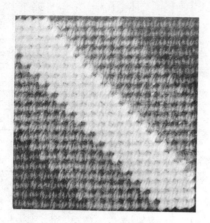

Basketweave is one of the most used and misused stitches in needlepoint. It is an excellent stitch to know and use. A durable backing, resembling a woven pattern, is created. This makes it a "must" for chairs, footstools, and other items that will receive lots of wear.

The finished piece is not distorted, but still needs blocking. (See page 81.) Basketweave allows a worked canvas to give a lot, yet still be strong. It can be worked without turning the canvas. Because it lacks maneuverability, it is not a good stitch for designing. (Use Continental for designing in very small areas if you want a Tent Stitch.)

Study the figure below. Note that, basically, the stitch fills the canvas in diagonal rows, starting at the upper right corner.

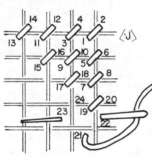

Basketweave

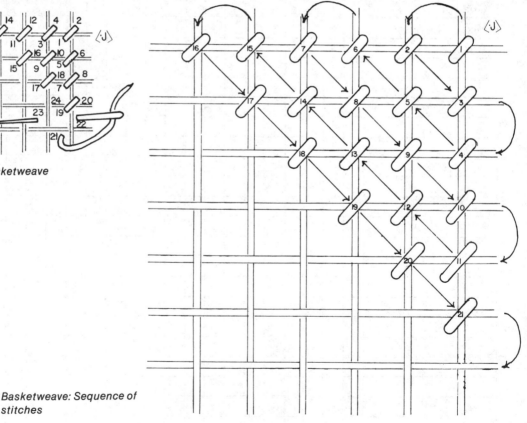

Basketweave: Sequence of stitches

As you work you will notice that a pattern is developing. In making an up row, the needle always goes straight across under two mesh. In making a down row, the needle always goes straight down under two mesh. Notice that the first of these two mesh is covered by a stitch in the preceding row. It is a very common error to go across or under three mesh by not counting the covered one.

At the end of each row there is what many students refer to as a turn stitch. Actually it is the first stitch of a new row. If it helps you to consider it a turn stitch, then do so. At the end of the up row this is a horizontal Continental Stitch and at the end of the down row this is a vertical Continental Stitch. The common error here is to leave the turn stitch out. Often students get carried away and make two turn stitches. If you have made an error somewhere, check to see if this is it.

When your yarn runs out and you must start another one, be sure to start **exactly** where you left off. If you do not, a line will show on the right side. For example, if your yarn runs out at the end of an up row, do not start the new yarn at the bottom of that up row you just finished, thus starting another up row. Instead you should be at the top of that last up row, ready to begin a down row. Most people tend to put their work away for the day when they have finished working the yarn on the needle. It might help you not to do this when working Basketweave. Leave the needle threaded with half a yarn and stick it into the canvas in position ready to take the next stitch. This way you will not lose your place. (See the figures to the right.)

When working Basketweave on Regular Mono canvas, note that at the intersections of mesh in a horizontal row, the vertical mesh alternate between being on top of and underneath the horizontal mesh. However, on the diagonal, the vertical mesh are always on top or underneath the horizontal mesh.

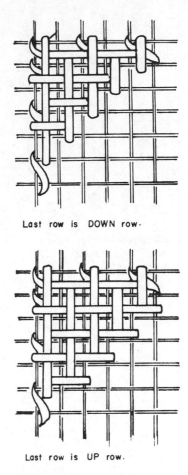

Last row is DOWN row.

Last row is UP row.

Basketweave: Wrong side—last row is down *row (top); last row is* up *row (bottom)*

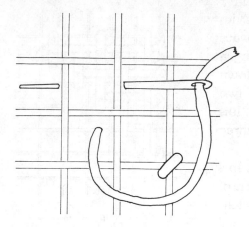

Basketweave: Right—up row
covering a horizontal
mesh intersection

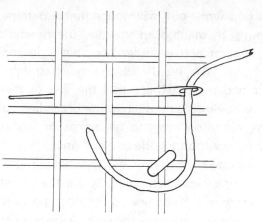

Basketweave: Wrong—up row
covering a vertical mesh
intersection

If you will take care always to cover the vertical mesh intersections with a down row and to cover the horizontal mesh intersections with an up row, you will produce a stitch that is very even in appearance on the right side. This will also help you to keep track of up rows and down rows. (See above.)

When you come to the end of each strand of yarn, weave it under the yarns on the back side of the canvas for about an inch. Follow the weave that the stitch makes. Clip closely. This will keep the back neat. If you work the beginning and ending tails under any other way, a ridge will form that will show on the right side.

Basketweave is not really frightfully complicated. It may take some study on your part, but once you get the hang of the stitch you will enjoy working it. It has a certain rhythm that develops easily. You can achieve a perfection with this stitch that is unique. Use it no matter how small the area. (When the area is absolutely too small and when outlining, use the Continental Stitch.)

The Continental Stitch has the next-best backing and it is the next most distinct stitch of the Tent Stitches. Its main drawback is that it pulls the canvas badly out of shape.

You really should use Basketweave wherever you can. But Continental will get the very small areas that Basketweave cannot.

If you insist on using Continental instead of Basketweave, you should try to make the stitches as even and uniform as possible. You may work Continental either horizontally (see below) or vertically (below right). Choose the direction that best fills the area you have. Work the stitch in that direction—for the whole space. Combinations of horizontally and vertically worked Continental will produce lines on the right side. Always work this stitch from right to left. If you are filling a large space, do not turn the canvas upside down for the second row; cut the yarn and begin the second row below the first on the right. The drawing does not show this because I do not recommend that you use this stitch in a large enough area to matter.

CONTINENTAL

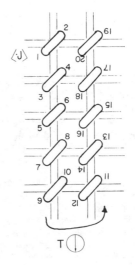

Continental: Vertical—work down

Continental: Horizontal—work left to right

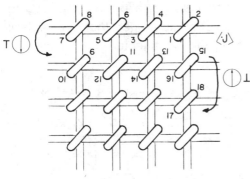

Continental: Reverse side

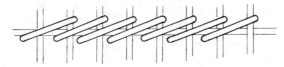

Diagonal Stitches 183

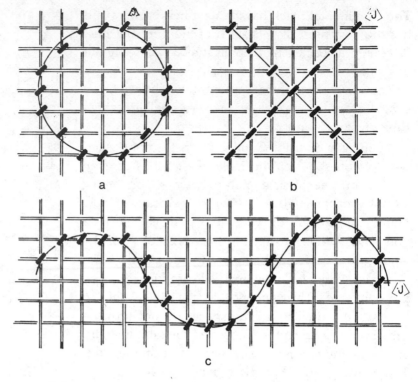

a   b

c

HALF-CROSS

The Half-Cross Stitch has the poorest backing and the stitch is not distinct. I do not allow my students to use this stitch and I strongly suggest that you replace it with Basketweave and Continental.

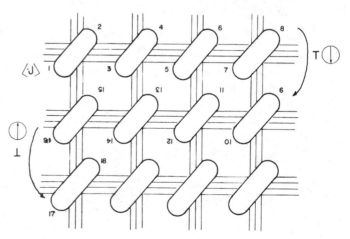

Half-Cross: Horizontal

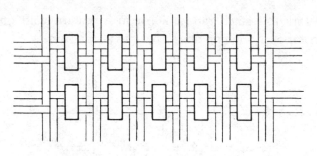

Half-Cross: Reverse side

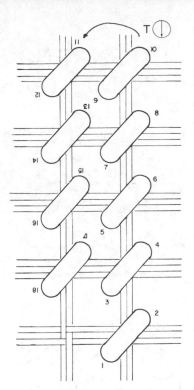

Half-Cross: Vertical

This stitch is excellent for shading. In working it, be sure to keep it a 1 x 1, 2 x 2, 3 x 3, 4 x 4, or 5 x 5 stitch. Count the mesh junctions diagonally (page 175). The rows will be irregular. The drawing is an example only. Do your own.

IRREGULAR CONTINENTAL

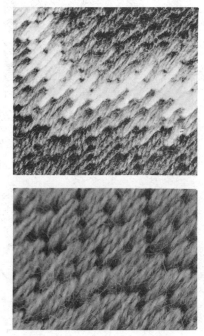

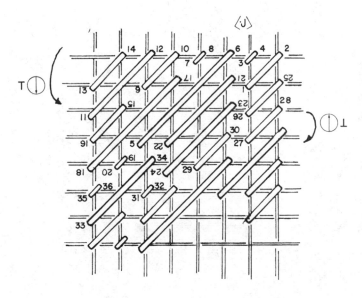

ALTERNATING CONTINENTAL

Work this stitch randomly or in a pattern with one color or more than one. It fits into a small area.

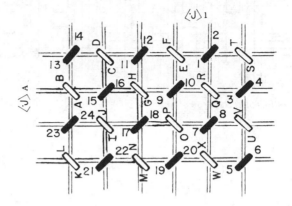

PADDED ALTERNATING CONTINENTAL

Work this stitch in three colors.

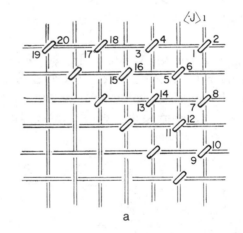

a

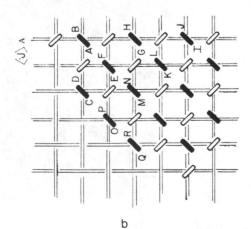

b

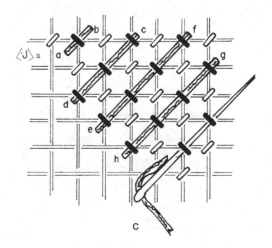

c

Split the vertical mesh of Penelope canvas and work Continental or Basketweave. Thin your yarn. This is difficult to get smooth and even on Penelope canvas. Use it only if one or two small areas of your design demand Petit Point. For a whole Petit Point picture, use Petit Point canvas (page 13). Most of the stitches in this book can be worked in Petit Point, too.

PETIT POINT

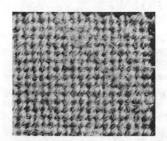

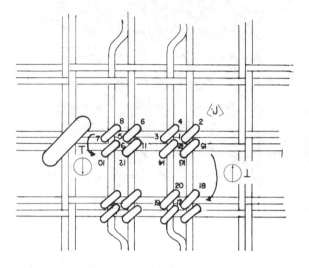

This makes a nice, small vertical stripe. In one color this is a good stitch. Work it vertically in two colors and make a pin-stripe fabric. Thin your yarn.

REP

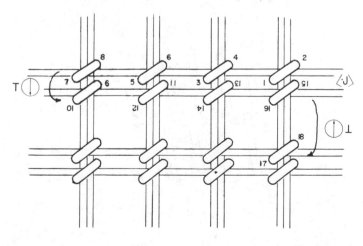

Diagonal Stitches   187

DIAGONAL STRIPE

The color arrangement can make this stitch appear as two different ones. Suit the color selection to your needs.

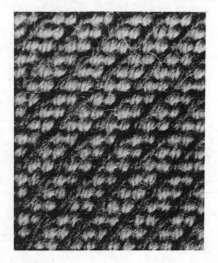

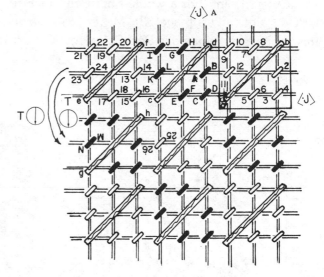

SLANTED GOBELIN

This stitch is versatile, for it can be worked between two and six mesh tall and one or two mesh wide. When the stitch is taller than two mesh, you will probably need to thicken your yarn.

Slanted Gobelin makes a horizontal row. It is good for dresser drawers or anything in rows.

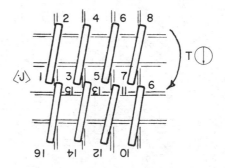

This is the stitch that I used as a divider on my samplers (Plates 32, 34, 36, and 38, for example).

SLANTED GOBELIN 2 × 2

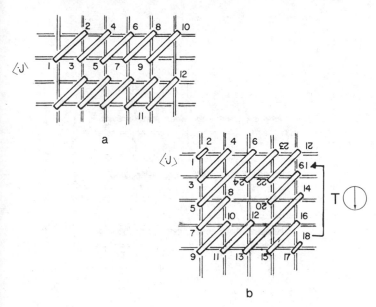

a

b

Thicken your yarn.

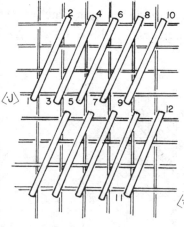

Slanted Gobelin:
4 x 2 (above);
5 x 2 (right)

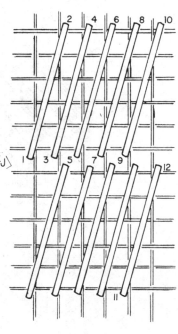

SLANTED GOBELIN 5 × 2

Slanted Gobelin: (top to bottom) 2 x 2; 3 x 2; 4 x 2; 5 x 2

PADDED SLANTED GOBELIN

The tramé adds a padding to Slanted Gobelin. Use it when you want a subtle texture.

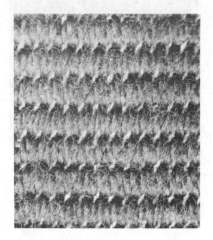

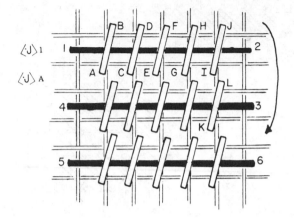

SPLIT SLANTED GOBELIN

This stitch is reminiscent of embroidery's Split Stitch. Use it for shading. It is tedious to work, but very pretty.

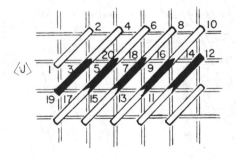

This stitch is similar to Split Gobelin. It, however, does not split the stitch on the row above; it merely rests beside it. It, too, can be worked two to five mesh tall and one to two wide.

INTERLOCKING GOBELIN

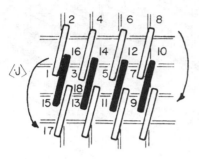

Thicken your yarn.

GIANT INTERLOCKING GOBELIN

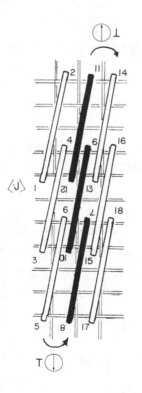

OBLIQUE SLAV

You will probably have to thicken your yarn for this stitch. There are two mesh between stitches and two mesh between rows.

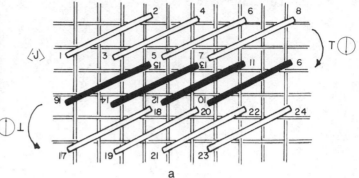

a

b

Oblique Slav: Horizontal (upper right); Vertical (lower right and photograph)

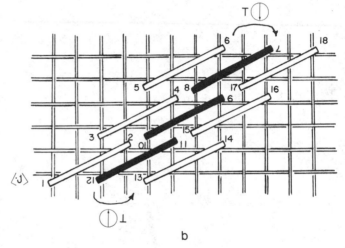

ENCROACHING OBLIQUE

This stitch is Interlocking Gobelin turned on its side. Thicken your yarn.

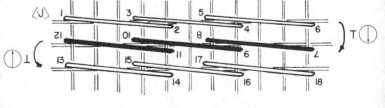

This stitch leaves a bare spot every now and then. Take an extra stitch to cover the hole. Doing this will not ruin the pattern. You may have to thicken your yarn.

DIAGONAL BEATY

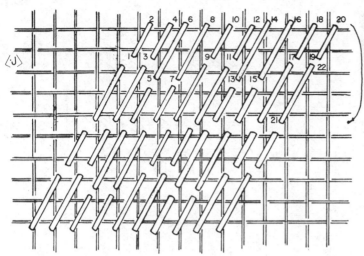

Take great care to get the tension even; otherwise it will look sloppy.

KNITTING

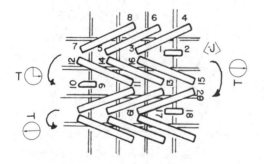

LAZY KNITTING

Do not confuse this stitch with Alternating Continental Stitch.

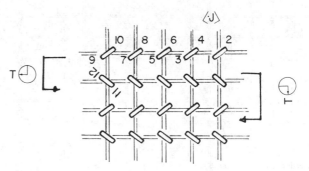

GIANT KNITTING

You will have to thicken your yarn.

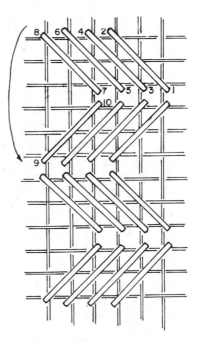

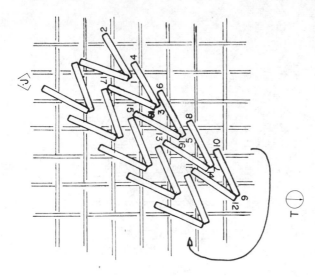

DIAGONAL
KNITTING

The Kalem Stitch looks like knitting. Be sure the tension is even.

KALEM

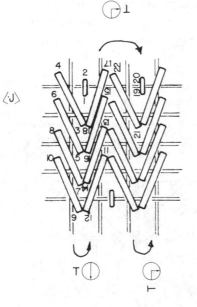

LAZY KALEM

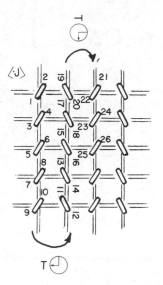

STEM

The Stem Stitch is usually best with two colors. Use a thinner yarn for the Back-Stitch. Complete one column of stitches at a time. Do a vertical Back-Stitch in a second color between the columns. This stitch makes good fences, columns, etc.

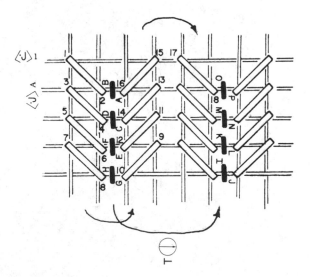

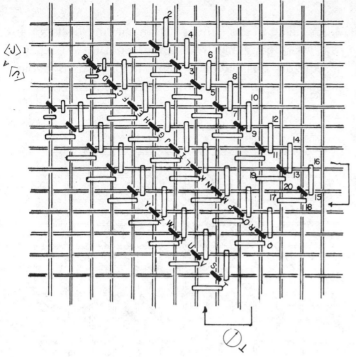

DIAGONAL
STEM

Byzantine makes good steps and fills in diagonally shaped areas well.

BYZANTINE #1

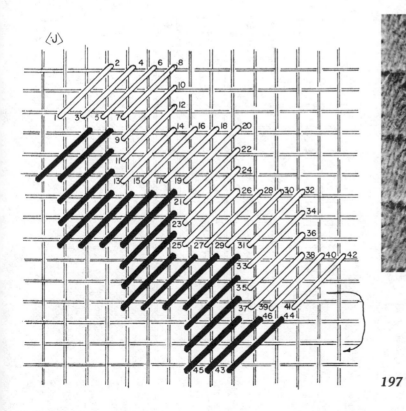

197

BYZANTINE #2

When filling in the canvas with a stitch in a diagonal row, work generally from upper right to lower left, as you do Basketweave. This helps you to avoid snagging the yarn in the row before as you stitch.

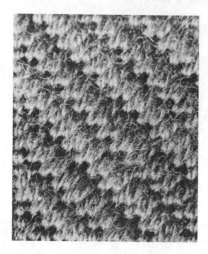

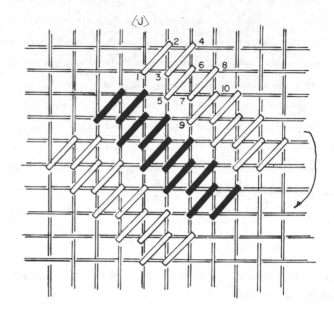

BYZANTINE #3

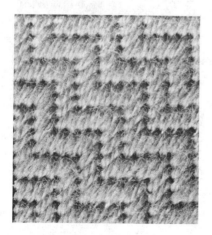

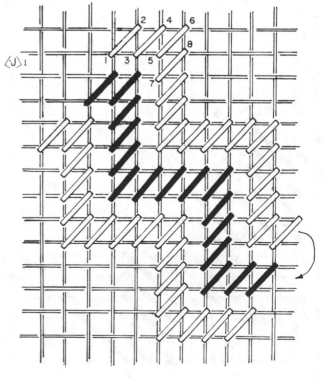

BYZANTINE #4

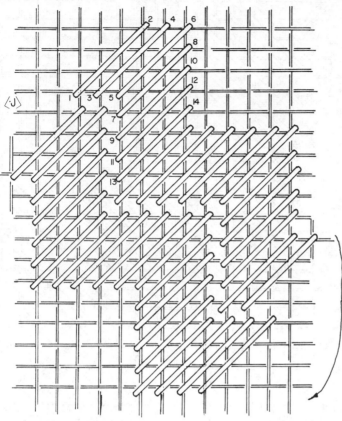

BYZANTINE #5

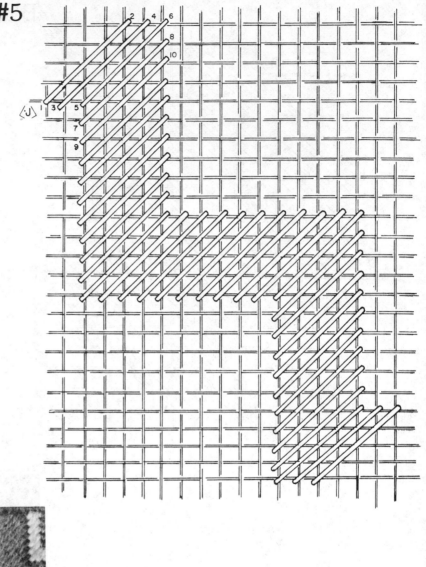

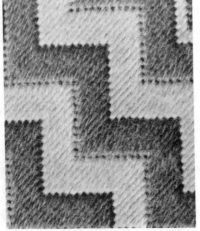

Work rows of Byzantine 1 x 1, 2 x 2, 3 x 3, and 4 x 4 in order or mix them up.

IRREGULAR BYZANTINE

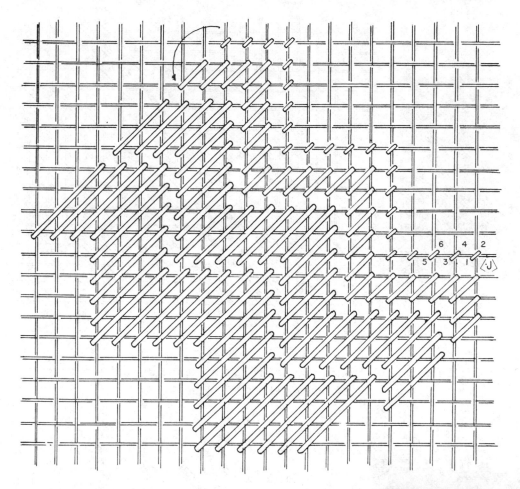

BYZANTINE
SCOTCH

Fill in between the Byzantine steps with a Scotch Stitch. This is a larger version of Diagonal Hungarian Ground.

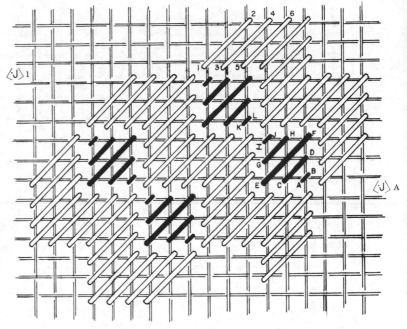

JACQUARD

Jacquard is very much like the Byzantine Stitch with a Continental Stitch divider.

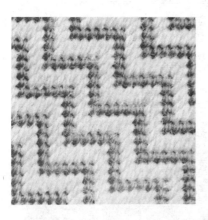

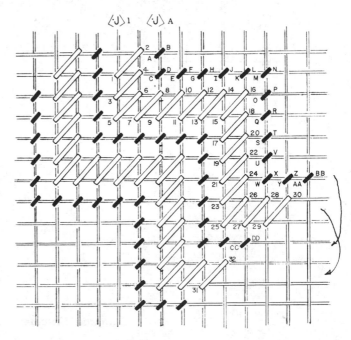

Do as many stitches as you want before turning the corner, but be consistent. Mix up the length of the stitches (2 x 2, 3 x 3, 4 x 4) or stitch them in order.

IRREGULAR JACQUARD

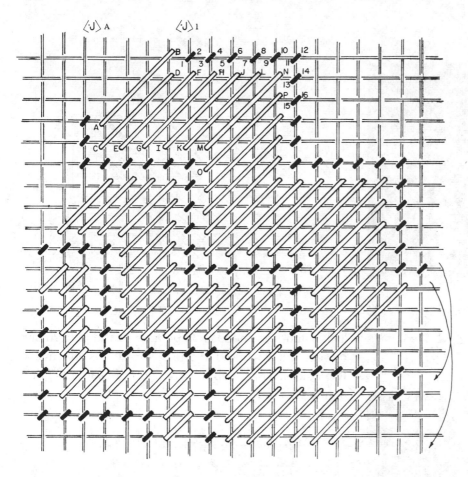

DIAGONAL HUNGARIAN GROUND

Work this stitch in two colors, or work a very large, uninterrupted area in one color. Otherwise the pattern is lost.

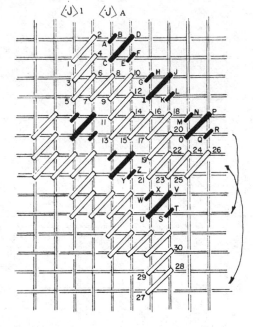

STAIRCASE

This stitch, too, needs a large area so the pattern can be seen if it is worked in one color. Or it is effective in two colors. This stitch is a variation of Diagonal Hungarian Ground.

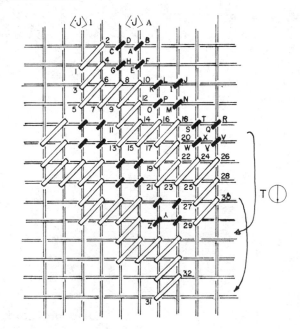

This is an especially pretty stitch, but it is difficult to work around lots of letters.

MILANESE

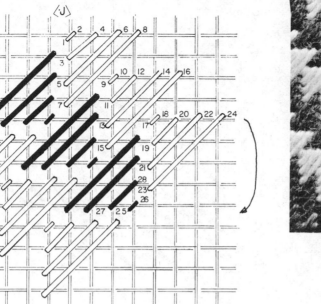

MILANESE COLOR VARIATION

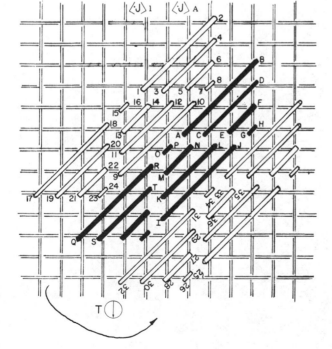

ORIENTAL

The Oriental Stitch is a good background in one color. It looks entirely different in two colors. Few stitches undergo such a change in appearance. Try it both ways.

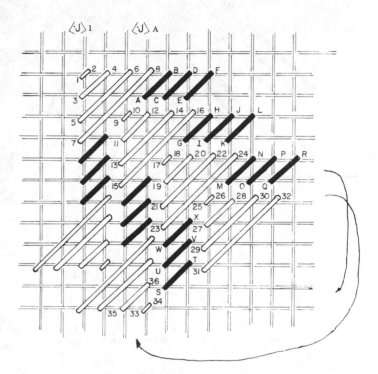

Mixed Milanese is easy to lose track of if you don't follow it carefully. It is a beautiful stitch, but I do not like it for large areas because it is very slow and it is quite a yarn hog.

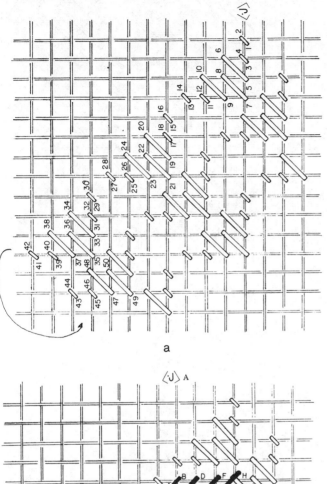

a

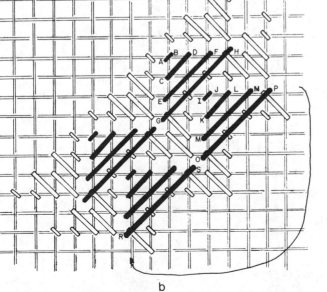

b

ARROWHEAD

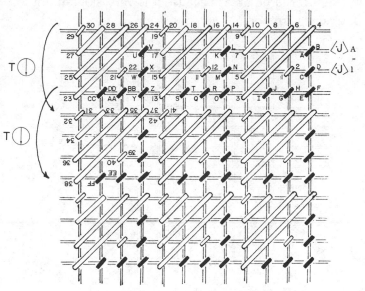

SIX:

Box Stitches

Box Stitches are a series of diagonal stitches that form squares or boxes. The diagonal box stitches are simply boxes laid in a diagonal line, with the corners overlapping. (See the Diagonal Scotch Stitch page 233). Note how the short stitch is shared.

Most of these stitches make excellent borders. They lend themselves to beautiful geometric patterns in several colors. I have only gone into a few color variations, for there are whole books that discuss color variations of just a few stitches.

The Box Stitch sampler was worked on Penelope 10, although it could have been done on Mono 10 canvas. Tapestry yarn was used throughout—and for all forty-three stitches I did not have to thicken or thin the yarn.

209

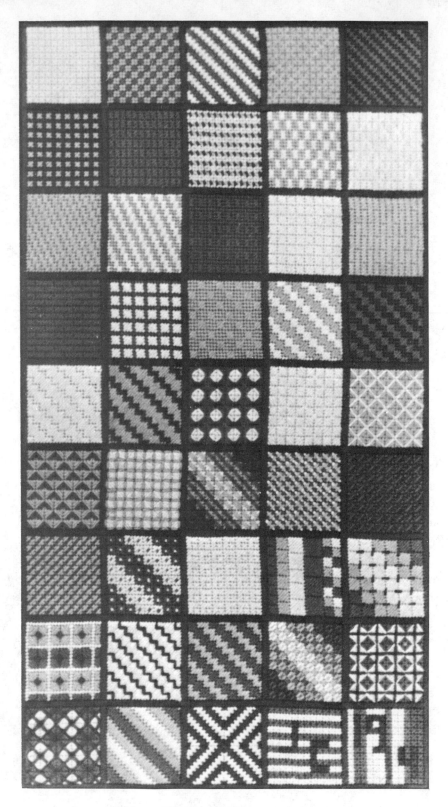

210   *The Stitches*

Key to Sampler Stitches

1. Mosaic
2. Mosaic Checker
3. Diagonal Mosaic
4. Reversed Mosaic
5. Mosaic Stripe
6. Framed Mosaic
7. Cashmere
8. Tied Cashmere
9. Cashmere Checker
10. Reversed Cashmere
11. Diagonal Cashmere
12. Framed Diagonal Cashmere
13. Framed Cashmere
14. Scotch
15. Elongated Cashmere
16. Horizontal Cashmere
17. Framed Scotch
18. Scotch Checker
19. Diagonal Scotch
20. Moorish
21. Giant Diagonal Scotch
22. Giant Moorish
23. Diamond Scotch
24. Reversed Scotch
25. Windowpane Scotch
26. Triangular Scotch
27. Framed Reversed Scotch
28. Crossed Scotch
29. Crossed Tied-Down Scotch
30. 1 – 3 – 5 Woven Scotch
31. Dotted Scotch
32. Tied Scotch
33. Divided Scotch
34. Giant Scotch
35. Half-Framed Scotch
36. Framed Scotch Variation
37. Framed Diagonal Scotch
38. Wide Moorish
39. Continuous 2 – 4 Woven Scotch
40. Point Russe #1
41. Point Russe #2
42. Giant Diagonal Mosaic
43. Four-Way Mosaic
44. Mosaic
45. 2 × 2 Slanted Gobelin

1	2	3	4	5
6	7	8	9	10
11	12	13	14	15
16	17	18	19	20
21	22	23	24	25
26	27	28	29	30
31	32	33	34	35
36	37	38	39	40
41	42	43	44	45

44

BOX STITCHES	Border	Good Backing	Poor Backing	Background	Design	Accent	Fast	Slow	Geometric Pattern	Shading	Yarn Hog	Snags	Snag-Proof	Little Texture	Medium Texture	High Relief	Flower Stitch	Weak Pattern	Medium Pattern	Strong Pattern	Distorts Canvas
Mosaic	•	•		•	•		•		•				•	•				•			•
Mosaic Checker	•	•		•	•		•		•				•	•				•			•
Reversed Mosaic	•	•		•	•		•		•				•	•				•			•
Framed Mosaic	•	•		•	•				•				•	•					•		•
Diagonal Mosaic		•		•	•		•		•	•			•	•				•			•
Four-Way Mosaic		•		•	•		•		•	•			•	•				•			
Mosaic Stripe		•		•	•				•				•	•					•		
Giant Diag. Mosaic		•		•	•		•		•	•	•			•				•			•
Cashmere	•	•		•	•		•		•				•	•				•			•
Tied Cashmere	•	•			•	•		•	•				•		•					•	•
Cashmere Checker	•	•		•	•		•		•				•	•					•		•
Reversed Cashmere	•	•		•	•		•		•				•	•				•			•
Framed Cashmere	•	•		•	•				•				•	•					•		•
Elongated Cashmere	•	•		•	•		•		•				•	•				•			•
Horizontal Cashmere	•	•		•	•		•		•				•	•				•			•
Diagonal Cashmere		•		•	•		•		•	•			•	•					•		•
Framed Diag. Cash.		•		•	•				•				•	•					•		•
Scotch	•	•		•	•		•		•					•				•			•
Giant Scotch	•	•		•	•		•		•			•		•				•			•
Tied Scotch	•	•			•	•			•				•		•					•	•
Dotted Scotch	•	•		•	•				•				•	•						•	•
Half-Framed Scotch	•	•			•		•		•			•		•					•		•
Cr. Tied-Down Scot.	•	•			•	•		•	•	•					•					•	•
Woven Scotch	•	•			•	•		•	•	•					•					•	•
Cont. 2-4 Wov. Scot.	•	•			•	•		•	•	•					•					•	•
Crossed Scotch	•	•			•	•		•	•	•		•	•							•	•
Divided Scotch	•	•		•	•				•			•		•					•		•
Scotch Checker	•	•		•	•		•		•					•					•		•
Framed Scotch	•	•		•	•		•		•					•					•		•
Reversed Scotch	•	•		•	•				•					•				•			
Framed Rev. Scotch	•	•			•			•	•			•			•				•		

BOX STITCHES (cont.)	Border	Good Backing	Poor Backing	Background	Design	Accent	Fast	Slow	Geometric Pattern	Shading	Yarn Hog	Snags	Snag-Proof	Little Texture	Medium Texture	High Relief	Flower Stitch	Weak Pattern	Medium Pattern	Strong Pattern	Distorts Canvas
Framed Scotch Var.	•	•		•	•	•	•		•						•				•		
Windowpane Scotch	•	•		•	•		•		•						•					•	
Triangular Scotch	•	•			•		•		•					•						•	
Diamond Scotch	•	•		•	•		•		•					•						•	
Point Russe #1	•	•			•	•		•	•			•			•					•	
Point Russe #2	•	•			•	•		•	•			•			•					•	
Diagonal Scotch		•		•	•		•							•				•			•
Framed Diag. Scotch		•			•			•	•			•			•				•		•
Giant Diag. Scotch		•		•	•		•		•			•		•				•			•
Moorish Stitch		•		•	•		•		•					•					•		•
Wide Moorish		•		•	•		•		•					•					•		•
Giant Moorish		•		•	•		•		•			•		•					•		•

MOSAIC

Mosaic is the smallest of the Box Stitches. It is just three diagonal stitches: short, long, short. It makes a box two by two mesh. Mosaic is an excellent background or design stitch. This stitch is a good background to work behind Continental letters. It can be worked horizontally, vertically, or diagonally.

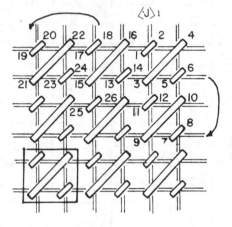

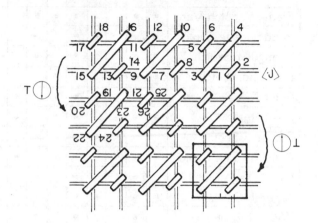

Mosaic: Horizontal

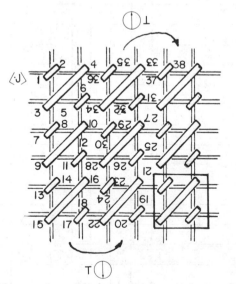

Mosaic: Diagonal

Mosaic: Vertical

Mosaic Checker must be worked in two colors. Do the Mosaic boxes in one color and fill in between them with Basketweave in another color. The Basketweave Stitches are lost in one color. This stitch wears well and creates a pretty pattern.

MOSAIC CHECKER

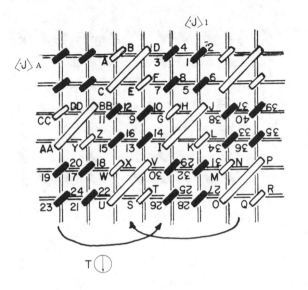

This stitch is worked most easily by doing a diagonal row from upper left to lower right. Then turn the canvas 90° so that the upper right now becomes the upper left. Work the same type of diagonal row, filling in the blank spaces. I think this stitch looks best in one color.

REVERSED MOSAIC

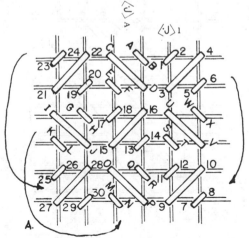

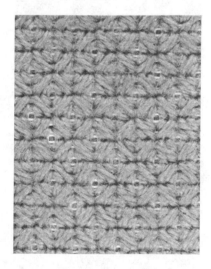

FRAMED MOSAIC

This stitch is simply a Mosaic Stitch with a frame of Continental all the way around. Work this stitch in one or more colors.

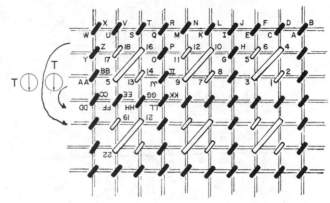

DIAGONAL MOSAIC

When Mosaic is worked diagonally, it becomes merely a line of short and long stitches. For this reason, you may use it for shading. Do this stitch in one or more colors.

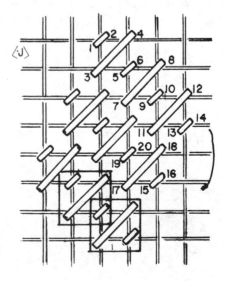

Combine Diagonal Mosaic with Reversed Diagonal Mosaic (bottom of facing page) to make a Four-Way Mosaic (below). This stitch is most successful if two or more colors are used.

FOUR-WAY MOSAIC

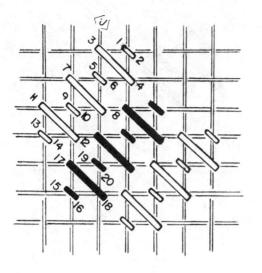

MOSAIC STRIPE

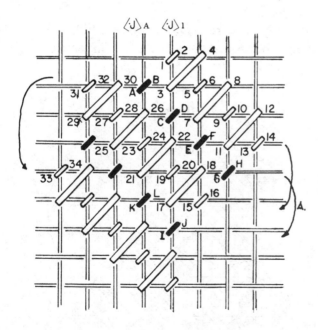

GIANT
DIAGONAL
MOSAIC

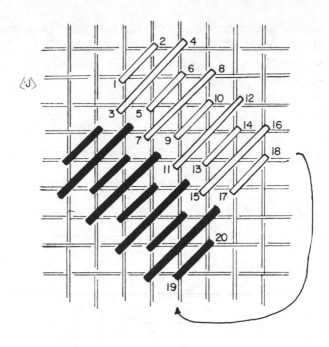

CASHMERE

Cashmere is a rectangular Mosaic Stitch. It can be worked horizontally, vertically, or diagonally.

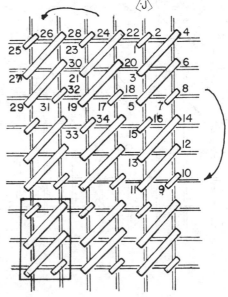

Cashmere: Diagonal

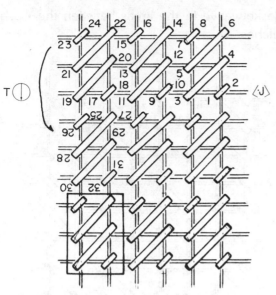

Cashmere: Horizontal

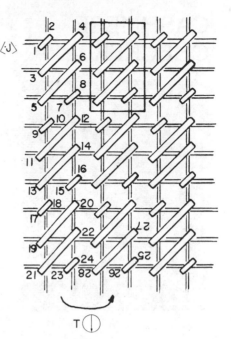

Cashmere: Vertical

Tie the two long stitches together. Use your thumbnail to move the yarns aside to see just where your needle must go. This tie creates a slight bump.

TIED CASHMERE

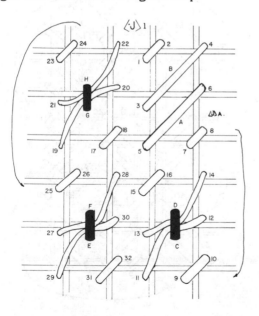

CASHMERE CHECKER

Work Basketweave in the areas between the Cashmere Stitches.

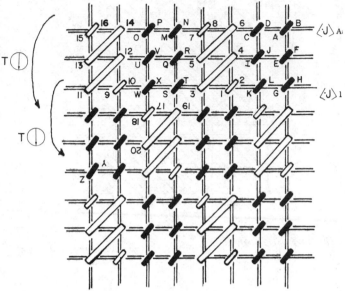

REVERSED CASHMERE

Work in diagonal rows. Turn canvas 90° for the next row. Start with the widest part of the area to be filled.

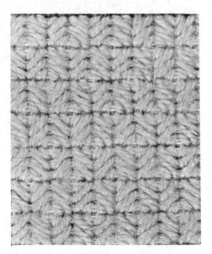

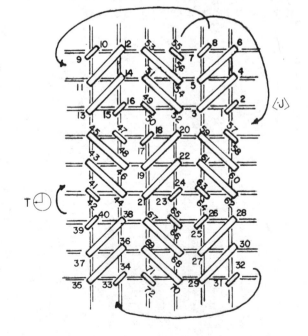

The Continental Stitch is used between the Cashmere boxes.

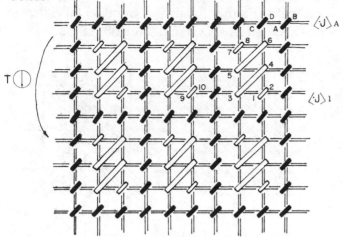

FRAMED CASHMERE

Elongated Cashmere is just an extra-long Cashmere Box. In alternating rows, it reminds me of the outside of a barn. The number of long stitches may vary.

ELONGATED CASHMERE

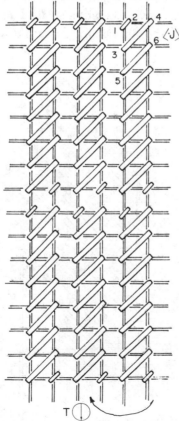

221

HORIZONTAL CASHMERE

Turn Cashmere on its side and lengthen a little, but not as much as Elongated Cashmere. This makes nice bricks. Frame it with the Continental Stitch in white and you have even more realistic bricks.

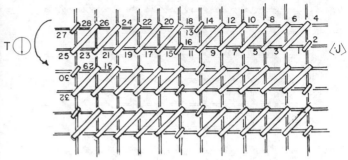

DIAGONAL CASHMERE

The second row of Diagonal Cashmere is a bit tricky to work. I try to remember that the first long stitch in the second row is diagonally below the last short stitch. After I have taken that stitch, I go back and pick up the first short stitch in the second row.

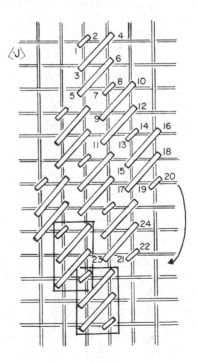

FRAMED
DIAGONAL
CASHMERE

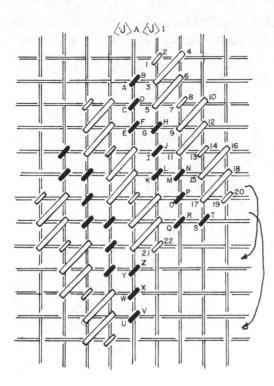

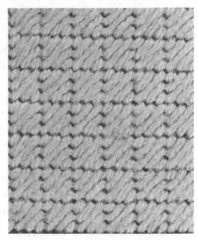

The Scotch Stitch is merely a large Mosaic Stitch. It has many lovely variations. This stitch can be worked three ways. (See Mosaic and Cashmere Stitches.)

SCOTCH

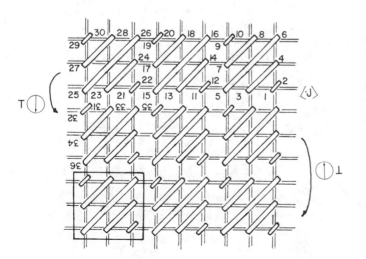

GIANT SCOTCH

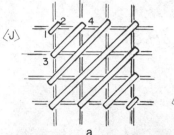

The Scotch Stitch can be worked in many sizes: five-stitch, seven-stitch, nine-stitch, and eleven-stitch. Keep in mind that the longer the stitches, the more likely they are to snag.

a

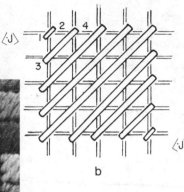

b

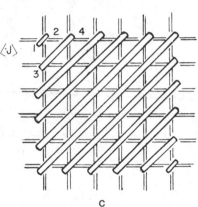

c

TIED SCOTCH

The tie is worked in the center of the longest stitch. This tie adds a bump and also reduces the likelihood of snagging.

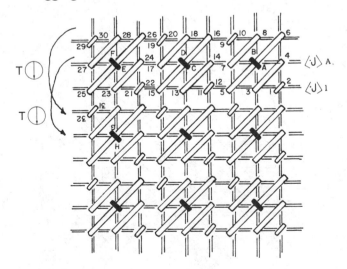

There are three Continental Stitches across the widest part of the Scotch. This cuts down on the snagging possibilities.

DOTTED SCOTCH

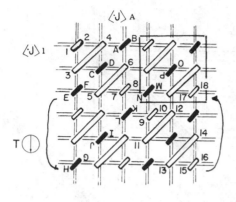

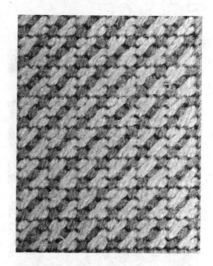

The small Straight Stitches make a most interesting pattern.

HALF-FRAMED SCOTCH

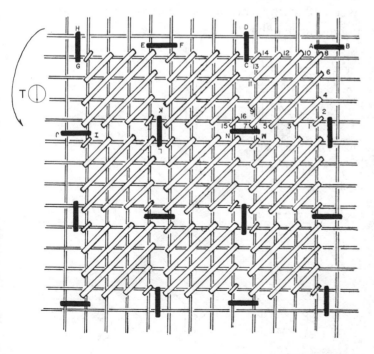

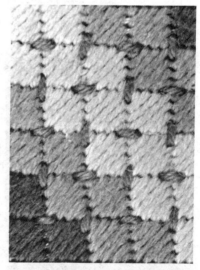

CROSSED TIED-DOWN SCOTCH

This stitch must be done in steps. First work stitches 1, 3, and 5. Next cross the whole thing. Then work stitches 2 and 4. Use three colors.

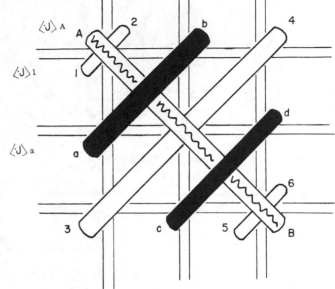

WOVEN SCOTCH

This stitch is worked like a regular Scotch Stitch, except that the contrasting-colored yarn is woven under the first, third, and fifth stitches.

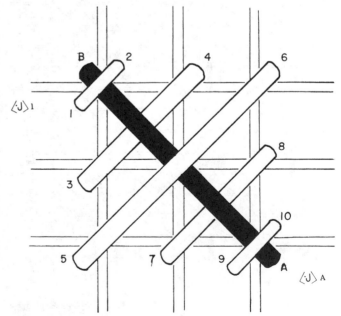

Weave a contrasting color under the second and fourth stitches for a whole diagonal row, coming up at A and down at B.

CONTINUOUS 2-4 WOVEN SCOTCH

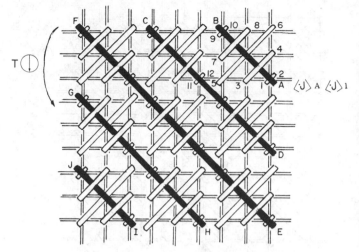

In working the basic foundation of the Scotch Stitch, omit the first and last stitches. Cross each Scotch Box by coming up at A and down at B. Without those short stitches, it is easy to miss the right hole. Study the drawing carefully. The A-B line is merely a large Back-Stitch. (See page 36.)

CROSSED SCOTCH

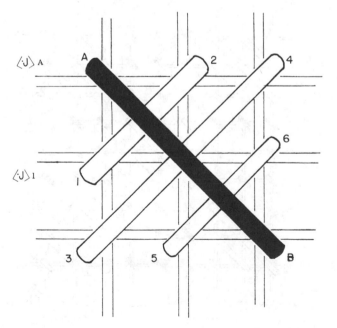

DIVIDED
SCOTCH

I like this stitch in one color, although it may be worked with more.

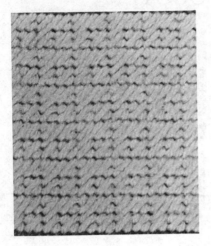

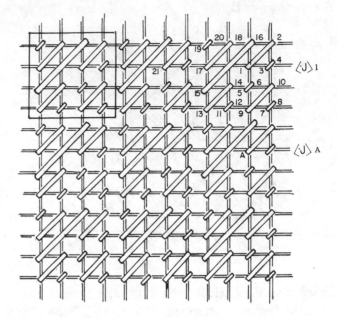

SCOTCH
CHECKER

This stitch is pretty in one or two colors. Fill in between each Scotch Box with Basketweave.

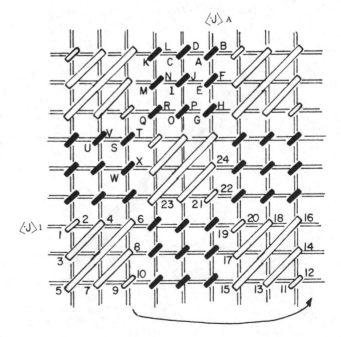

Stitch the frame in the Continental Stitch. Work all the horizontal rows first. Work the vertical rows next, skipping the stitches that have been worked. Work a portion of vertical rows to ease turning the corner to the next row. Work missed areas as convenient.

FRAMED SCOTCH

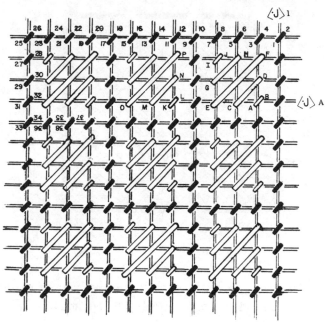

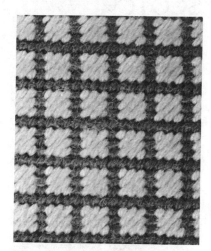

Try this stitch in one color. See Reversed Mosaic for hints on working Reversed Scotch.

REVERSED SCOTCH

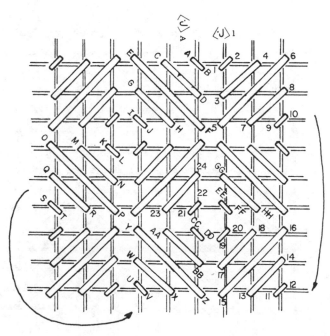

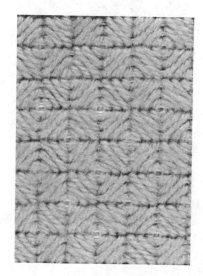

FRAMED REVERSED SCOTCH

Work a ground of Reversed Scotch and then frame. This frame is made by making one straight stitch per side of each Scotch Box.

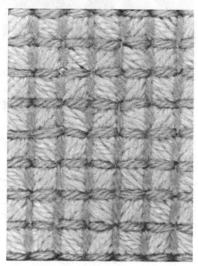

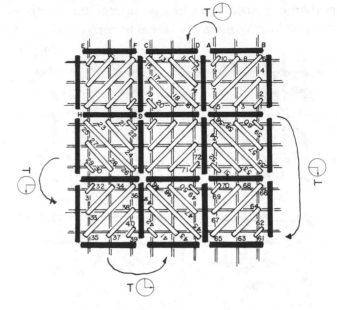

FRAMED SCOTCH VARIATIONS

This is only one stitch of the many that can be made by combining Scotch, frames, filling stitches, and color. Experiment and see how many pretty patterns you can come up with.

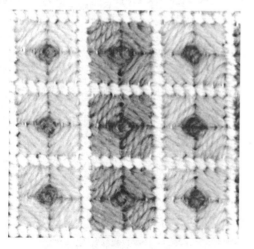

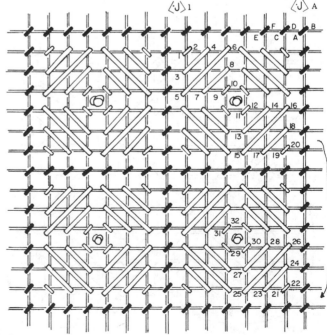

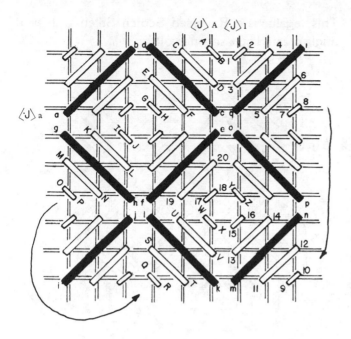

WINDOWPANE
SCOTCH

This is merely a Reversed Scotch Stitch, with a triangle of color used for a different look.

TRIANGULAR
SCOTCH

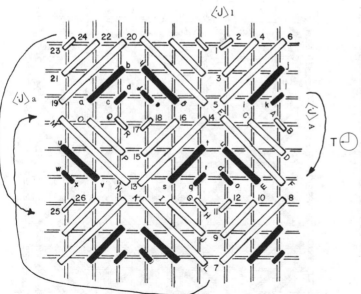

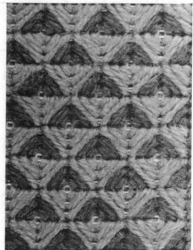

DIAMOND
SCOTCH

This, again, is a Reversed Scotch Stitch with a triangle created by a second color.

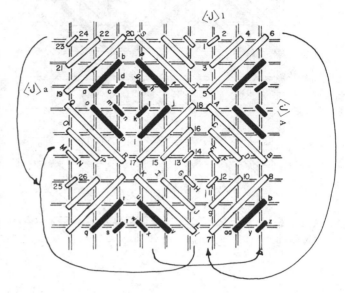

POINT RUSSE
#1

This stitch must be worked in at least three colors in order for it all to show up.

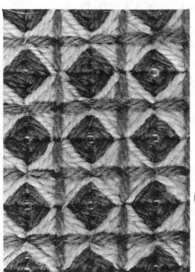

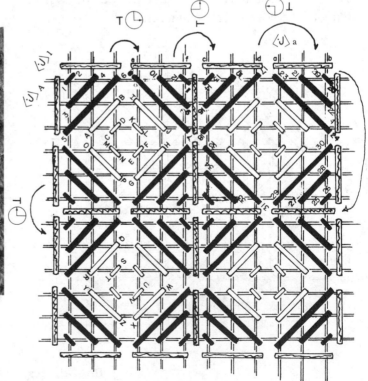

This stitch, too, needs a minimum of three colors to be seen well.

POINT RUSSE #2

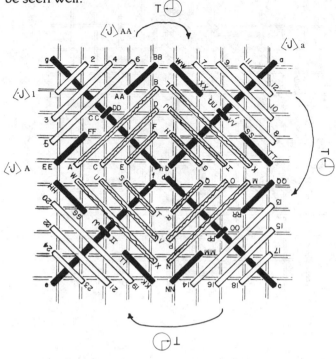

Share the short stitch when making the next box.

DIAGONAL SCOTCH

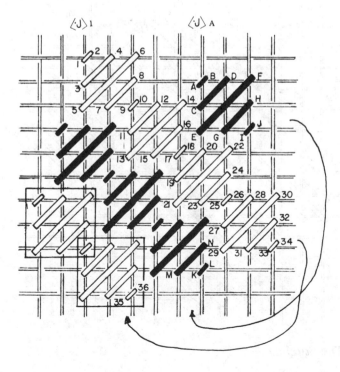

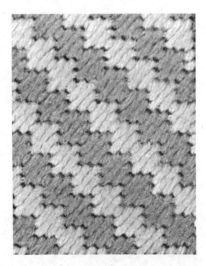

FRAMED
DIAGONAL
SCOTCH

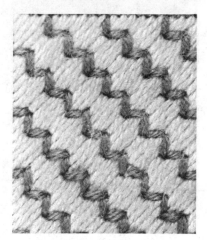

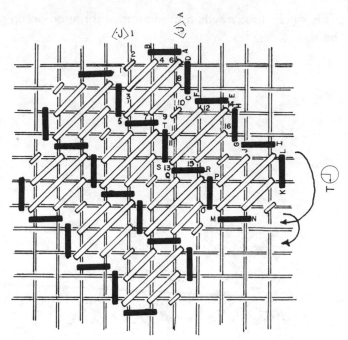

GIANT
DIAGONAL
SCOTCH

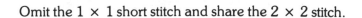

Omit the 1 × 1 short stitch and share the 2 × 2 stitch.

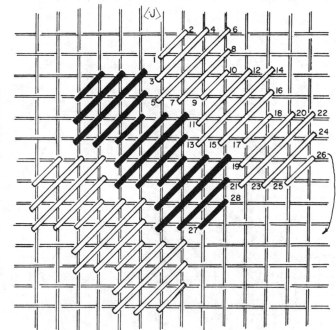

This is simply a Diagonal Scotch with a separating row of Continental Stitch. It resembles stairs; it can be used for rooftops and geometric designs.

MOORISH

A 2 × 2 Slanted Gobelin separates the rows of Diagonal Scotch.

WIDE MOORISH

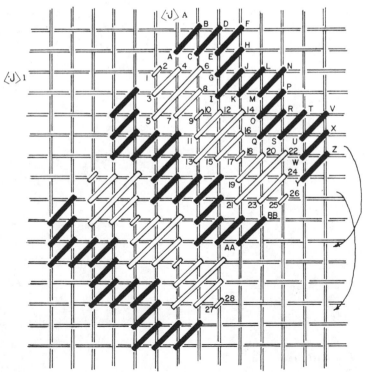

GIANT
MOORISH

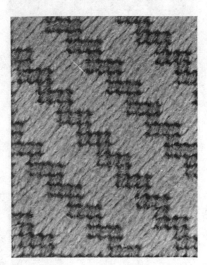

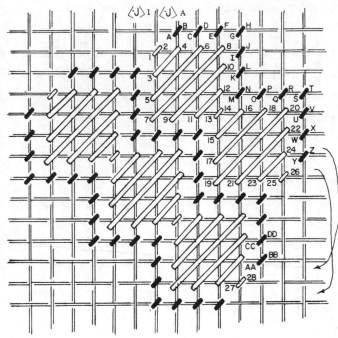

SEVEN:

Cross Stitches

Cross Stitches make pretty filling, design, and border stitches. They often stand alone to represent flowers.

When worked on Regular Mono canvas, the Cross Stitch must be crossed as you go. Watch the numbering as you go through this section.

It does not matter whether you cross the right arm over the left or the left arm over the right—but you must be consistent. I find it easier to work the whole area in half of the cross first. Then I go back and cross those stitches. I manage to ruin it every time if I don't do this.

The Cross-Stitch sampler was worked on Penelope 7 canvas with Persian yarn. Many of the Cross Stitches did not need thickening; however, many did. When the Cross Stitch is worked on smaller canvas it is not distinct. Larger crosses can be worked successfully on smaller canvas.

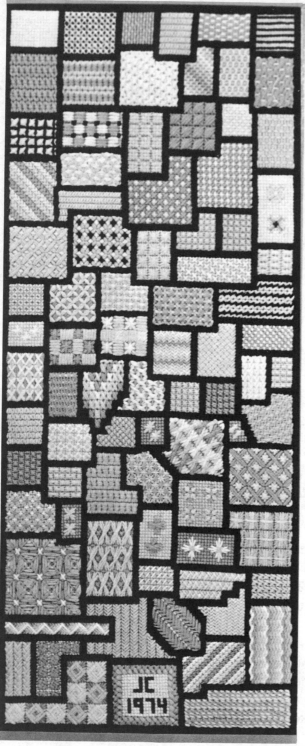

Key to Sampler Stitches

1. Cross Stitch
2. Double Cross Tramé
3. 1 x 1 Spaced Cross Tramé
4. Oblong Cross
5. 1 x 3 Spaced Cross Tramé
6. Tied Oblong Cross
7. Giant Tied Oblong Cross
8. Double Tied Oblong Cross
9. Flying Cross
10. Alternating Oblong Cross
11. Double Stitch
12. Hourglass Cross
13. Italian Cross
14. Barred Square
15. Woven Square
16. Bound Cross
17. Upright Cross
18. Long Upright Cross
19. Diagonal Upright Cross
20. Cross Diagonal
21. Slanted Cross
22. Checkerboard Cross
23. Combination Crosses
24. Medallion
25. Double Cross
26. Trellis Cross
27. Double Leviathan
28. Smyrna
29. Reversed Smyrna Cross
30. Staggered Crosses
31. Horizontal Elongated Smyrna
32. Rice
33. Giant Rice
34. Straight Rice
35. Double Straight Rice
36. Hitched Cross
37. Lone Slashed Cross
38. Patterned Crosses
39. Patterned Scotch Crosses
40. Herringbone
41. Herringbone Gone Wrong

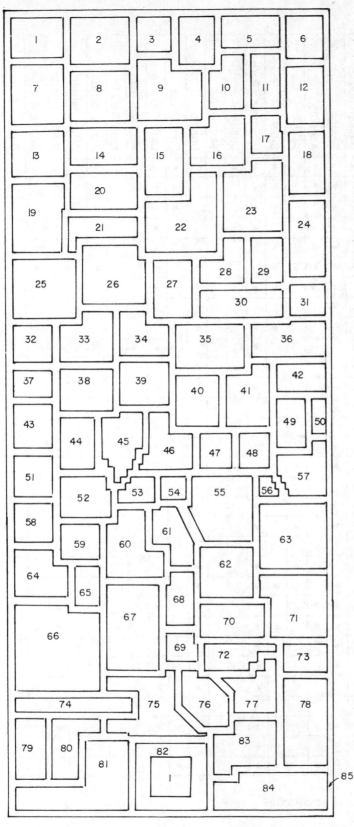

239

CROSS STITCHES	Border	Good Backing	Poor Backing	Background	Design	Accent	Fast	Slow	Geometric Pattern	Shading	Yarn Hog	Snags	Snag-Proof	Little Texture	Medium Texture	High Relief	Flower Stitch	Weak Pattern	Medium Pattern	Strong Pattern	Distorts Canvas
Cross Stitch				•	•			•	•	•			•	•			•	•			
Dotted Stitch					•			•	•				•	•					•		
Three-Stitch Cross				•	•			•	•				•		•		•		•		
Crossed Mosaic	•	•			•				•					•				•			
Rice	•				•	•		•	•					•			•			•	
Giant Rice	•				•	•		•	•			•		•			•			•	
Straight Rice	•				•	•		•	•			•		•			•			•	
Double Cross Tramé	•			•	•				•					•				•			
Raised Cross					•			•	•			•			•					•	
Oblong Cross				•	•				•					•				•			
Obl. Cr. Color Var.					•	•			•	•				•				•			
1 x 1 Sp. Cr. Tramé					•	•			•					•				•			
1 x 3 Sp. Cr. Tramé					•	•			•			•		•				•			
Oblong Cross Tramé					•	•			•					•				•			
Sleeping Obl. Cross					•	•			•			•		•				•			
Alt. Oblong Cross					•	•			•	•				•				•			
Flying Cross					•	•			•			•			•				•		
Hourglass Cross					•	•			•			•			•				•		
Van Dyke	•		•	•	•		•		•			•		•					•		
Tied Oblong Cross					•	•			•						•				•		
Gt. Tied Obl. Cross					•	•			•			•		•					•		
Dbl. Tied Obl. Cross					•	•			•					•					•		
Hitched Cross	•				•	•	•		•					•					•		
Knotted Cross	•				•	•		•	•		•		•			•			•		
Italian Cross	•			•	•				•			•		•				•			
Roman Cross					•	•			•			•		•				•			
Floral Cross					•				•	•		•		•						•	
Double Stitch					•	•			•						•	•			•		
Staggered Crosses					•	•			•					•					•		
Barred Square	•			•	•	•		•	•			•		•	•				•		
Woven Square	•			•	•	•		•	•				•	•						•	

240   The Stitches

CROSS STITCHES (cont.)	Border	Good Backing	Poor Backing	Background	Design	Accent	Fast	Slow	Geometric Pattern	Shading	Yarn Hog	Snags	Snag-Proof	Little Texture	Medium Texture	High Relief	Flower Stitch	Weak Pattern	Medium Pattern	Strong Pattern	Distorts Canvas
Bound Cross	•			•	•	•			•			•			•					•	
Braided Cross	•		•	•	•	•	•		•			•			•				•		
Upright Cross				•	•				•	•			•	•				•			
Slashed Cross				•	•	•						•			•		•		•		
Long Upright Cross				•	•	•			•					•					•		
Diag. Upright Cross				•	•				•					•						•	
Cross Diagonal				•	•				•			•		•					•		
Mini-Cross Diagonal				•	•				•				•	•				•			
Checkerboard Cross				•	•				•					•					•		
Combination Crosses				•	•				•				•	•					•		
Slanted Cross	•			•	•				•					•				•			
Fern			•	•	•		•			•					•				•		
Binding Stitch	•							•					•			•				•	
Plaited Stitch			•	•	•		•			•					•				•		
Diagonal Fern			•	•	•	•						•			•				•		
Herringbone			•	•	•		•			•					•				•		
H'bone Gone Wrong			•	•	•		•								•				•		
Two-Color H'bone	•		•									•			•				•		
Six-Trip H'bone	•		•						•	•		•			•				•		
Greek	•		•	•	•							•			•				•		
Diagonal Greek			•	•	•	•									•				•		
Plaited Gobelin	•			•	•					•	•	•			•				•		
Waffle	•		•			•					•	•				•				•	
Double Cross				•	•	•			•			•			•		•				
Trellis Cross				•	•	•		•	•			•		•			•		•		
Windowpane				•	•	•			•			•			•		•			•	
Fancy Cross				•	•	•		•	•			•			•		•			•	
Slanting Star					•							•			•		•	•			
Double Str. Cross				•	•	•						•			•		•			•	
Leviathan	•			•	•				•			•			•					•	
Double Leviathan	•				•	•			•			•			•	•	•		•		

CROSS STITCHES (cont.)	Border	Good Backing	Poor Backing	Background	Design	Accent	Fast	Slow	Geometric Pattern	Shading	Yarn Hog	Snags	Snag-Proof	Little Texture	Medium Texture	High Relief	Flower Stitch	Weak Pattern	Medium Pattern	Strong Pattern	Distorts Canvas
Triple Leviathan				•	•	•		•	•			•		•			•			•	
Medallion						•			•			•		•			•			•	
Triple Cross						•			•			•				•	•			•	
Triple Oblong Cross				•	•	•			•			•			•					•	
Windmill						•			•			•				•	•		•		
Tied Windmill						•			•			•			•		•			•	
Butterfly	•			•	•	•	•	•				•			•				•		
Tied Star				•	•	•	•	•				•			•		•			•	
Lone Tied Star						•									•		•		•		
Smyrna Cross	•			•	•	•			•							•	•			•	
Rev. Smyrna Cross	•			•	•	•			•							•	•			•	
Horiz. Elon. Smyrna	•			•	•	•			•			•				•	•			•	
Vert. Elon. Smyrna	•			•	•	•			•			•				•	•			•	
Alternating Smyrna				•	•	•			•							•	•			•	
Long-Arm Smyrna	•			•	•	•			•			•				•	•			•	
Patterned Crosses	•			•	•	•			•			•			•					•	
Pat. Scotch Crosses	•			•	•	•			•			•			•					•	
Woven Cross	•			•	•	•			•		•	•			•		•			•	
Point de Tresse	•			•	•	•			•			•			•					•	
Woven Band	•											•	•							•	
Railway	•			•								•	•							•	

On Mono canvas, each Cross must be crossed right away. It is faster, however, to work Penelope with a Cross Stitch. Both look alike.

CROSS STITCH

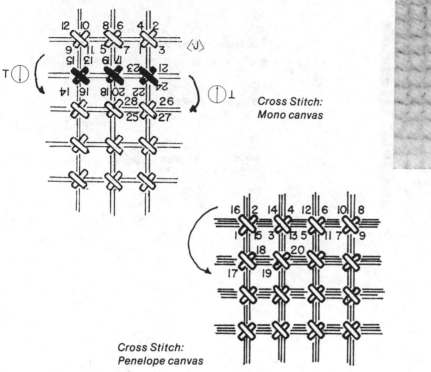

Cross Stitch:
Mono canvas

Cross Stitch:
Penelope canvas

Cross in a contrasting color. Note that the stitch pattern is basically Basketweave.

DOTTED STITCH

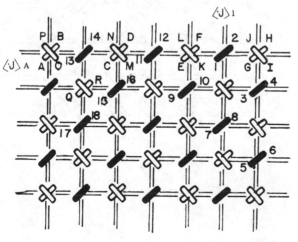

THREE-STITCH CROSS

You may need a tramé to cover the canvas.

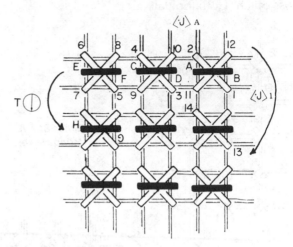

CROSSED MOSAIC

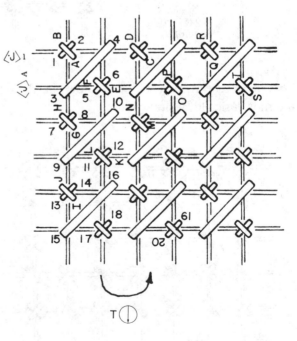

Use this stitch for a border of varying widths.

RICE

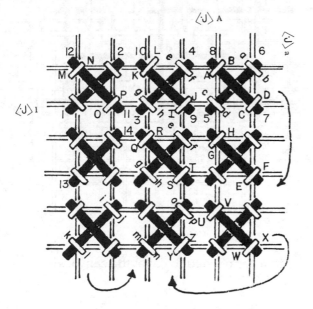

GIANT RICE

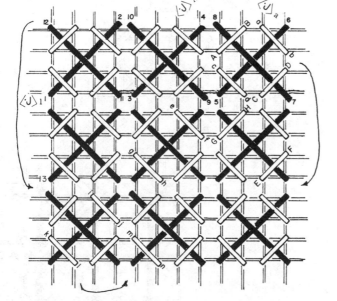

STRAIGHT RICE

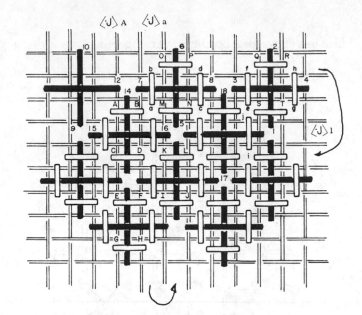

DOUBLE CROSS TRAMÉ

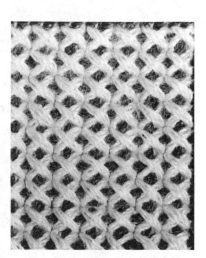

The tramé is needed to cover the canvas.

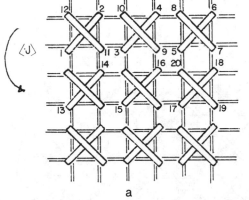

a

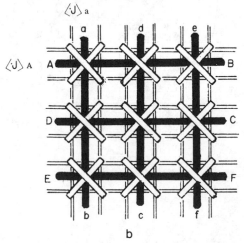

b

Thicken the yarn for the vertical stitches. Use three colors.

RAISED CROSS

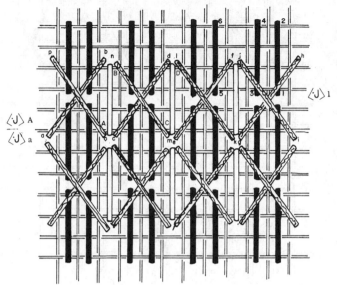

OBLONG CROSS

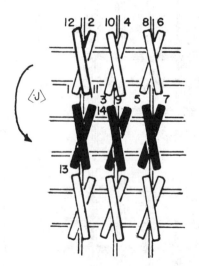

OBLONG CROSS COLOR VARIATION

This is just one way to show how color can vastly change the looks of a stitch.

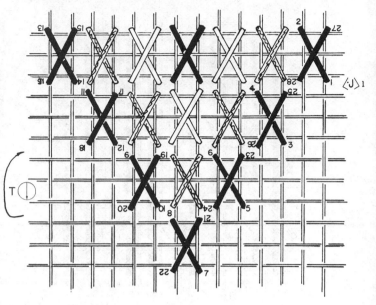

1 x 1 SPACED CROSS TRAMÉ

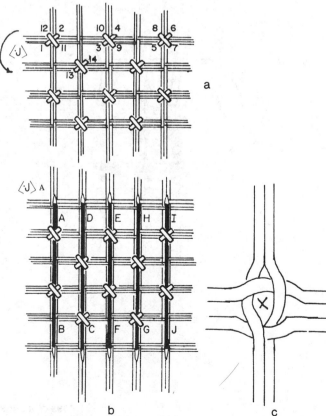

a

b

c

248

This stitch is worked most easily by stitching a checkerboard pattern of Oblong Cross Stitches first and then by running a tramé under them.

When the tramé is worked in a dark shade of green and the Oblong Cross in a lighter shade of green, this stitch resembles grass.

The tramé and Cross-Stitches may run horizontally or vertically. Suit it to your needs.

1 x 3 SPACED CROSS TRAMÉ

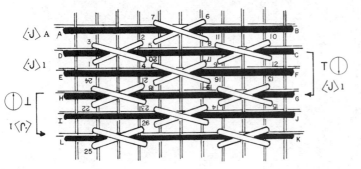

You might need to thicken the yarn for the tramé.

OBLONG CROSS TRAMÉ

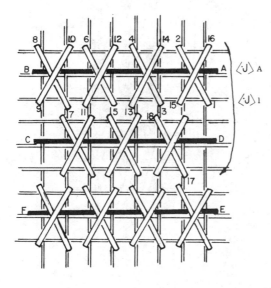

SLEEPING OBLONG CROSS

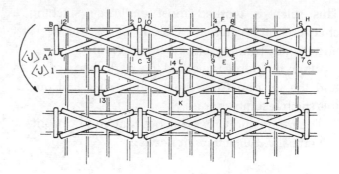

ALTERNATING OBLONG CROSS

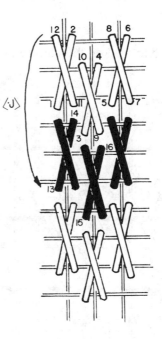

Thicken the yarn.

FLYING CROSS

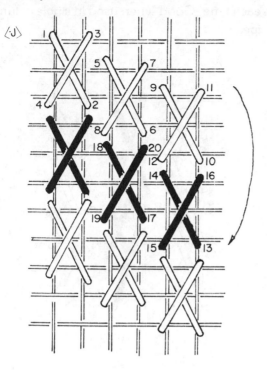

HOURGLASS CROSS

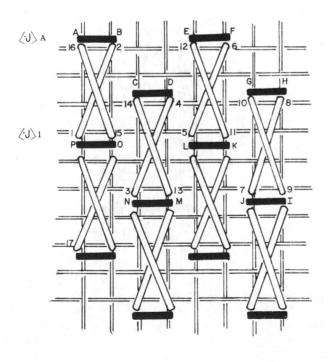

VAN DYKE

Always start the next row at the top. End and cut yarn each time. Good when used in single columns or as stripes.

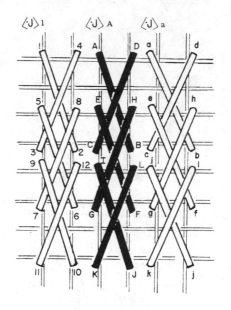

TIED OBLONG CROSS

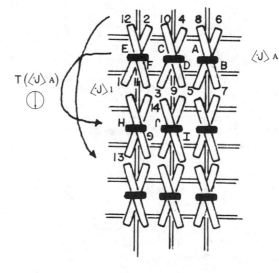

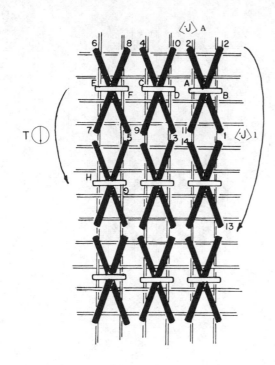

GIANT TIED OBLONG CROSS

Cross and tie before going on to the next motif.

DOUBLE TIED OBLONG CROSS

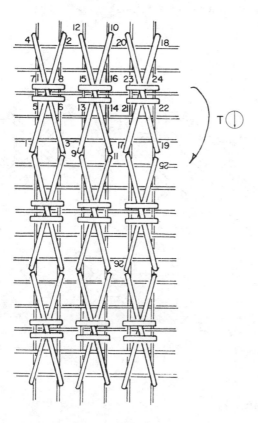

HITCHED
CROSS

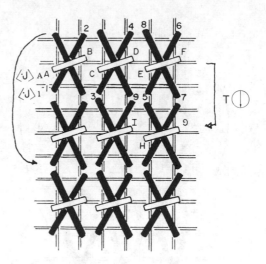

KNOTTED
CROSS

This stitch is quite slow to do. You may need to poke.
Cross and knot each stitch as you go.

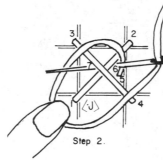

Step 2.

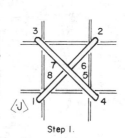

Step 1.

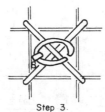

Step 3.

Work this stitch 4 x 4, 3 x 3, or 2 x 2.

ITALIAN CROSS

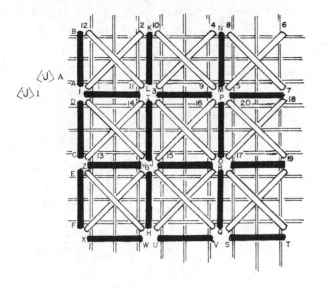

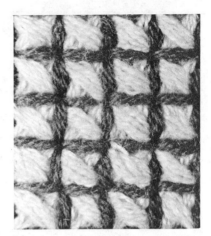

ROMAN CROSS

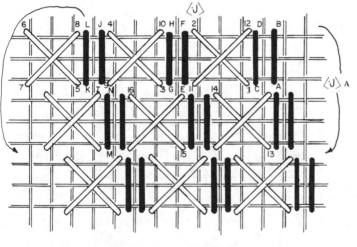

FLORAL CROSS

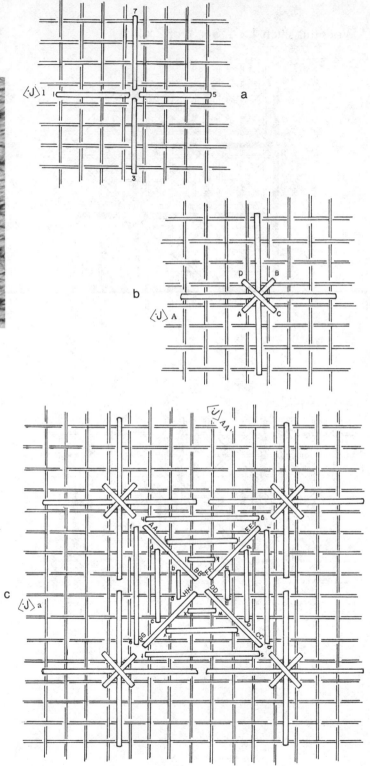

This is a good stitch for bumpy texture. When worked in one color it resembles tree bark. It is also good for polka dots.

DOUBLE STITCH

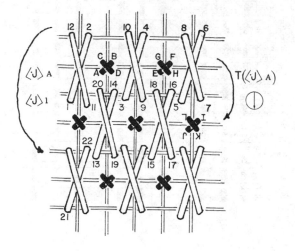

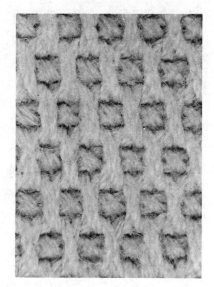

STAGGERED CROSSES

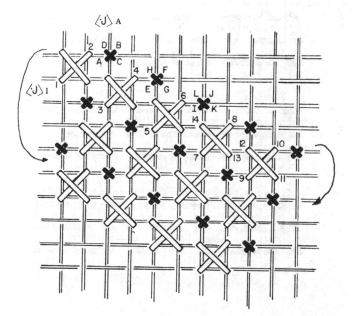

BARRED
SQUARE

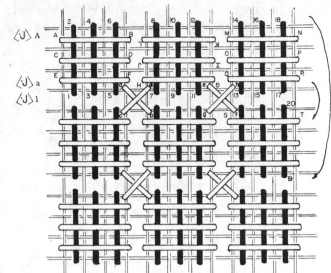

WOVEN
SQUARE

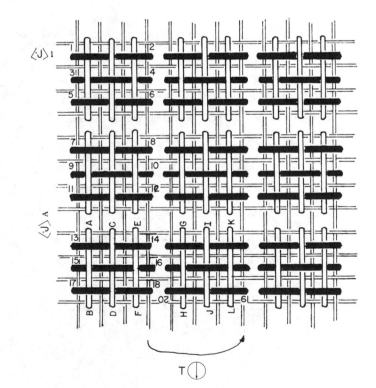

Alternate direction of crosses.

BOUND CROSS

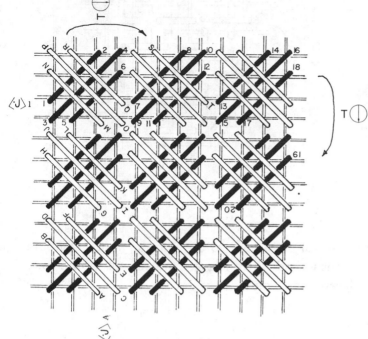

Thicken your yarn for this stitch. The French Knot in the center is decorative. It could, however, cover bare canvas.

In going from #5 to #6, slip the needle under stitch #1–2. In going from #7 to #8, slip the needle under stitch #3–4.

BRAIDED CROSS

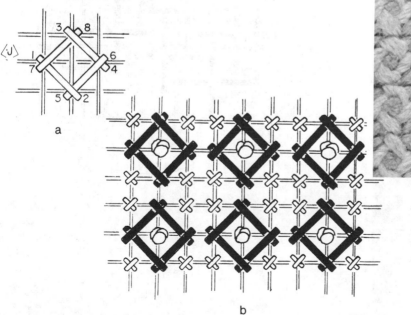

a

b

UPRIGHT
CROSS

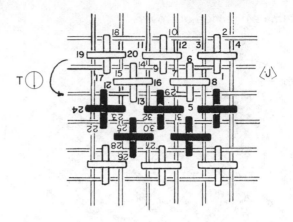

SLASHED
CROSS

You will often have to use your finger to move the yarns to find where to place the difficult second row. It can stand alone.

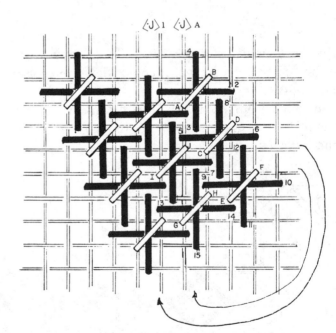

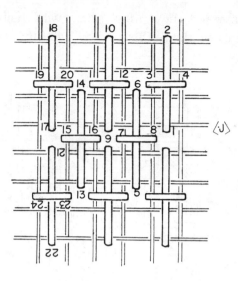

LONG UPRIGHT CROSS

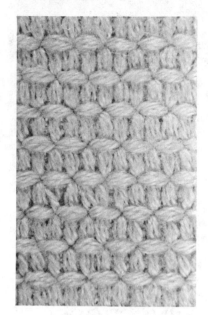

DIAGONAL UPRIGHT CROSS

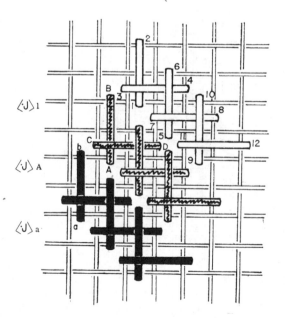

CROSS DIAGONAL

The diagram shows the stitch with half of the diagonals worked; the photo, with the diagonals completed.

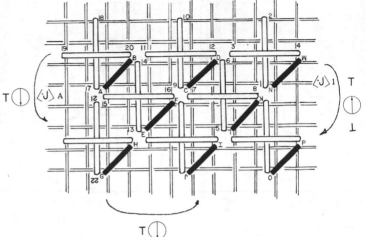

MINI-CROSS DIAGONAL

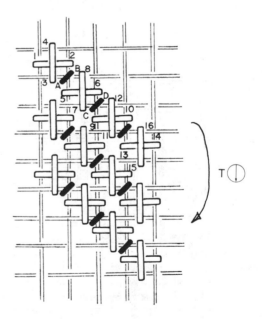

This stitch resembles a basket.

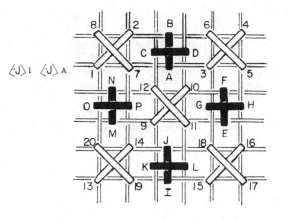

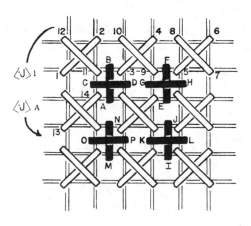

CHECKER-BOARD CROSS

COMBINATION CROSSES

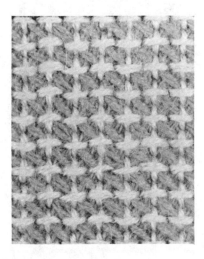

SLANTED CROSS

The first part of the stitch is the same as the Cross Stitch, but the return is like Straight Gobelin.

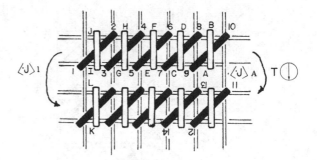

FERN

Work this stitch in vertical columns from top to bottom only. Do not turn the canvas upside down for the next row. It makes a fat, neat braid. Fill the space at the top of the column with a Cross Stitch.

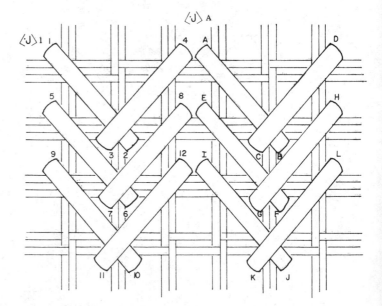

The Binding Stitch is not only useful; it is attractive, too. It finishes edges and sews seams (page 108). It is worked only on the edge of canvas. You will need two threads of the canvas to secure it properly. On Penelope this is one mesh; on Mono, two mesh.

It is worked much like the Fern Stitch and it, too, produces a braid.

BINDING STITCH

Correct sewing or binding of a seam

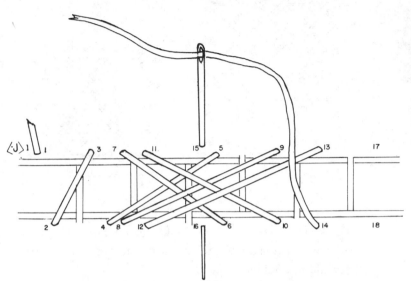

Correct way

Wrong way

Cross Stitches   265

PLAITED STITCH

The Plaited Stitch is worked in the same way as the Fern Stitch, but with overlapping rows. It covers Penelope 7 better than the Fern Stitch does. When finished, it looks somewhat like Herringbone and it is done less painfully.

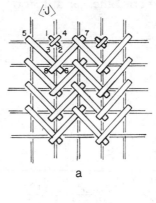

a

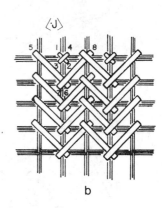

b

DIAGONAL FERN

Thicken your yarn to stitch Diagonal Fern. This is one of those stitches that must be started with compensating stitches.

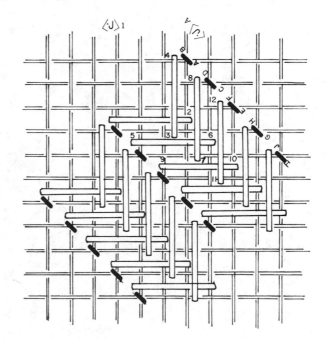

Work Herringbone from left to right only. Cut the yarn at the end of the first row and begin the second row directly beneath the first stitch of the first row, one mesh below.

You will have to move the yarn in the row above with your fingers in order to find the holes for the second row. This stitch is very tedious to work.

The common error is skipping a row. If you are having trouble, check to be sure every hole is filled along the edge of the stitch.

HERRINGBONE

This stitch is worked like Herringbone except that you turn the canvas upside down to work the second row.

It is easier to learn if you end with a stitch that slants upward.

You still have to move the yarns in the row below to find the holes for the second row.

It is a common error to skip every other row. (See Herringbone.)

HERRINGBONE GONE WRONG

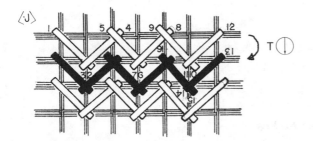

267

TWO-COLOR
HERRINGBONE

Stitch the darker color first.

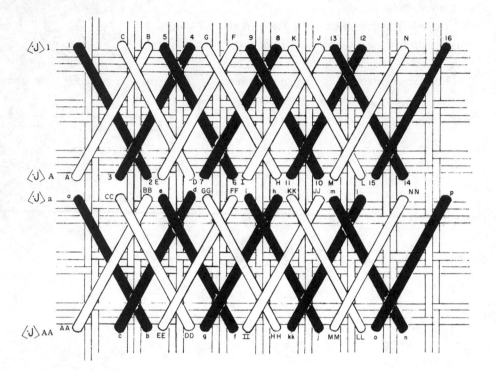

This is excellent border stitch. Work it on Interlock Mono or Penelope canvas **only**—use all one color or many shades of one color. Put the darkest color down first. With only five colors, make the first and second trips in the darkest color.

SIX-TRIP HERRINGBONE

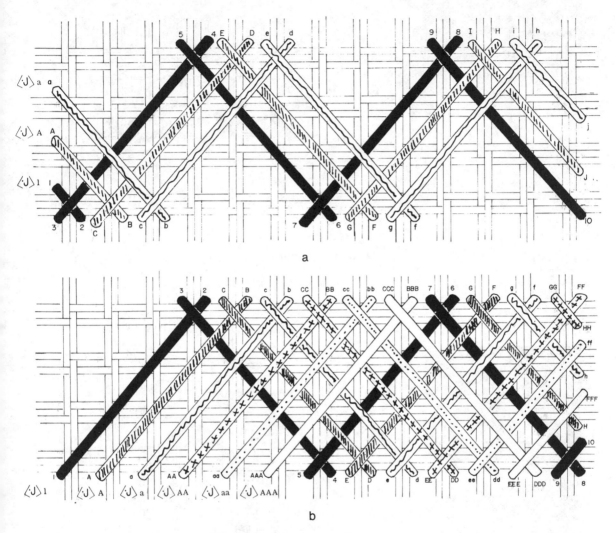

a

b

GREEK

Work the Greek Stitch from **left to right only.** Break the yarn at the end of the row and begin again below the first stitch. It is actually a Cross Stitch with one short arm and one long arm. Each cross is intertwined with the next one.

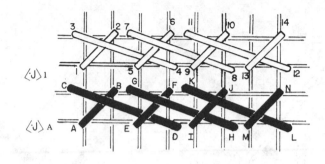

DIAGONAL GREEK

Work from left to right only.

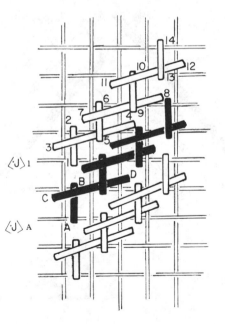

Be sure your yarn will cover the canvas. Experiment. Use your thumb to push the yarn back to find the holes for the next stitch. Work from top to bottom only. Cut the yarn at the end of the first row and begin the second row at the top. Do the compensating stitches last.

PLAITED GOBELIN

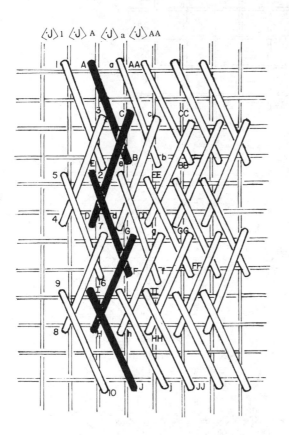

WAFFLE

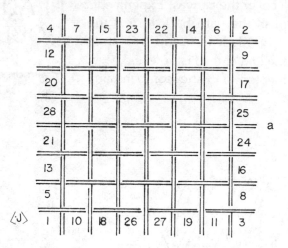

a

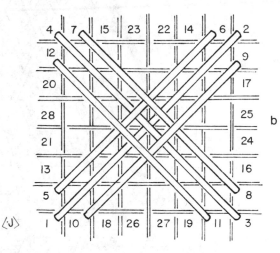

b

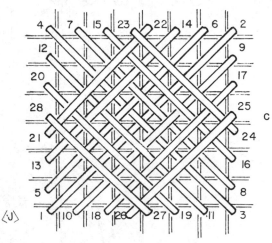

c

This stitch makes a woven basket look.

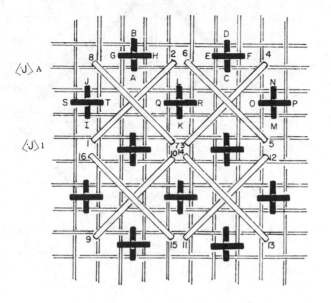

DOUBLE CROSS

This stitch resembles a basket.

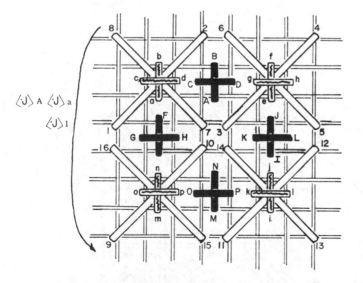

TRELLIS CROSS

WINDOWPANE

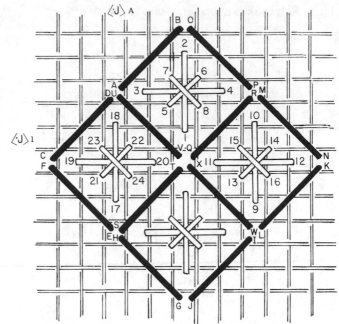

FANCY CROSS

You may need a tramé to make this stitch cover the canvas.

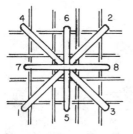

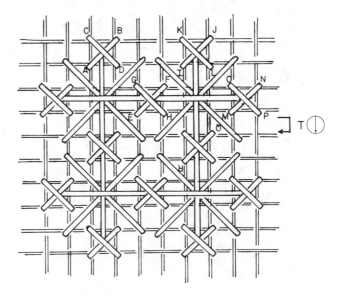

The Slanting Star stands alone on a ground of Cross Stitch. It is actually an upright cross with a Knotted Stitch super-imposed on it.

SLANTING STAR

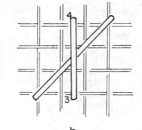

a

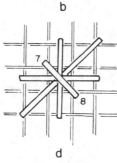

b

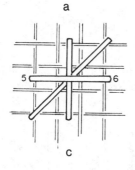

c

d

DOUBLE STRAIGHT CROSS

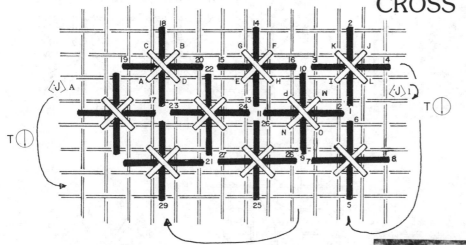

LEVIATHAN

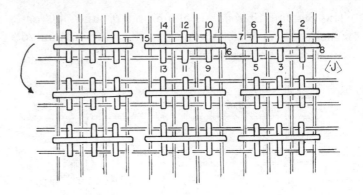

DOUBLE
LEVIATHAN

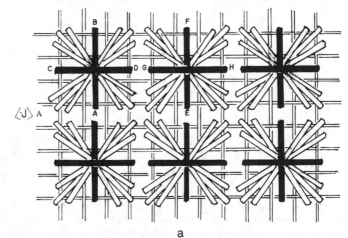

a

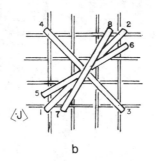

b

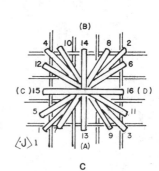

c

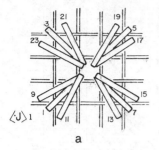

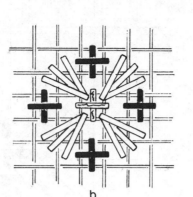

a

b

TRIPLE LEVIATHAN

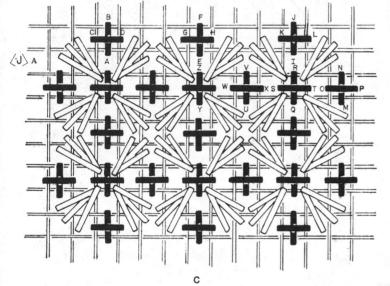

c

MEDALLION

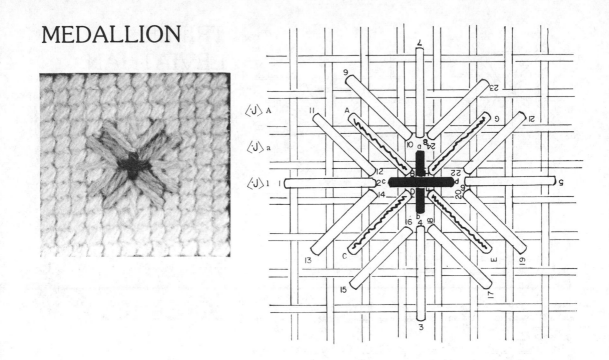

TRIPLE CROSS

Triple Cross stands alone. It is similar to Triple Leviathan.

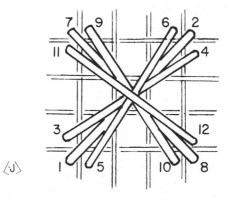

TRIPLE OBLONG CROSS

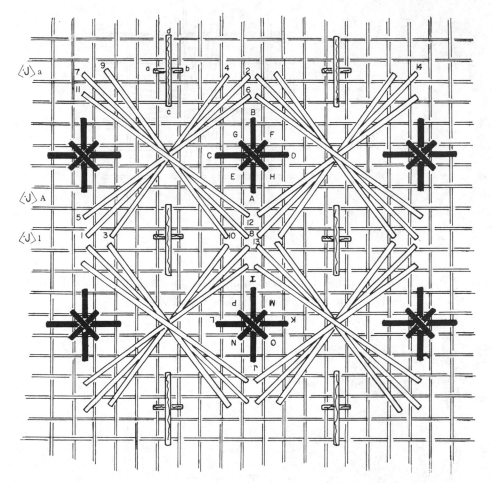

Cross Stitches   **279**

WINDMILL

This stitch stands alone. Fill the spaces with Cross.

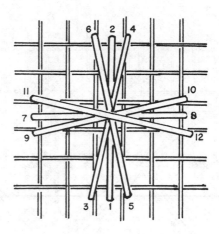

TIED WINDMILL

The Tied Windmill also stands alone. Put it on a ground of Cross Stitch, if you wish.

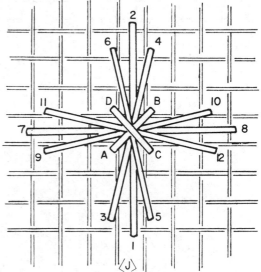

The Butterfly Stitch looks like a basket. When stitch E-F is worked in the same color as the numbered stitches and stitches A-B and C-D are on top, it resembles a butterfly.

BUTTERFLY

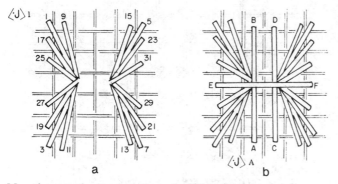

Use this stitch diagonally in both directions.

TIED STAR

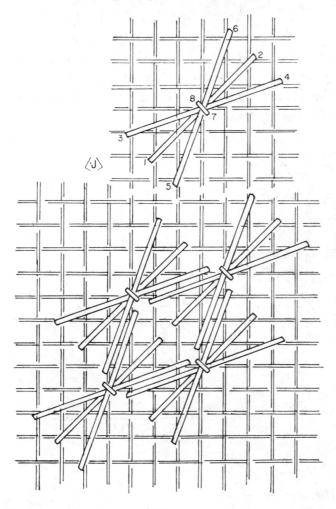

LONE TIED STAR

This stitch stands alone. Fill with Continental, Upright Cross, or Cross Stitches. It resembles a bow or a bow tie.

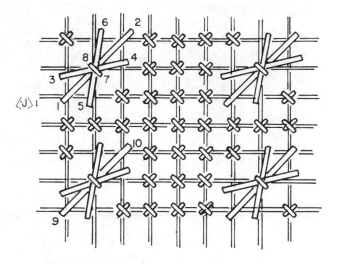

SMYRNA CROSS

Make the x first, then the +. Smyrna Cross makes a good bump. When the + is worked in a light color, the stitch resembles hot cross buns. It is good for buttons, polka dots, etc.

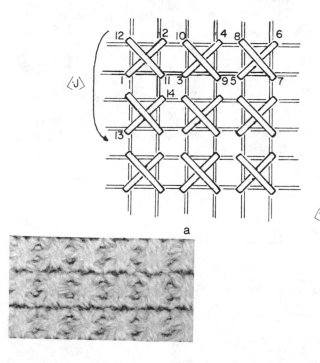

a

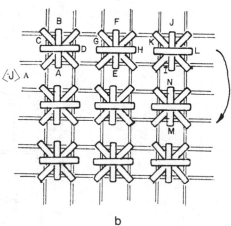

b

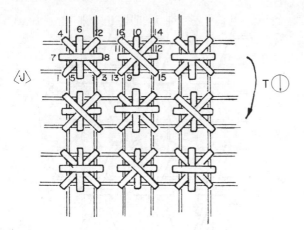

REVERSED
SMYRNA
CROSSES

HORIZONTAL
ELONGATED
SMYRNA

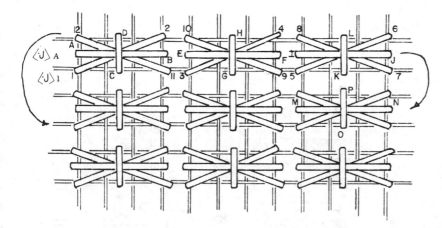

Cross Stitches   283

VERTICAL
ELONGATED
SMYRNA

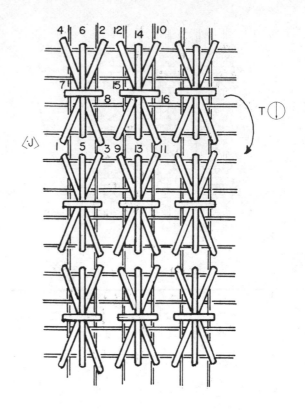

ALTERNATING
SMYRNA

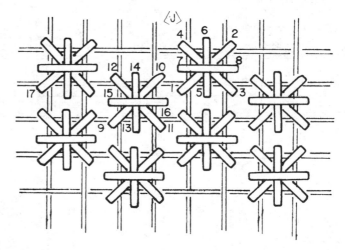

The last stitch of the + covers two Smyrna Crosses, giving an interesting reflection of light.

LONG-ARM SMYRNA

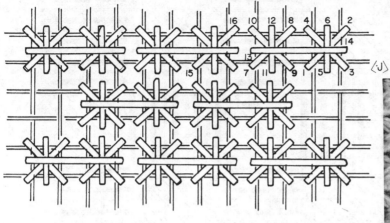

This stitch and the Patterned Scotch Crosses are examples of Diaper Patterns. These are combinations of stitches. Use these or make up your own.

PATTERNED CROSSES

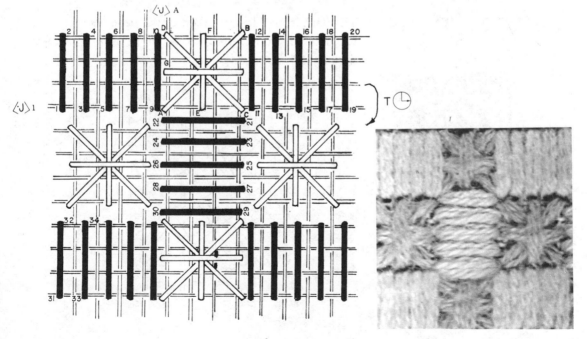

PATTERNED SCOTCH CROSSES

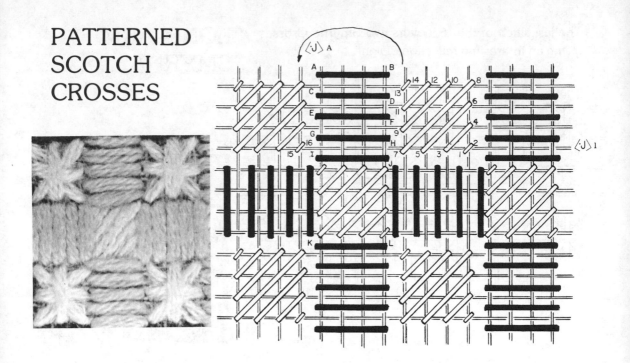

WOVEN CROSS

The yarn from #15 is worked under yarn #9–10 on its way to #16. Do not try to work compensating stitches; they cannot be readily done.

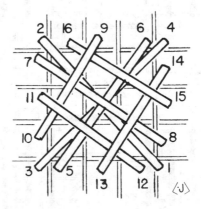

This makes a long column, suitable for a border.

POINT DE TRESSE

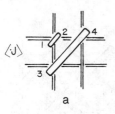

a

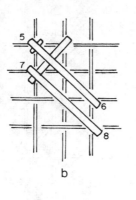

b

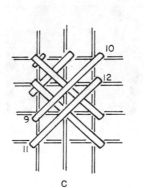

c

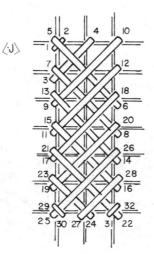

d

e

WOVEN BAND

This is an excellent border.

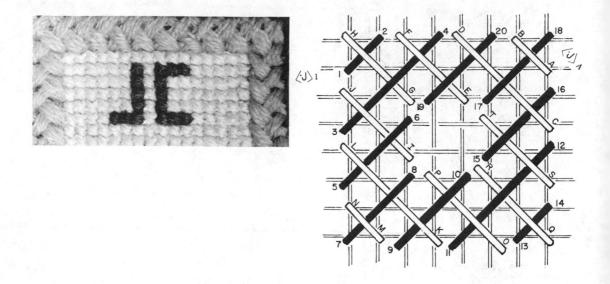

RAILWAY

Each lettered stitch is woven under every other numbered stitch. This, too, makes an excellent border. Make sure it covers.

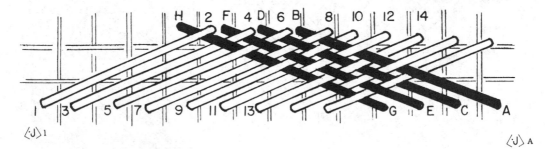

EIGHT:

Tied Stitches

The Tied Stitches are pretty and many are good stitches for shading. The Periwinkle Stitch was especially designed to be accented with beads.

These stitches are somewhat slow, but they mostly give good backings with little snagging on the right side of the canvas.

It is **most** important that you tie each stitch or group of stitches as you go. Each of the drawings is numbered; follow them closely.

The sampler showing the Tied Stitches was worked on Mono 10 with a full strand of tapestry yarn. Some of the stitches did not cover completely. Thickening the yarn made them bulky; for them I recommend a smaller canvas, perhaps Mono 12 or 14. Remember, this decision is yours, because it depends on the kind, color, and brand of yarn, as well as the canvas you use. Test each stitch you plan to use. You may also consider painting the canvas (page 66).

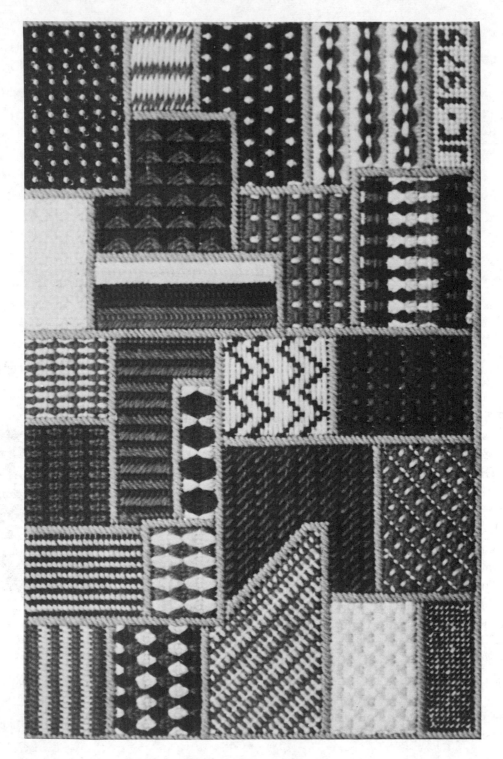

290   The Stitches

Key to Sampler Stitches

1. Knotted Stitch
2. Interlocking Parisian Cross
3. French
4. Paris
5. French Variation
6. Periwinkle
7. Rococo
8. Long Rococo
9. Giant Rococo
10. Long and Short Oblique
11. Fly Stitch
12. Arrowhead Fly
13. Roumanian Couching
14. Diagonal Roumanian
15. Interlocking Roumanian
16. Bokhara Couching
17. Wheat
18. Alternating Wheat
19. Interlocking Wheat
20. Web
21. Diagonal Wheat
22. Rounded Wheat Columns
23. Alternating Rounded Wheat Columns
24. Shell
25. Web
26. 2 x 2 Slanted Gobelin

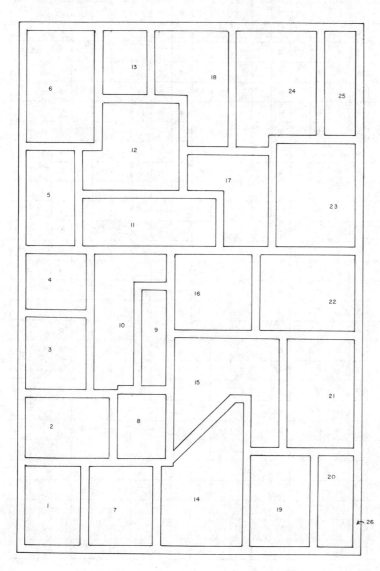

TIED STITCHES	Border	Good Backing	Poor Backing	Background	Design	Accent	Fast	Slow	Geometric Pattern	Shading	Yarn Hog	Snags	Snag-Proof	Little Texture	Medium Texture	High Relief	Flower Stitch	Weak Pattern	Medium Pattern	Strong Pattern	Distorts Canvas
Knotted Stitch		•		•	•			•		•			•	•					•		
Inter. Pars. Cross		•		•	•			•		•			•	•					•		
French		•		•	•			•		•			•	•					•		
Paris		•		•	•			•					•	•					•		
French Variation				•	•			•					•	•					•		
Periwinkle				•	•			•								•				•	
Rococo		•		•	•	•		•					•	•					•		
Long Rococo		•		•	•	•		•					•	•					•		
Giant Rococo		•		•	•	•		•					•	•					•		
Long and Short Obl.	•	•		•	•	•		•				•		•					•		
Fly				•	•									•					•		
Arrowhead Fly	•			•	•	•		•				•		•					•		
Couching			•		•	•	•					•		•				•			
Roumanian Couching			•	•	•	•	•					•		•					•		
Diagonal Roumanian				•	•					•			•	•					•		
Inter. Roumanian				•	•					•		•		•					•		
Bokhara Couching			•	•	•	•	•		•			•		•					•		
Wheat	•	•		•	•	•		•				•			•				•		
Alternating Wheat		•		•	•	•		•				•			•				•		
Interlocking Wheat		•		•	•	•		•				•			•				•		
Diagonal Wheat		•		•	•	•		•				•			•				•		
Rounded Wheat Cols.		•		•	•	•		•							•				•		
Alt. Rnd. Wh. Cols.		•		•	•	•		•							•				•		
Shell	•	•			•	•		•			•	•				•				•	
Web					•	•		•		•			•	•				•			

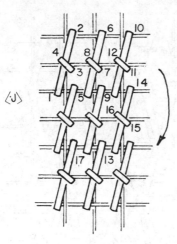

KNOTTED
STITCH

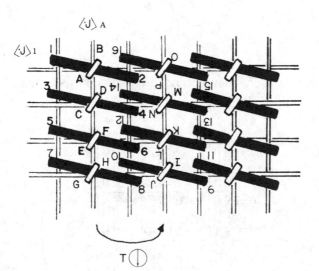

INTERLOCKING
PARISIAN
CROSS

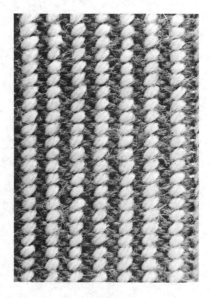

FRENCH

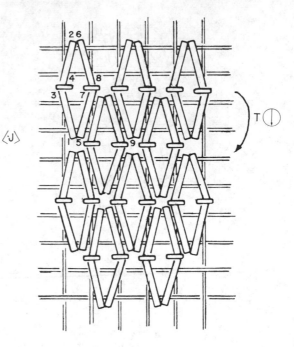

PARIS

Try this stitch when you need a woven basket look.

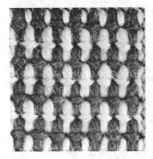

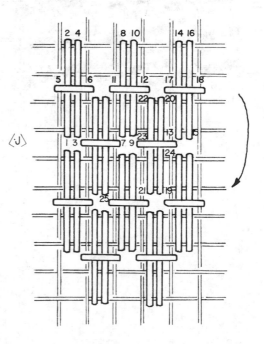

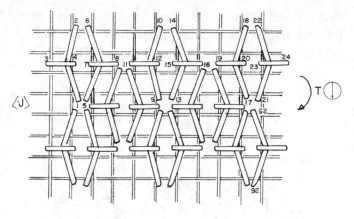

FRENCH
VARIATION

PERIWINKLE

Because this stitch was designed to be used with beads, it does not cover the canvas unless beads are used. Use long, thin beads; one round one, large enough to cover; or three, as I have done. This stitch would make a particularly attractive background for an evening purse, especially if worked with metallic thread.

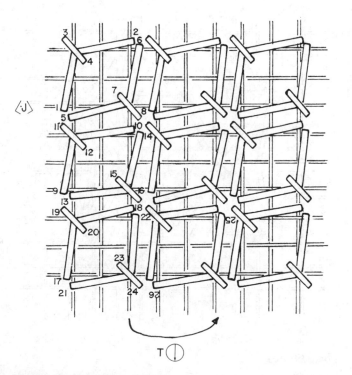

ROCOCO

When used alone, this stitch makes a good ball, balloon, button, or anything else round. When turned 90° (on its side) and with a stem added, the Rococo becomes a nice replica of a musical note.

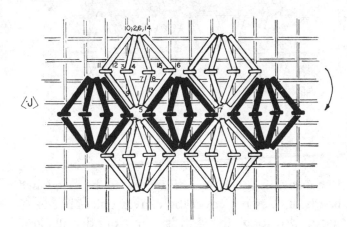

LONG ROCOCO

The Long Rococo has a diamond shape.

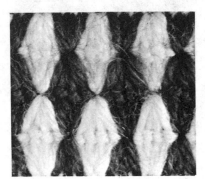

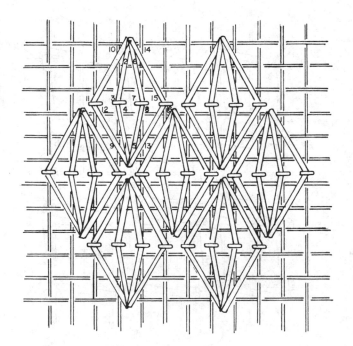

Make the Rococo any size you wish. Simply add a stitch on the far right of center and the far left of center. For every pair of stitches you add, add one mesh at the top and one at the bottom. This technique will keep the Rococo round. When extra stitches are not added, Long Rococo results.

GIANT ROCOCO

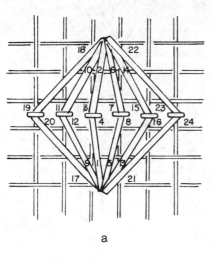

a

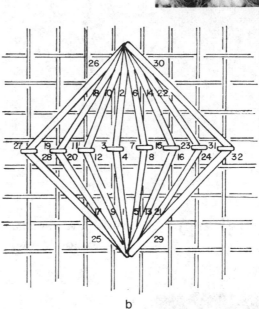

b

LONG AND SHORT OBLIQUE

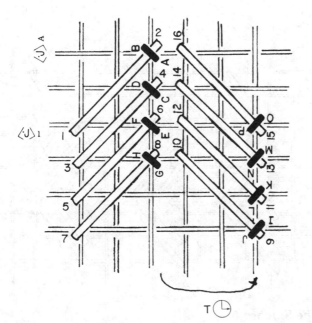

297

FLY

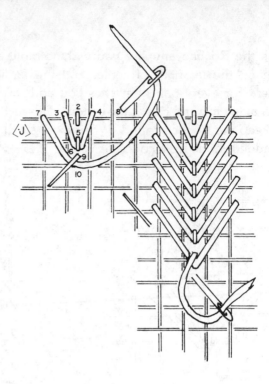

ARROWHEAD FLY

Two "Arrowheads," placed in vertical column and/or in a horizontal row, make an attractive border.

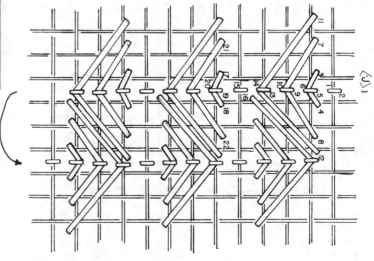

Couching is laying one yarn where you want it and tacking it down with another yarn. It curves well. Thread two needles. Try to tie at even intervals.

COUCHING

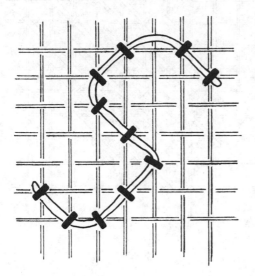

You may vary the placement of the ties, but every tie stitch is always a 1 x 3 stitch.

ROUMANIAN COUCHING

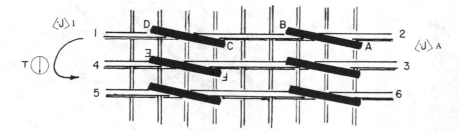

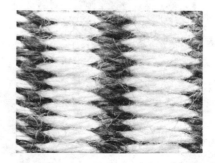

DIAGONAL
ROUMANIAN

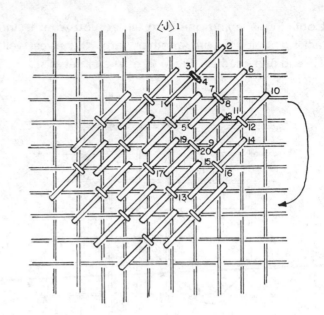

INTERLOCKING
ROUMANIAN

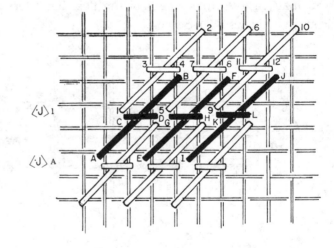

Use the tie stitch to create any pattern, regular or
irregular, that you like.

BOKHARA
COUCHING

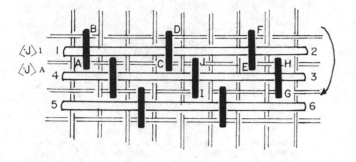

WHEAT

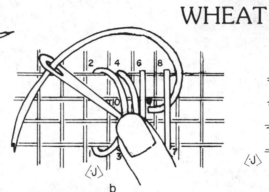

a

b

c

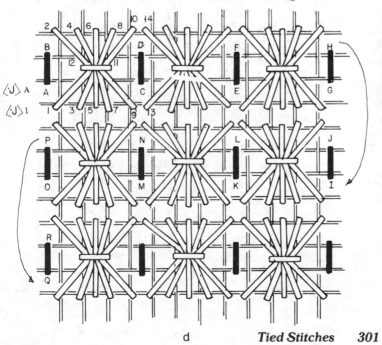

d   *Tied Stitches*   **301**

ALTERNATING
WHEAT

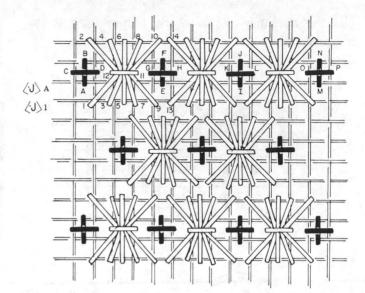

INTERLOCKING
WHEAT

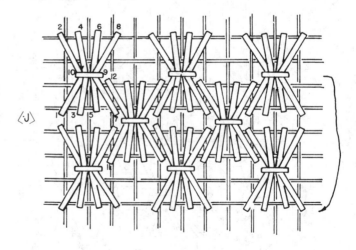

Diagonal Wheat may slant both ways.

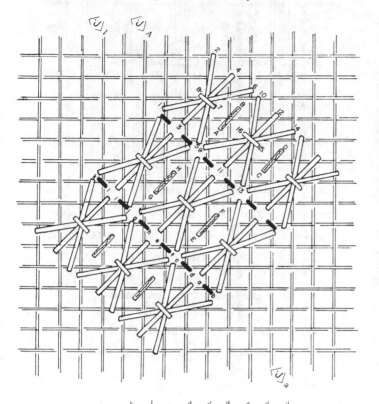

DIAGONAL
WHEAT

ROUNDED
WHEAT
COLUMNS

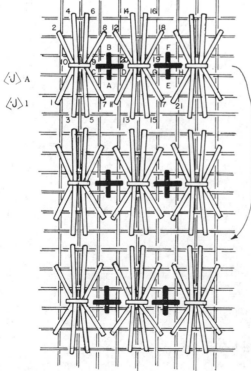

303

ALTERNATING ROUNDED WHEAT COLUMNS

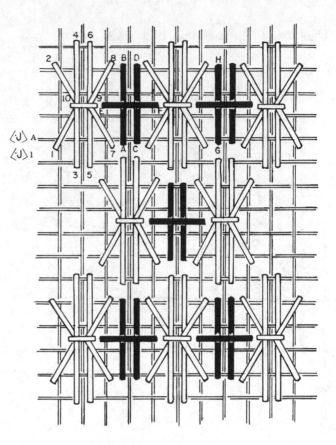

SHELL

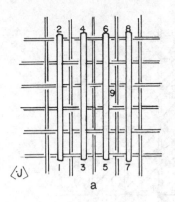

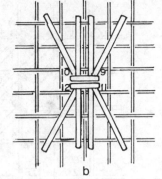

a

b

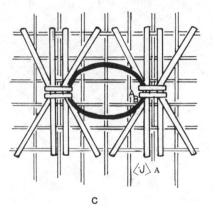

c

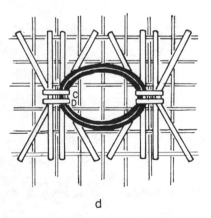

d

WEB

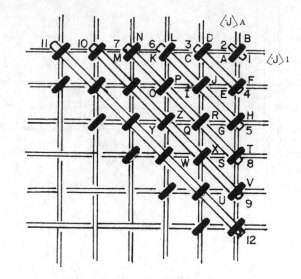

NINE:

Eye Stitches

Eye Stitches are those that are made by putting several stitches into one hole. This technique creates a hole, a dimple, or an eye.

The sampler of Eye Stitches on the following page was made on Interlock Mono 10, using a full strand of tapestry yarn (except for Algerian Eye, which needed a 2-ply yarn).

Eye Stitches are very pretty and interesting to do, but slow to work up. In stitching them, work from the outside to the center and **always** go **down** into the center. This will prevent splitting or snagging the yarn of the stitches you have already worked.

As you put what seems an impossible number of stitches into one small hole, take care that each of these stitches goes into the hole smoothly. If you are working on Regular Mono canvas, this task will be a little easier. It is a great help to enlarge the center hole by poking the point of a pair of embroidery

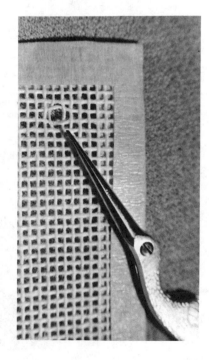

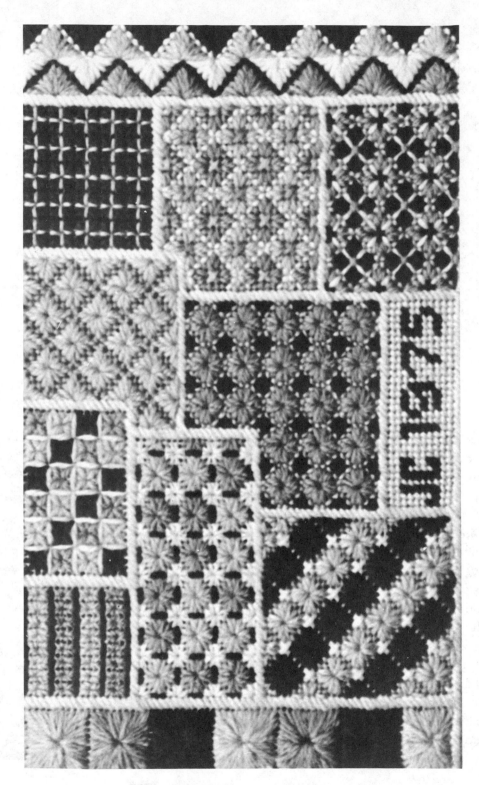

308   *The Stitches*

Key to Sampler Stitches

1. Square Eyelet
2. Algerian Eye
3. Framed Star
4. Diamond Eyelet
5. Double Star
6. Triangular Ray
7. Squared Daisies
8. Ringed Daisies
9. Crossed Diamond
10. Crossed Daisies
11. Double Crossed Diamond
12. Continental and Basketweave

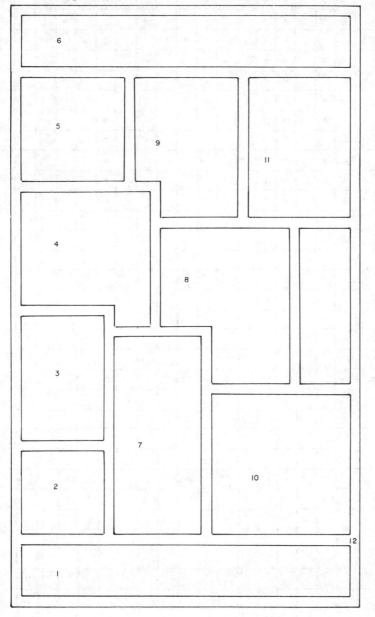

scissors into it. Spread the mesh gently to enlarge the hole. This works **only** on Regular Mono canvas. Use 2-ply Persian yarn on other kinds.

You may need to pull the yarn more tightly as each eye forms. This helps to make the stitch smooth, but be careful not to pull the canvas out of shape.

Note that Eye Stitches usually begin with an Upright Cross, going from the outside into the center. Next, one stitch is taken in each quadrant in a circular motion until all the remaining stitches have been taken. The even-numbered stitches are all in the center of the eye, and because they do not fit easily, they have been omitted.

Eye Stitches lend themselves to broad borders, backgrounds, and pillows. Single motifs or clusters of two or three eyes make lovely flowers.

Because the Eye Stitches have good backing, most of them will wear well. Those that will not are those that have long yarns on top, such as Triangular Ray and Square Eyelet. (Refer to "Covering the Canvas," on page 35.)

EYE STITCHES	Border	Good Backing	Poor Backing	Background	Design	Accent	Fast	Slow	Geometric Pattern	Shading	Yarn Hog	Snags	Snag-Proof	Little Texture	Medium Texture	High Relief	Flower Stitch	Weak Pattern	Medium Pattern	Strong Pattern	Distorts Canvas
Framed Star	•	•			•	•		•	•			•			•		•		•		
Double Star	•	•			•	•		•	•						•		•		•		
Algerian Eye	•	•		•	•			•	•				•	•				•			
Square Eyelet	•	•			•	•		•	•		•	•			•			•			
Diamond Eyelet	•	•		•	•	•		•	•			•		•						•	
Triangular Ray	•	•			•	•		•	•			•			•					•	
Crossed Diamond	•				•	•		•	•						•		•			•	
Double Crossed Dia.	•				•	•		•	•						•		•			•	
Squared Daisies	•	•		•	•	•		•	•						•		•			•	
Ringed Daisies	•	•		•	•	•		•	•						•		•			•	
Crossed Daisies	•	•		•	•	•		•	•						•		•			•	

Without the frame, this is simply the Star Stitch. The frame is necessary to cover the canvas, except on Mono 14.

FRAMED STAR

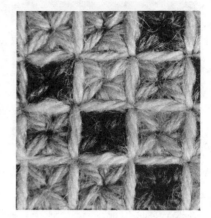

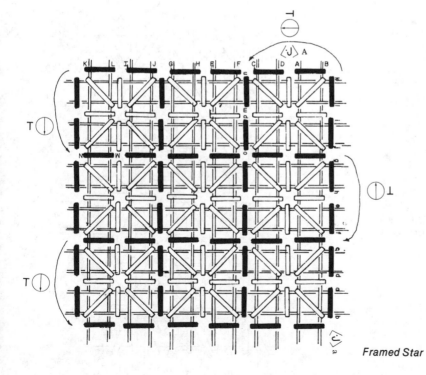

Star

Framed Star

DOUBLE STAR

This stitch is actually a framed Reversed Mosaic. I think you will find it easier to get a smooth finish if you follow the numbers given. This stitch is particularly attractive in two colors.

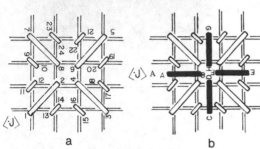

a

b

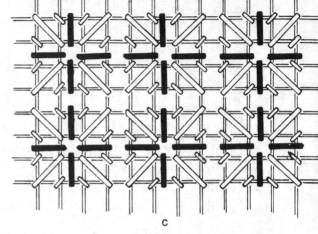

c

ALGERIAN EYE

You may find it necessary to thin your yarn to work this stitch.

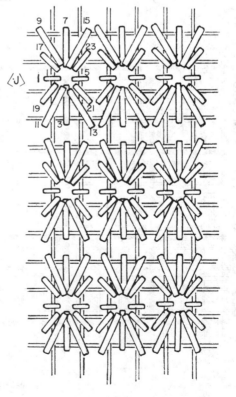

The Square Eyelet Stitch shown here covers an area 10-mesh square. It may cover 6 x 6 or 8 x 8.

SQUARE EYELET

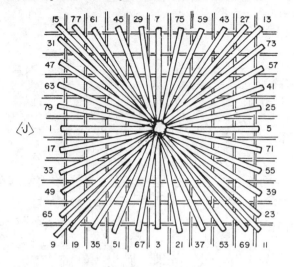

Diamond Eyelet lets you put a pearl or bead in the center. The Back-Stitch and Frame Stitch fill in between the diamonds. This stitch makes a good border, background, or geometric design with many color possibilities.

DIAMOND EYELET

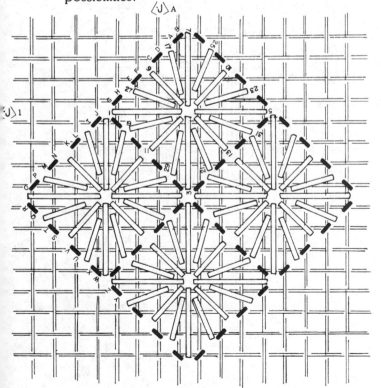

313

TRIANGULAR RAY

This stitch makes a nice border. Arrangement of color can create rick-rack. Use a Back-Stitch, if it does not cover.

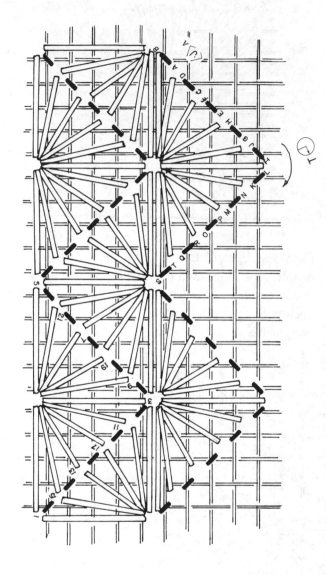

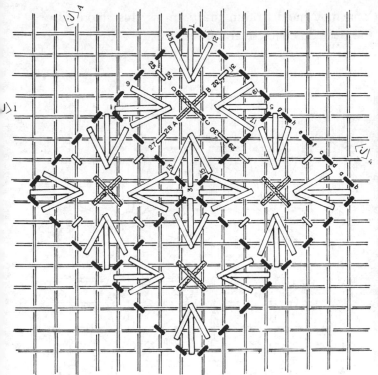

CROSSED DIAMOND

DOUBLE CROSSED DIAMOND

315

SQUARED
DAISIES

You may need to thin the yarn for this stitch. Use the Back Stitch to cover the canvas.

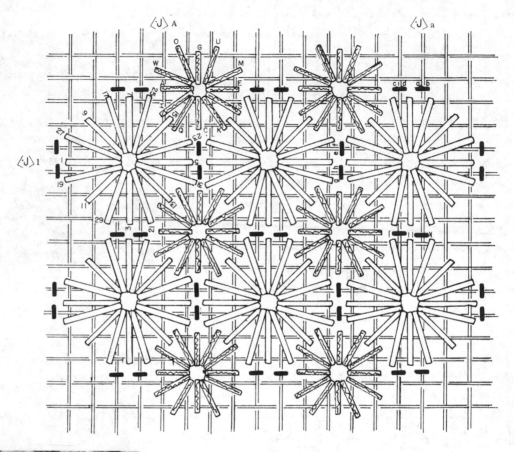

This is the same round eye as in Squared Daisies—except that the areas between the eyes are filled differently. This gives a changed look to the stitch.

RINGED DAISIES

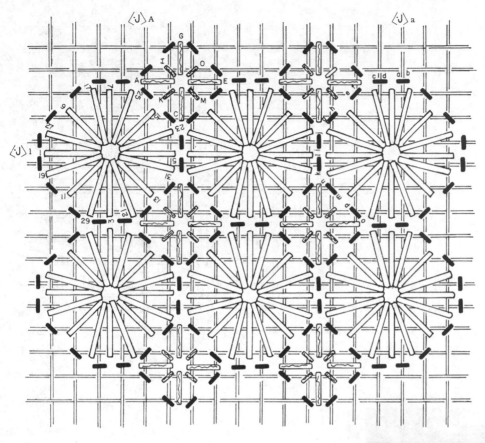

CROSSED
DAISIES

Here again is the round eye, but this time in alternating rows instead of columns.

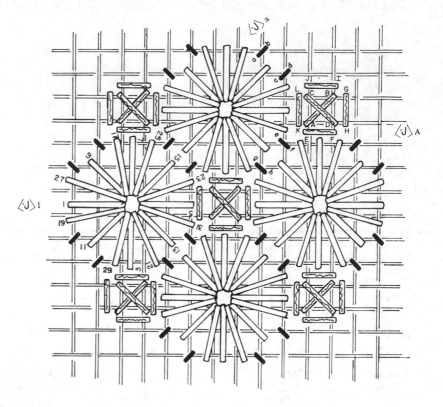

TEN:

Leaf Stitches

Leaf Stitches have a charm all their own; they complement lovely flowers. Given on the following pages are a few of those you can use. Mix them up, use one or two favorites, or make up your own.

Use the Leaf Stitches as overall patterns, singly, or in pairs. Turn Leaf Stitches sideways or upside down to make feathers. They may be worked in three three ways and are labeled #1, #2, #3, accordingly:

1. From the top, one stitch to the right, one stitch to the left, etc.
2. From the bottom, one stitch to the right, one stitch to the left, etc.
3. From the bottom, up one side, and down the other.

These stitches will also work up well in geometric patterns. Have fun with color. Most lend themselves well to shading.

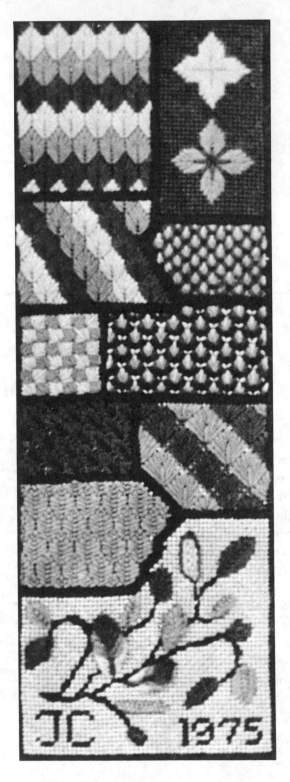

320   The Stitches

Key to Sampler Stitches

1. Leaf #1
2. Basketweave
3. Four-Way Leaf
4. Leaf #3
5. Leaf #2
6. Diamond Ray
7. Ray Stitch
8. Mini Leaf
9. Diagonal Leaf
10. Diamond Leaf
11. Roumanian Leaf
12. Raised Close Herring-
    bone
13. Free-Form Van Dyke
14. Diagonal Roumanian
    Leaf
15. Cretan
16. Rose Leaf
17. Close Herringbone
18. 2 x 2 Slanted Gobelin

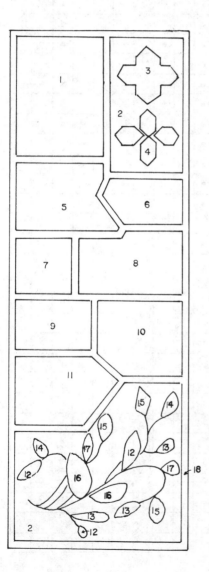

LEAF STITCHES	Border	Good Backing	Poor Backing	Background	Design	Accent	Fast	Slow	Geometric Pattern	Shading	Yarn Hog	Snags	Snag-Proof	Little Texture	Medium Texture	High Relief	Flower Stitch	Weak Pattern	Medium Pattern	Strong Pattern	Distorts Canvas
Diamond Ray		•		•	•	•			•	•					•		•				
Mini Leaf	•	•			•	•			•	•	•			•			•		•		
Ray Stitch	•	•				•			•	•	•					•	•		•		
Leaf #1	•	•		•	•	•			•	•		•		•					•		
Leaf #2	•	•		•	•	•			•	•		•		•					•		
Leaf #3	•	•		•	•	•			•	•		•		•					•		
Diamond Leaf		•		•	•	•			•	•		•		•					•		
Four-Way Leaf		•				•			•	•		•		•					•		
Diagonal Leaf		•		•	•	•			•	•		•		•					•		
Roumanian Leaf	•	•				•	•					•			•				•		
Diag. Roum. Leaf		•				•	•					•			•				•		
Cretan	•	•				•	•					•			•					•	
Close Herringbone						•						•				•			•		
Raised Close H'bone						•					•	•				•			•		
Free-Form Van Dyke						•					•	•				•				•	
Rose Leaf						•		•		•	•	•				•				•	

The Diamond Ray Stitch makes a most interesting pattern and has a good backing. I generally like something faster to work up for a background, but you might want to use it that way. The longest stitch is not likely to snag.

DIAMOND RAY

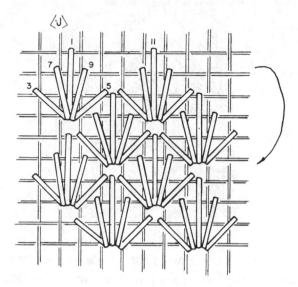

The Mini-Leaf Stitch is just a small version of the Leaf Stitch.

MINI-LEAF

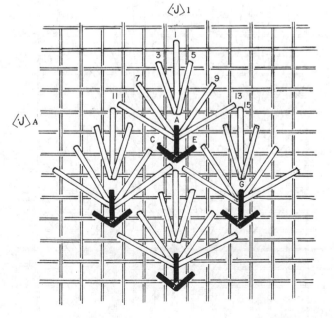

RAY

These Ray Stitches are worked in one color

The Ray Stitch is also very slow to work up and is hard on the fingers. Try spreading the base hole with a pair of scissors as described on page 319. In spite of its drawbacks, this Stitch is worthwhile, for it is lovely when finished. It makes a good, bumpy border but not recommended for large areas.

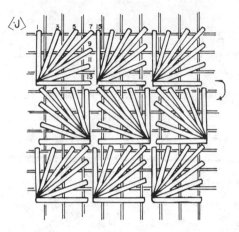

LEAF #1

This is the basic and most familiar Leaf Stitch. It makes an interesting pattern. It is lovely when shaded within each leaf. An optional vein may be added as in Leaf #3. This has a good backing and makes a pretty border or vertical stripe.

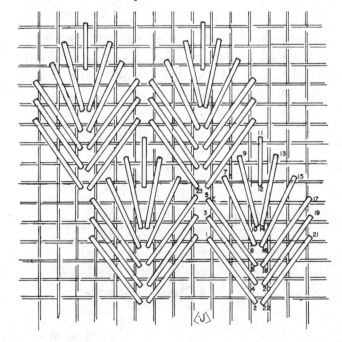

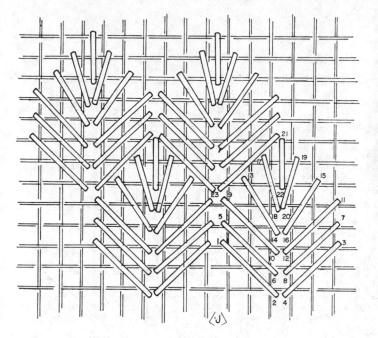

LEAF #2

Do the vein last in another color, if you wish.

LEAF #3

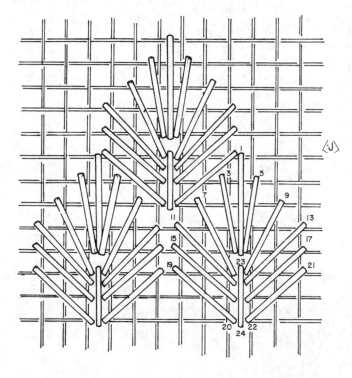

DIAMOND LEAF

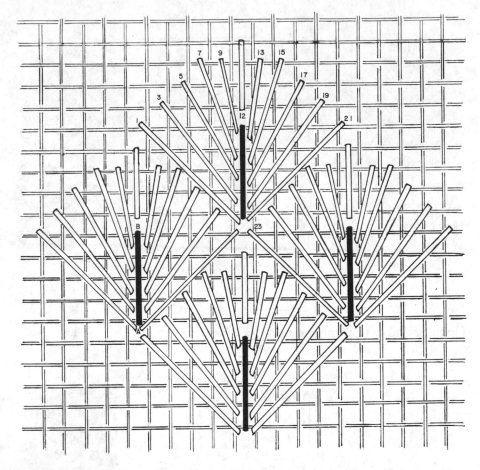

Fill in around the leaves with Basketweave. When placed in an arrangement of several leaves, a pretty overall pattern with good backing occurs.

FOUR-WAY LEAF

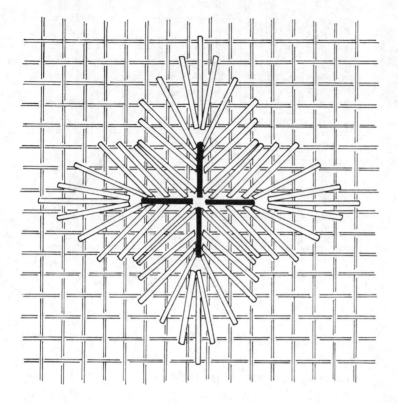

DIAGONAL LEAF

Use this Leaf Stitch in groups or singly. The resulting pattern is pleasing to the eye.

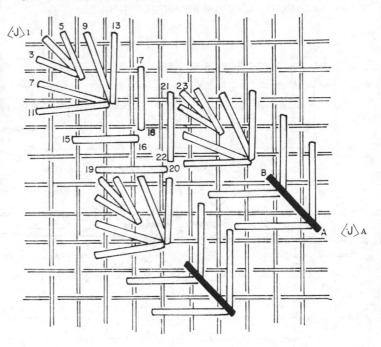

ROUMANIAN LEAF

The Roumanian-type stitches (Roumanian Leaf; Diagonal Roumanian Leaf, below; and Fly Stitch) are fast and fun to work. Refer to the Fly Stitch, page 298. Shading within the leaf can be done but then the speed of the stitch is lost.

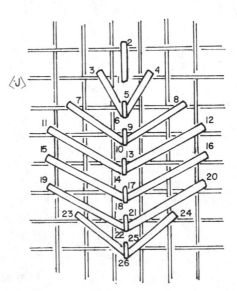

In order to give this more of a leaf shape, two stitches share one of the center stitches. Stitch #7 slips under #5-6 and goes down at #8. The pattern is then resumed.

DIAGONAL ROUMANIAN LEAF

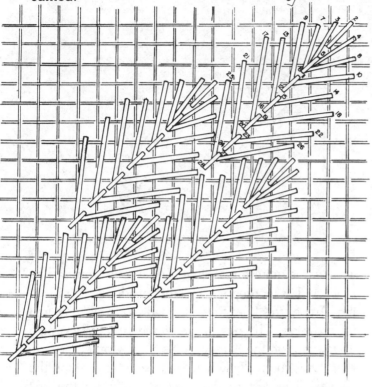

This stitch forms a neat braid down the center. It can be worked with long or short spaces from the center to the edges. This is a very pretty Leaf Stitch and is usually used singly. There is no backing behind the braid.

CRETAN

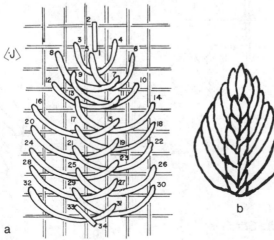

a

b

CLOSE HERRINGBONE

This makes a slightly raised leaf, made by crossing stitches over each other. There is some backing, but not a great deal. This stitch stands alone and makes a long, smooth leaf.

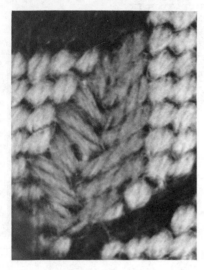

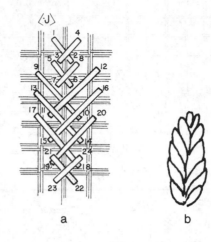

a　　　　　b

RAISED CLOSE HERRINGBONE

This leaf is quite three-dimensional and is interesting to work. It is worked in steps that produce a fair backing. Again, this Leaf Stitch is used alone as an accent for a design. The needle penetrates the canvas only at the tip of the leaf and as it is worked to the rear. Only the first stitch at the base goes through the canvas. The rest of the stitches go under the first stitch on top of the canvas. The size and shape can be readily varied.

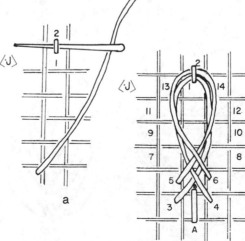

a

c

b

The Van Dyke can be worked in just about any slant or curve you wish. I have pictured a traditional leaf shape for you, but you may work it on top of your background in a looser arrangement that resembles a fern leaf. The size can be varied.

This stitch is fun to work and goes quickly. It is used alone or in groups. A pretty, raised braid is formed down the center.

Slip the needle from #6–7, #10–11, 14–15 etc. without penetrating the canvas.

FREE-FORM VAN DYKE

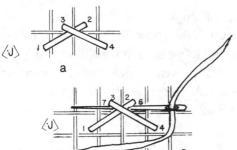

a

b

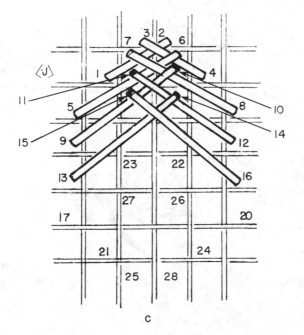

c

ROSE LEAF

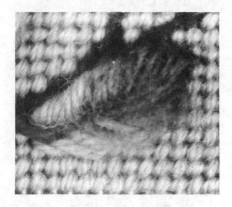

The Rose Leaf Stitch looks more difficult than it really is. If you follow the diagrams and instructions step by step, I don't think you will have any trouble.

1. Fold over a piece of light-weight cardboard that is 1″ to 2″ wide after folding. Experiment with the size of the loops. This will depend on how big you want your leaf and how thick your yarn is.

2. As you take your needle from #1-2 and from #3-4, etc., wrap it over the cardboard. When you have made all the stitches, carefully remove the cardboard.

3. Using your finger or a crochet hook, pull the last loops through the "tunnel," reversing their order.

4. Arrange the loops so that they resemble a pointed leaf with a broad base. Tack the last loop at the point in place with a short stitch.

5. Using a Straight Stitch, make a vein.

a

b

c

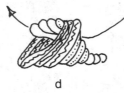

d

e

f

ELEVEN

Decorative Stitches

These Decorative Stitches have many uses, some quite specialized and some more broad. They are not related in construction technique.

This sampler was worked on Interlock Mono 10 with tapestry yarn. I did not have to thicken or thin the yarn for any of the stitches in this section.

Key to Sampler Stitches

1. Buttonhole
2. Buttonhole in Half-Circle
3. Chain
4. Laced Chain
5. Diagonal Chain
6. Perspective
7. Basketweave—Wrong Side
8. Cut Turkey Work
9. Looped Turkey Work
10. Surrey
11. Hollie Point
12. Velvet
13. Loop
14. Loop
15. Continental and Basketweave
16. Twisted Chain
17. Thorn
18. Wound Cross
19. French Knots on Stalks
20. Ridged Spider Web
21. Woven Spider Web
22. Starfish
23. French Knot
24. Bullion Knot
25. Smooth Spider Web
26. 2 × 1 Slanted Gobelin
27. 2 × 2 Slanted Gobelin

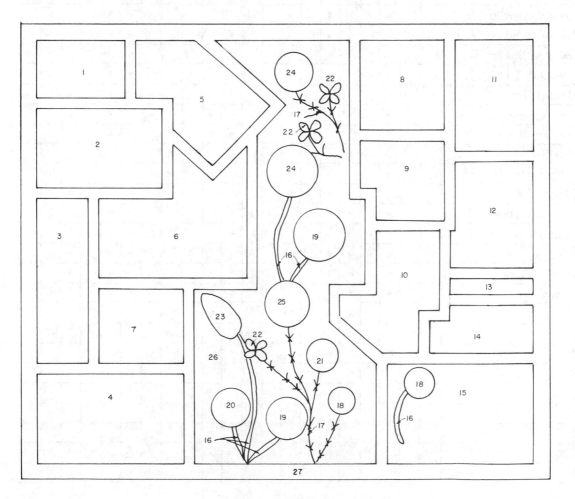

DECORATIVE STITCHES	Border	Good Backing	Poor Backing	Background	Design	Accent	Fast	Slow	Geometric Pattern	Shading	Yarn Hog	Snags	Snag-Proof	Little Texture	Medium Texture	High Relief	Flower Stitch	Weak Pattern	Medium Pattern	Strong Pattern	Distorts Canvas
Buttonhole	•			•	•	•			•			•		•				•			
B'hole in Half-Circ.				•	•	•		•	•			•			•					•	
Chain	•		•		•	•								•					•		
Laced Chain				•	•				•	•			•	•				•			
Diagonal Chain	•		•		•	•								•						•	
Perspective	•			•	•	•			•	•				•						•	
B'weave—Wrong Side	•	•			•	•								•					•		
Woven Spider Web		•				•		•			•					•	•			•	
Smooth Spider Web		•				•		•			•					•	•			•	
Ridged Spider Web		•				•		•			•					•	•			•	
Wound Cross		•				•		•			•					•	•			•	
French Knot		•				•		•					•		•		•		•		
Fr. Knots on Stalks		•				•		•				•			•		•		•		
Bullion Knot		•				•		•			•	•				•	•			•	
Starfish					•	•								•						•	
Thorn		•				•		•				•		•						•	
Twisted Chain		•				•		•				•				•			•		
Looped Turkey Work		•	•		•	•				•	•	•				•	•		•		
Cut Turkey Work		•	•		•	•				•	•	•				•	•	•			
Surrey		•	•		•	•				•	•	•				•	•			•	
Hollie Point		•			•	•		•			•	•			•		•		•		
Velvet		•			•	•		•			•	•				•	•			•	
Loop		•			•	•		•			•	•				•	•			•	

The Buttonhole Stitch has many variations. There are only two given here.

This stitch creates a smooth area and a ridge. Arrange these areas to suit your purposes. Disregard the mesh. Treat the canvas as if it were fabric and stitch. When worked as shown here, horizontal stripes are created.

Work the rows from bottom to top and from left to right. To change from one strand of yarn to the next, you will need two needles, threaded with the same color yarn. If, for example, your yarn runs out at #8 on the drawing, insert the needle into the canvas at #8, leaving the yarn from #7 to #8 a little loose. Let this needle dangle on the wrong side of the canvas. Bury the tail of the yarn on the second needle on the wrong side. Bring the needle up at #9. Let this second needle dangle. Adjust the tension on the first needle and bury the tail. Continue with the second needle.

BUTTONHOLE

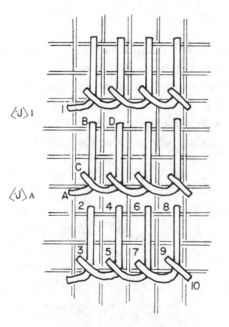

BUTTONHOLE IN HALF-CIRCLE

This stitch makes a lovely filler for a field or faraway flower garden.

Make sure that the stitches that go into the middle are even. (See Eye Stitches, page 307-18.)

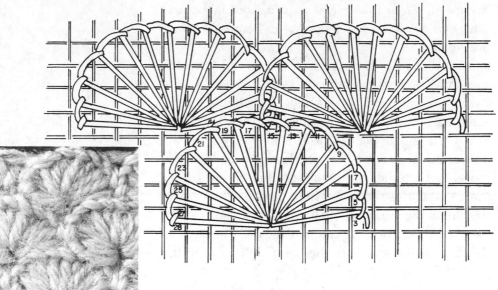

CHAIN

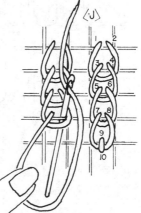

The Chain Stitch is quite a versatile stitch. It is one of a few stitches that curves. You may work it on top of the background or leave a space in the background to work the Chain Stitch.

This stitch is easier to work if you turn the canvas so that you are working horizontally and from right to left.

Laced Chain is a snag-proof stitch that is fun to work. After the first row of Straight Gobelin is worked, the rest is simply lacing one Chain Stitch onto the one above it in the preceding row. Note: the rows are worked horizontally, not vertically.

LACED CHAIN

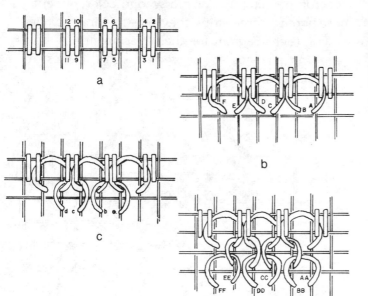

a

b

c

d

DIAGONAL CHAIN

PERSPECTIVE

Make a Diagonal Stitch, 2 x 2, upward and to the right. Place two more similar stitches below the first. From the holes where the first three stitches ended, begin three more diagonal stitches—this time downward and to the right. You will have a three-stripe chevron pointing up. With a second color, superimpose another three-stripe chevron—this time pointing down. (See diagram for their placement.) A box, seen in perspective, is created. This makes an interesting pattern.

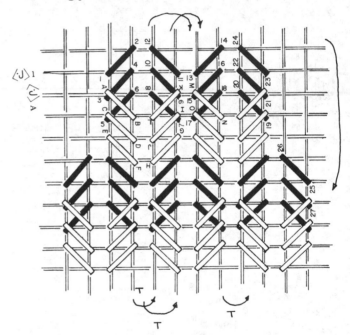

BASKETWEAVE—WRONG SIDE

Turn the canvas over. Carefully work Basketweave. Bury the tails on the wrong side of the canvas.

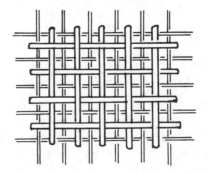

SPIDER WEBS

There are some instructions for working Spider Webs that are basic to all three versions.

Lay one of the foundations shown in the figure below. Only the Woven Spider Web **must** have an odd number of spokes. If these spokes are not **well secured**, the whole thing will come undone.

Bring the needle up as close to the center as you can without actually coming through the center. Work this yarn in the pattern of the stitch you are doing. Do not penetrate the canvas until you are through. Keep going around and around until the spokes are no longer visible. When you think you cannot possibly get one more round in, do two more—then you are through.

To make a high ball, pull the yarn tightly, but not so tightly that the spokes become misshapen. As you take each stitch, pull the yarn toward the center. This helps to tighten the stitch.

Spider Web foundations

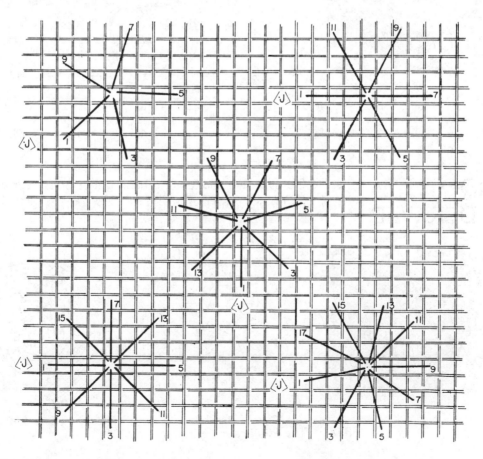

You may change colors or techniques midstream. For example, you can make a wheel by working Woven Spider Web (for the hub), Ridged Spider Web (for the spokes), and Smooth Spider Web (for the rim).

Use Spider Webs for grapes, apples, other fruit, wheels, balls, buttons, flowers, ladybugs, spiders, and other insects—anything round.

WOVEN SPIDER WEB

Lay the spokes. You must have an odd number. Weave the yarn over and under the spokes. When you think you cannot possibly get one more row in, do two more. Then you are through.

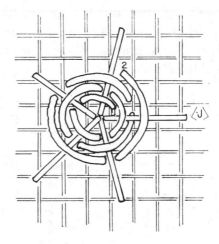

SMOOTH SPIDER WEB

Go over two spokes and back under one; over two, under one, and so forth.

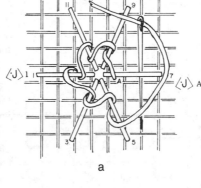

a

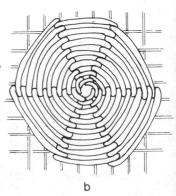

b

Reverse the process of the preceding stitch. Go under two spokes and back over one; under two, over one.

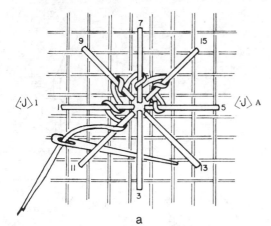

a

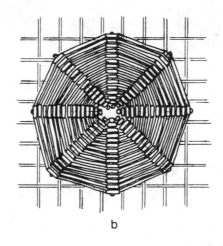

b

This is another good round stitch. Make it as fat as you like. Wind the yarn under all the spokes without penetrating the canvas.

WOUND CROSS

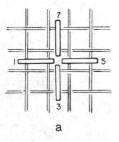

a

b

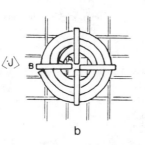

Decorative Stitches 343

FRENCH KNOT

French Knots are handy. They fill bare canvas, make polka dots, flower centers, whole flowers, and so forth.

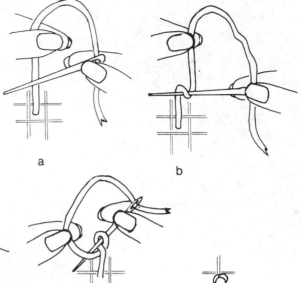

a

b

c

d

e

FRENCH KNOTS ON STALKS

These are an expanded version of the French Knot. They make lovely flowers.

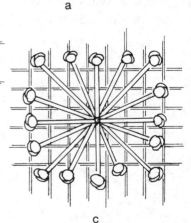

a

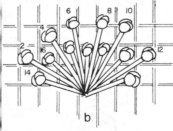

b

c

The Bullion Knot is worked by laying a thread and wrapping a yarn around it—without penetrating the canvas. Be sure that the tail is well-secured. Pull tightly and it will curl. Worked loosely, this stitch resembles finger curls.

BULLION KNOT

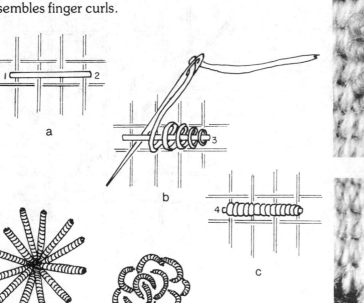

STARFISH

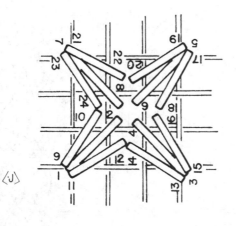

THORN

This stitch is good for making ferns and stems with small leaves or thorns. Curve it to suit your purposes.

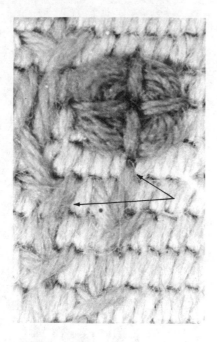

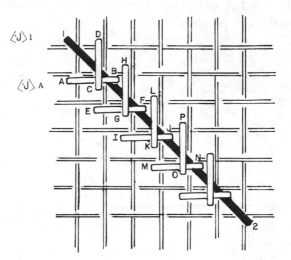

TWISTED CHAIN

This stitch can be worked in a single row and curved to meet your purpose. It may also be worked side by side to fill an area. It is **imperative** that your tension be even. Work from the top to bottom only.

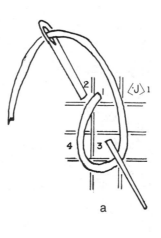

a

b

Stitch the **bottom** row first and work **up.** Work from left to right only. This means that you must cut your yarn at the end of every row. There is no tail to bury; it becomes part of the stitch. You may skip rows on a small canvas if it is too crowded.

Use a strip of paper to help you get the loops even (see following page). In working Looped Turkey Work, try not to run out of yarn in the middle of a row unless you have to.

Turkey Work should be worked on an even number of mesh. However, when you get to the end of a row, there often is a mesh left over. Work the last three mesh by leaving the extra one in the center of the stitch. (You are actually skipping a mesh.)

Work your whole design first, then put this stitch in. If you do not, you will never be able to move this stitch aside to get the others in.

LOOPED TURKEY WORK

Turkey Work

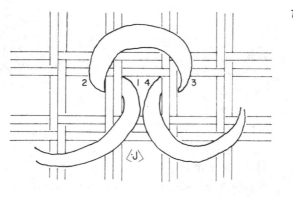

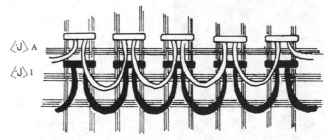

Looped Turkey Work

CUT TURKEY WORK

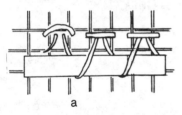

Work just as in Looped Turkey Work, but cut the loops as you go. After working Row 2, clip Row 1; after working Row 3, clip Row 2. If you cut each row immediately after it is worked, the pieces can be easily caught in the next row as you stitch it. However, if you wait until you have completely finished the area, it is quite hard to do a good cutting job. Cut as shown in Figure B, below.

Cutting the loops too short causes the rows to show. See top photo (right) and bottom photo (wrong).

It does not matter if you end a yarn in the middle of a row.

Persian yarn makes a fluffier Cut Turkey Work.

Work your whole design first; then put this stitch in. If you do not, you will never be able to move this stitch aside to get the others in.

To fluff your turkey work, pick at it with the point of the needle. Trim carefully.

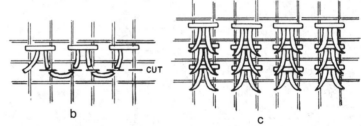

a   b   c

SURREY

This is similar to Turkey Work, but is worked diagonally. Leave the loops or cut them.

Work your whole design first; then put this stitch in. If you do not, you won't be able to move this stitch aside to get the others in.

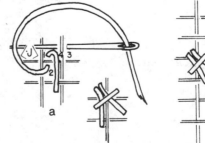

a

b

c

Hollie Point is an interesting stitch to work and it makes a pretty pattern. However, it is very difficult to get even. It is attached to the canvas along the top and side edges only; therefore, there is no backing at all. The stitches are completely detached from the canvas. The bottom row of stitches may be left loose or tacked down. For increased fullness, simply take two stitches in the same loop until the area is as full as you like. (See the parasol in Plate 11.)

Increase a little and leave the bottom loose to create a little girl's dress. The bottom row may be tacked down.

HOLLIE POINT

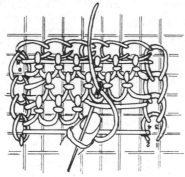

This stitch is worked like Turkey Work—bottom up and left to right except you must bury the yarn tails on wrong side of canvas. Skip one mesh between rows. Do not lift your thumb off the loop until the "x" is completed; it will all come apart. Cut it or leave it looped.

The Velvet Stitch makes a nice thatched roof or a flapper's fringe. If the loops are cut it makes a good shag rug for a doll house.

VELVET

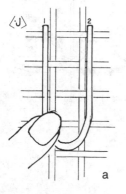

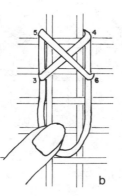

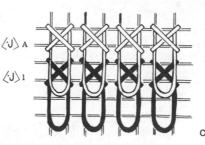

Work your whole design first, then put this stitch in. If you do not, you won't be able to move this stitch aside to get the others in.

LOOP

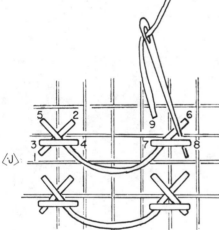

This stitch reminds me of Austrian drapes. Two rows of it, the second placed between the loops of the first, make a nice ruffle or lace trim (see at left). You may want the loop longer in this case.

In going from #5 to #6, slip the needle under the horizontal bar created by stitch #3-4. The next stitch begins at #6. Let the loop hang down three or so mesh between #5 and #6. Place subsequent rows in the next holes up.

Work your whole design first; then put this stitch in. If you do not, it will be impossible to move this stitch aside to get the others in.

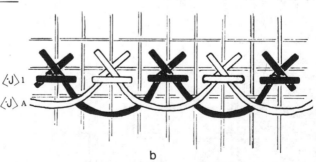

Appendix

The drawings in this section identify the various stitches used in the completed needlepoint projects illustrated in the color plates and in a few of the black-and-white photographs in Chapters 1 and 2. The diagram for Plate 17, for example, will be identified here as "Plate 17(A)"; the diagram for Figure 2-22 will be "Figure 2-22(A)." The drawings of the color plates are given as a group before those of the black-and-white photographs.

PLATE 1(A):
Wheel—Basketweave
Background—
    Hungarian Ground

PLATE 2(A):
1. Roumanian Leaf
2. Rococo
3. Turkey Work
4. French Knots
5. Wound Cross
6. Ridged Spider Web
7. Scotch
8. Basketweave

PLATE 3(A):
Background—
   Diamond Eyelet
Remainder—
   Cross Stitches

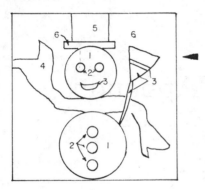

PLATE 4(A):
1. Smooth Spider Web
2. French Knot
3. Straight Stitch
4. Cross Stitch
5. Scotch
6. Continental

PLATE 5(A):
Stocking—
   1-3-5 Woven Scotch
Top, toe, and heel—
   Mosaic

PLATE 6(A):
Design—Bargello
Background—Mosaic

PLATE 7(A):
1. Cashmere
2. Mosaic
3. Half-Smooth Spider
   Web
4. Basketweave
5. Diagonal Mosaic
6. Smyrna
7. Woven Spider Web
8. Scotch

352

PLATE 8(A):
1. Scotch
2. Oblong Cross
3. Lone Tied Star
4. French Knot
5. Cashmere

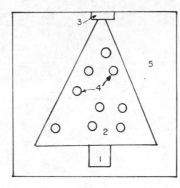

PLATE 9(A):
1. Smooth Spider Web
2. Straight Stitch
3. French Knot
4. Chain
5. Couching
6. Wound Cross
7. Roumanian Leaf
8. Basketweave

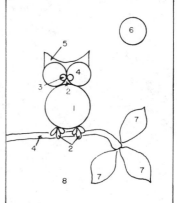

PLATE 10(A):
1. Mosaic
2. Buttonhole
3. French Knot
4. Chain
5. Smooth Spider Web
6. Couching
7. Milanese
8. Lone Tied Star

9. Cashmere
10. Smyrna Cross
11. Binding Stitch

PLATE 11(A):
Not shown; too complex
   to diagram

PLATE 12(A):
1. Basketweave
2. Mosaic
3. Turkey Work
4. Continental
5. Straight Gobelin
6. Petit Point
7. Rep
8. French Knot
9. Fly

PLATE 14(A):
Letters—Continental
Background—Scotch

PLATE 15(A):
Bargello

PLATE 16(A):
Cross Stitch

PLATE 17(A):
1. 3 x 1 Spaced Cross
   Tramé
2. Chain
3. Bullion Knot
4. Brick
5. Looped Turkey Work
6. Wound Cross
7. Twisted Chain
8. Ringed Daisy
9. French Knot

PLATE 13(A):
1. Roumanian Leaf
2. Chain
3. Bullion Knots
4. Looped Turkey Work
5. French Knots on Stalks
6. French Knots
7. Cut Turkey Work
8. Lone Tied Star
9. Couching
10. Basketweave
11. Mini Leaf
12. Milanese
13. Binding Stitch

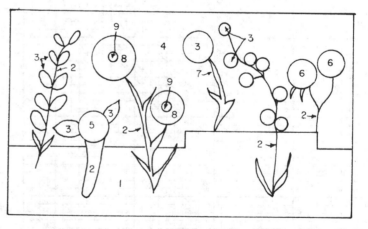

PLATE 18(A):
See Plate 17(A)

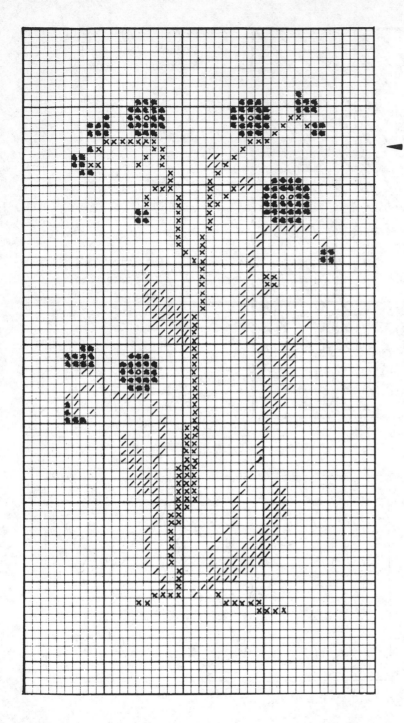

PLATE 19(A):
Letters—Cross Stitch
Background—Beaty

PLATE 20(A):
Design—Continental
Background—Basketweave

PLATE 21(A):—
  eyeglass case:
  1. Moorish
  2. Diagonal Hungarian
     Ground
  3. Oriental
  4. Jacquard
  5. Diagonal Scotch
  6. Byzantine
  7. Basketweave

356   Appendix

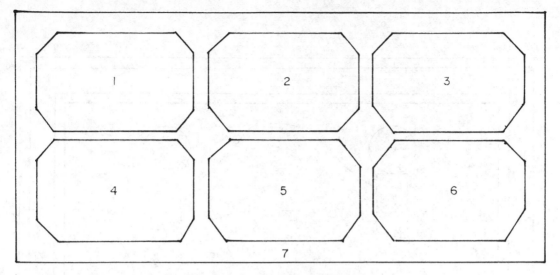

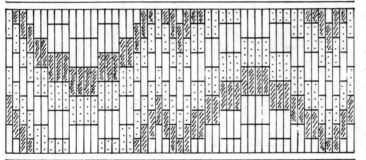

◄ PLATE 21(A)—belt:
Bargello

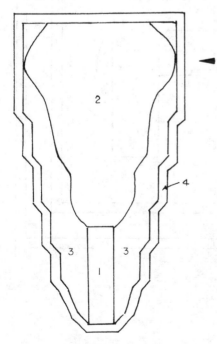

PLATE 22(A):
1. Fern
2. Leaf
3. Cross Stitch
4. Binding Stitch

◄

PLATE 23(A):
Trunk—Fern ►
Remainder—Cross Stitch

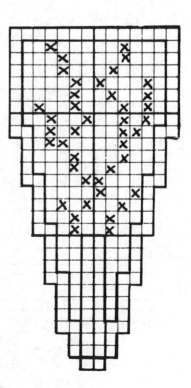

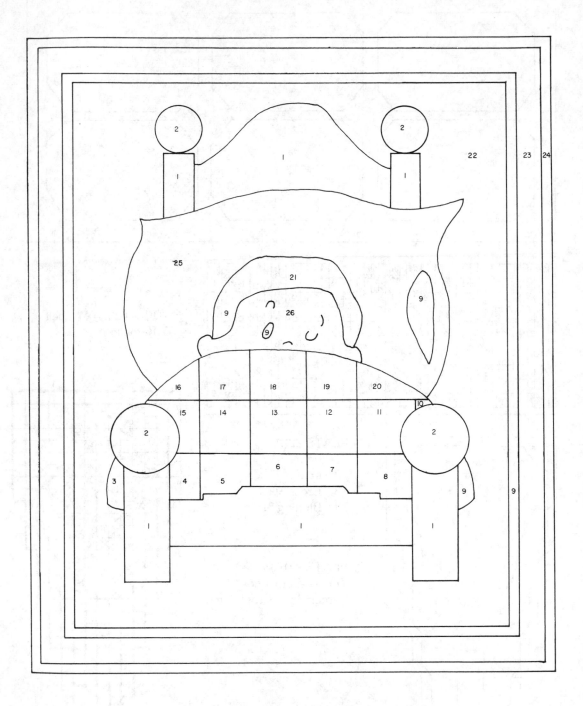

PLATE 24(A):
1. Mosaic
2. Smooth Spider Web
3. Cross Stitch
4. Reversed Mosaic
5. Dotted Stitch
6. Kalem
7. Combination Crosses
8. Hitched Cross
9. Continental
10. Checkered Cross
11. Double Stitch
12. Brick
13. Framed Mosaic
14. Diagonal Mosaic
15. Alternating Oblong
    Cross
16. Lazy Knitting
17. Smyrna
18. Tied Oblong Cross
19. Web
20. Rice
21. Cut Turkey Work
22. Diagonal Cashmere
23. Scotch
24. Binding Stitch
25. Jacquard
26. Basketweave

PLATE 25(A):
1. Mosaic
2. Smooth Spider Web
3. Looped Turkey Work
4. Trellis Cross
5. Cashmere
6. Bullion Knots
7. Basketweave
8. Flying Cross
9. Oriental
10. Continental
11. Scotch
12. Binding Stitch

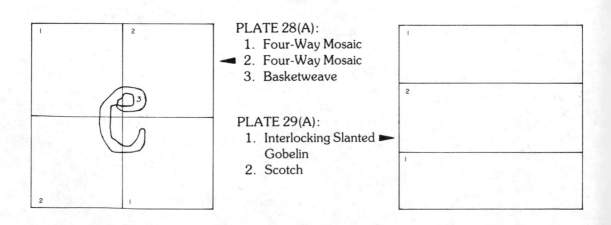

PLATE 26(A): ▲
  1. Basketweave
  2. Mosaic
  3. Turkey Work
  4. Framed Scotch

  5. Kalem
  6. Diagonal Mosaic
  7. French Knots
  8. Scotch
All outlines—Continental

PLATE 27(A):
Not shown; too complex
  to diagram

PLATE 28(A):
  1. Four-Way Mosaic
◀ 2. Four-Way Mosaic
  3. Basketweave

PLATE 29(A):
  1. Interlocking Slanted ▶
    Gobelin
  2. Scotch

PLATE 30(A):
Not shown; too complex
   to diagram

PLATE 31(A):
Letters—Continental
Background—Mosaic

PLATE 32(A):
See beginning of Chapter 5
   for diagram

PLATE 33(A):
Letters and flag—
   Cross Stitch
Background—Jacquard

PLATE 34(A):
See beginning of Chapter 8
   for diagram

PLATE 35(A):
Not shown; too complex
   to diagram

PLATE 36(A):
See beginning of Chapter 9
   for diagram

PLATE 37(A):
Letters—Cross Stitch
Boy and border—
   Basketweave
Background—
   Irregular Byzantine

PLATE 38(A):
See beginning of Chapter 7
   for diagram

PLATE 39(A):
See Plate 40(A)

PLATE 40(A):
Trellis Cross

PLATE 41(A):
Jacquard

PLATE 42(A):
  1. Bullion Knots
  2. Woven Spider Web
  3. French Knots on Stalks
  4. Chain (one loop)
  5. Looped Turkey Work
  6. Cashmere
  7. Chain
  8. Wound Cross
  9. Basketweave

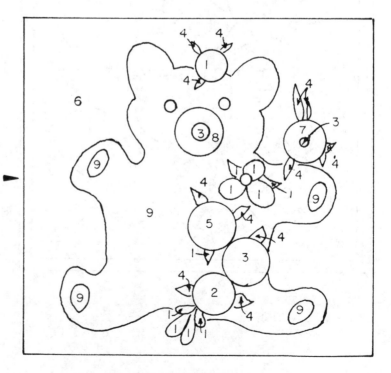

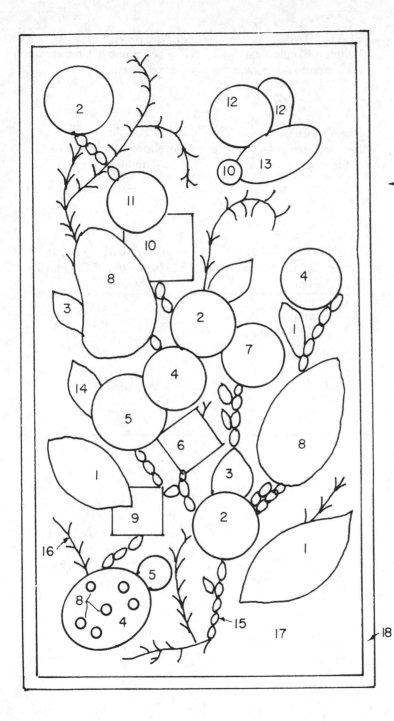

PLATE 43(A):
1. Roumanian Leaf
2. Ridged Spider Web
3. Leaf #1
4. Smooth Spider Web
5. Wound Cross
6. Smyrna Cross
7. Rococo
8. French Knots
9. Square Eyelet
10. Smyrna Cross
11. Medallion
12. Couching
13. Bullion Knot
14. Mini Leaf
15. Chain
16. Thorn
17. Basketweave
18. Binding Stitch

PLATE 44(A):
Not shown; too complex
    to diagram

PLATE 45(A):
1. Byzantine Scotch
2. Straight Gobelin
3. Hourglass Cross
4. Scotch Checker
5. Chain
6. Pavillion Diamonds
7. Pavillion Boxes
8. Oriental
9. Arrowhead
10. Mosaic
11. Crossed Diamond
12. 3 x 1 Spaced Cross
    Tramé
13. Diagonal Cashmere
14. Twisted Chain
15. Interlocking Slanted
    Gobelin
16. Jacquard

17. Fly
18. Rounded Wheat Columns
19. Byzantine
20. Hungarian
21. Cross Tramé
22. Mixed Milanese
23. Double Cross
24. Oblique Slav
25. Roumanian Leaf

26. Basketweave
27. Moorish
28. Scotch
29. Mini Leaf
30. Milanese
31. Old Florentine
32. Cashmere
33. Jacquard
34. Willow
35. Reversed Mosaic

36. Diagonal Leaf
37. Giant Brick
38. Rep
39. Reversed Scotch
40. Framed Scotch
41. 1 x 1 Spaced Cross Tramé
42. Diagonal Roumanian
43. Slashed Cross
44. Fern
45. Leaf #1
46. Herringbone
47. Double Brick
48. Basketweave—Wrong Side
49. Herringbone Gone Wrong
50. Bound Cross
51. Laced Chain
52. Diagonal Fern
53. Slanted Gobelin
54. Crossed Daisies
55. Two-Color Herringbone
56. Van Dyke
57. Knitting
58. Diagonal Scotch
59. Crossed Scotch
60. Framed Star
61. Hungarian
62. Diamond Eyelet
63. Mosaic Checker
64. Diagonal Mosaic
65. Mosaic
66. Woven Band

1	2	3	4	5	6	7	8
9	10	11	12	13	14	15	16
17	18	19	20	21	22	23	24
25	26	27	28	29	30	31	32
33	34	35	36	37	38	39	40
41	42	43	44	45	46	47	48
49	50	51	52	53	54	55	56
57	58	59	60	61	62	63	64

65 66

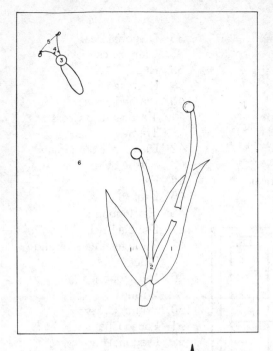

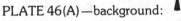

PLATE 46(A) —background: ▲

1. Chain
2. Slanted Gobelin
3. Smooth Spider Web

4. Couching
5. French Knots
6. Irregular Jacquard

▲ PLATE 46(A) —
  attached elements:
   1. Diagonal Mosaic
   2. Buttonhole
   3. Hungarian
   4. Chain
   5. Ridged Spider Web
   6. Smyrna Cross
   7. French Knots
   8. Reversed Mosaic
   9. Cut Turkey Work

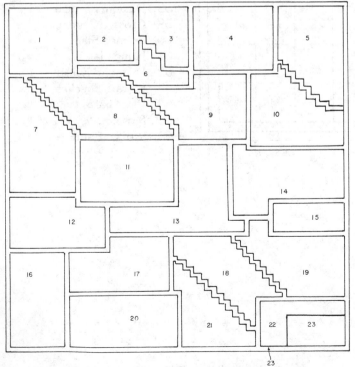

PLATE 47(A):
   1. Mosaic Checker
   2. Fern
   3. Divided Scotch
   4. Pavillion
◄ 5. Byzantine
   6. Cashmere
   7. Milanese
   8. Moorish
   9. Mosaic Stripe
   10. Diagonal Scotch
   11. Parisian

12. Diagonal Cashmere
13. Triangle
14. Oriental
15. Herringbone
16. Old Florentine
17. Scotch Checker
18. 1-3-5 Woven Scotch
19. Van Dyke
20. Pavillion Diamonds
21. Diagonal Hungarian Ground
22. Framed Scotch
23. Basketweave

FIGURE 1.38(A):
1. Do-Your-Own Bargello
2. Upright Cross
3. Binding Stitch
4. Petit Point
5. Buttonhole
6. Reversed Scotch
7. Reversed Mosaic
8. Basketweave
9. Byzantine

PLATE 48(A):
Not shown; too complex to diagram

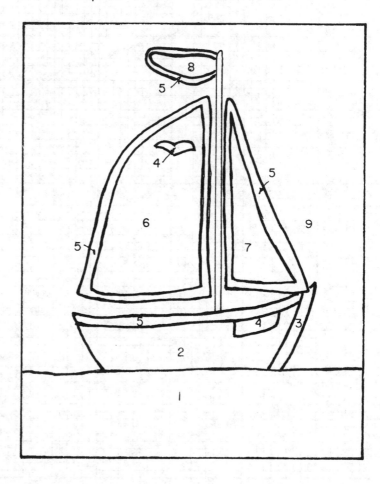

FIGURE 2.16(A):
Continental

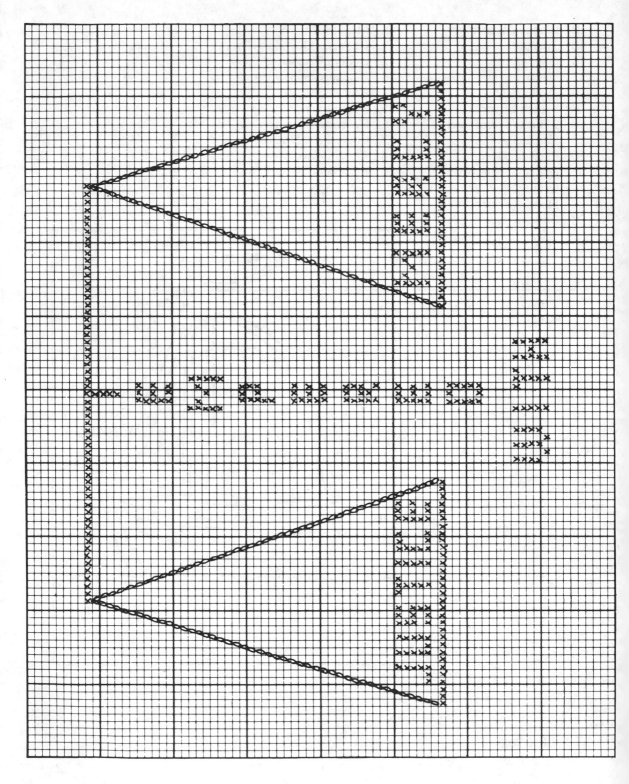

FIGURE 2.17(A):
Letters—Continental
Background—Byzantine

FIGURE 2.19(A):
Letters—Continental
Background—Diagonal
    Scotch

FIGURE 2.20(A):
Letters—Continental
Background—Scotch

FIGURE 2.21(A):
Letters—Cross Stitch
Background—Diagonal
    Scotch

FIGURE 2.22(A):
1. Scotch
2. Cross Stitch
3. Lone Tied Star
4. Couching
5. Byzantine

FIGURE 2.23(A):
1. Cross Stitch
2. Sleeping Oblong Cross
3. Double Stitch
4. Diagonal Mosaic

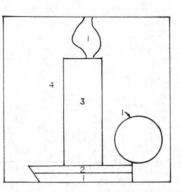

FIGURE 2.24(A):
Letters—Continental
Border—Reversed
    Mosaic
Background—Jacquard

LETTERS:
All letters shown in
Continental or Cross
Stitches

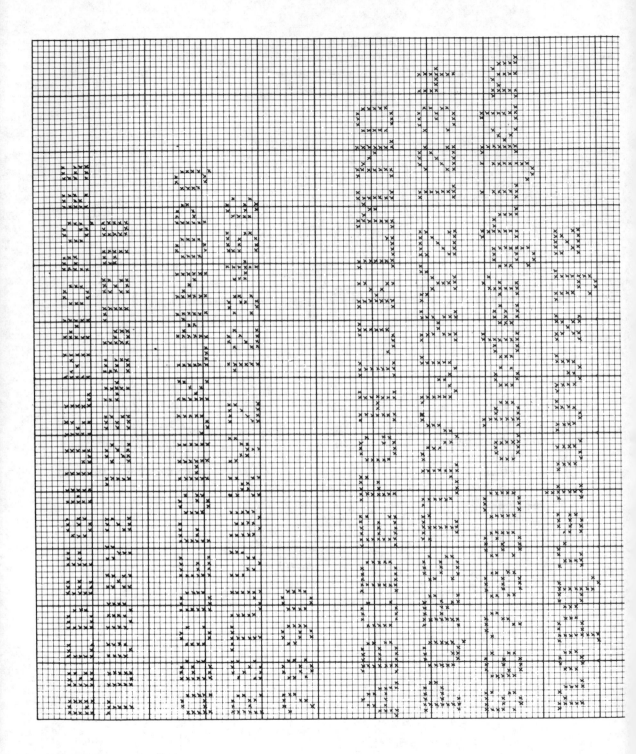

368   *Appendix*

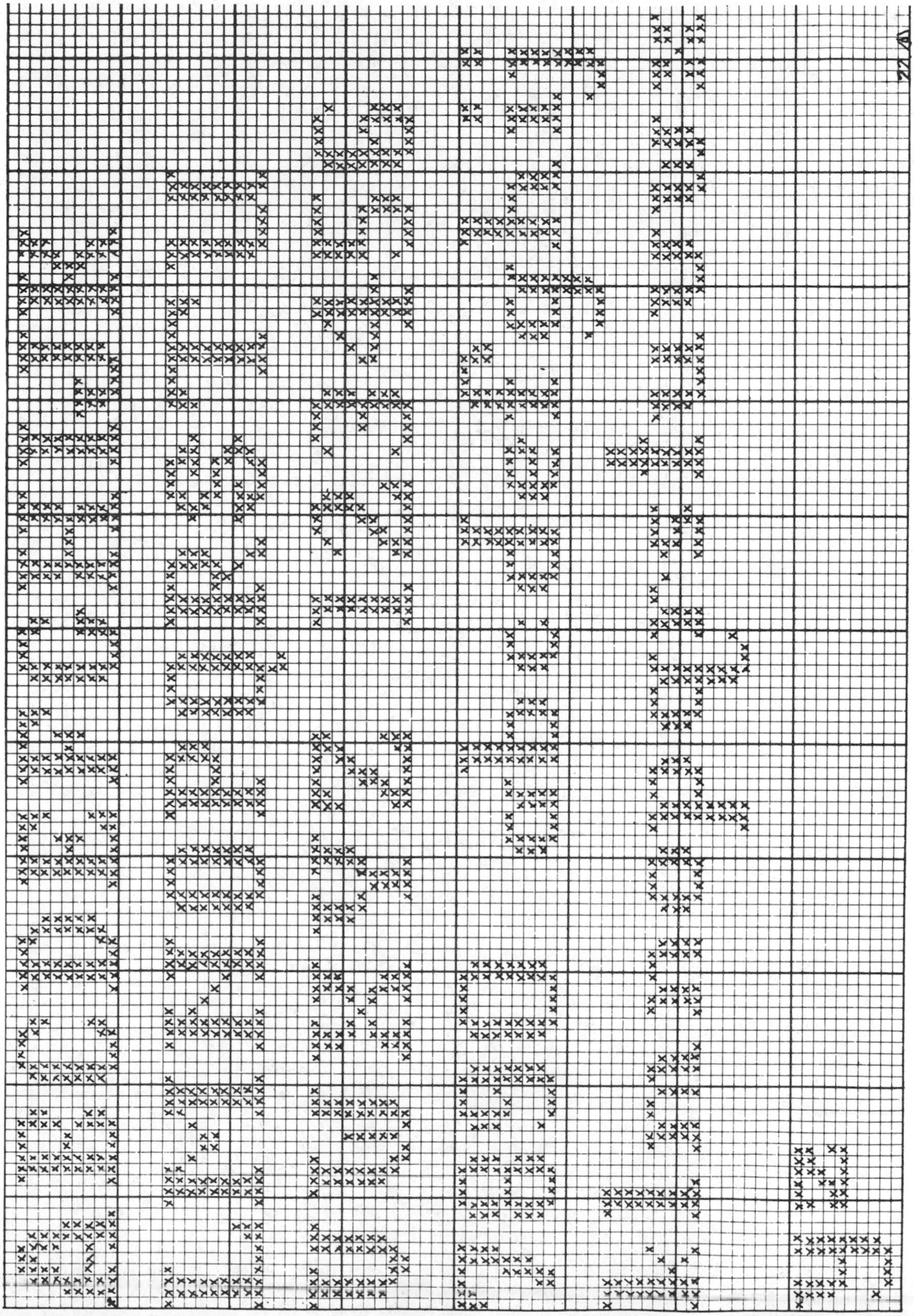

Bibliography

AMBUTER, CAROLYN, *Complete Book of Needlepoint.* New York: Thomas Y. Crowell Company, 1972.

BAKER, MURIEL, BARBARA EYRE, MARGARET WALL, and CHARLOTTE WESTERFIELD, *Needlepoint: Design Your Own.* New York: Charles Scribner's Sons, 1974.

BEINECKE, MARY ANN, *Basic Needlery Stitches on Mesh Fabrics.* New York: Dover Publications, Inc., 1973.

BUCHER, JO, *Complete Guide to Creative Needlepoint.* Des Moines, Iowa: Meredith Corporation, 1973.

BURCHETTE, DOROTHY, *Needlework Blocking and Finishing.* New York: Charles Scribner's Sons, 1974.

371

CHRISTENSEN, JO IPPOLITO, and SONIE SHAPIRO ASHNER, *Bargello Stitchery.* New York: Sterling Publishing Co., Inc., 1972.

————, *Cross Stitchery.* New York: Sterling Publishing Co., Inc., 1973.

————, *Needlepoint Simplified.* New York: Sterling Publishing Co., Inc., 1971.

DONNELLY, BARBARA H., *The Crewel Needlepoint World.* New York: Gullers International, Inc., 1973.

DRAKE, DORIS J., *Needlework Designs.* Thomasville, Georgia, 1967.

————, *Needlepoint Designs II.* n. p., 1971.

DYER, ANNE, and VALERIE DUTHOIT, *Canvas Work from the Start.* London: G. Bell & Sons, 1972.

FISCHER, PAVLINE, and ANABEL LASKER, *Bargello Magic.* New York: Holt, Rinehart and Winston, 1975.

GRIER, ROSEY, *Needlepoint for Men.* New York: Walker and Company, 1973.

HALL, NANCY, and JEAN RILEY, *Bargello Borders.* Franklin, Michigan: Needlemania, Inc., 1974.

HANLEY, HOPE, *Needlepoint.* New York: Charles Scribner's Sons, 1964.

————, *New Methods in Needlepoint.* New York: Charles Scribner's Sons, 1966.

IREYS, KATHARINE, *The Encyclopedia of Canvas Embroidery Stitch Patterns.* New York: Thomas Y. Crowell Company, 1972.

————, *Finishing and Mounting Your Needlepoint Pieces.* New York: Thomas Y. Crowell Company, 1973.

KAESTNER, DOROTHY, *Four Way Bargello.* New York: Charles Scribner's Sons, 1974.

KATZENBERG, GLORIA, *Needlepoint and Pattern.* New York: Macmillan Publishing Co., Inc., 1974.

KENYON, CAROL, and LYNNE MALPELI, *Custom Designs for Creative Needlepoint.* West Bloomfield, Michigan, 1973.

LAMPTON, SUSAN SEDLACEK, ED., *Needlepoint.* Menlo Park, California: Lane Books, 1973.

LANTZ, SHERLEE, *A Pageant of Pattern for Needlepoint Canvas.* New York: Atheneum, 1973.

LONG, EDITH, and SARA SCHLINTZ, *To the Point about Needlepoint.* New York: Cornerstone Library, 1974.

MARTIN, MARY, *Mary Martin's Needlepoint.* New York: Galahad Books, 1969.

PERRONE, LISBETH, *Needlepoint Workbook.* New York: Random House, 1973.

———, *The New World of Needlepoint.* New York: Random House, 1972.

RHODES, MARY, *Ideas for Canvas Work.* Newton, Massachusetts: Charles T. Branford Company, 1971.

ROME, CAROL CHENEY, *A New Look At Bargello.* New York: Crown Publishers, Inc., 1973.

———, and GEORGIA FRENCH DEVLIN, *A New Look at Needlepoint.* New York: Crown Publishers, Inc., 1973.

SCOBEY, JOAN, *Needlepoint from Start to Finish.* New York: Lancer Books, 1972.

———, and LEE PARR McGRATH, *Do-It-All-Yourself Needlepoint.* New York: Essandess Special Edition, 1971.

SIDNEY, SYLVIA, *Sylvia Sidney Needlepoint Book.* New York: Galahad Books, 1968.

SLATER, ELAINE, *The New York Times Book of Needlepoint.* New York: Quadrangle/The New York Times Book Co., 1973.

SNOOK, BARBARA, *The Craft of Florentine Embroidery.* New York: Charles Scribner's Sons, 1971.

_____, *Needlework Stitches.* New York: Crown Publishers, Inc., 1975.

WILLIAMS, ELSA S., *Bargello.* New York: Van Nostrand Reinhold Company, 1967.

_____, *Creative Canvas Work.* New York: Van Nostrand Reinhold Company, n. d.

WILSON, ERICA, *Embroidery Book.* New York: Charles Scribner's Sons, 1973.

ZIMMERMAN, JANE D., *An Encyclopedia of 375 Needlepoint Stitch Variations.* n.p., 1973.

Index to
Stitches

General Index

Gingham fabric, for blocking board, 82-83
Graphs, 67-68
Grid method, 64-65

Hand-painted designs, 4-5
Horizontal lines, 60, 61

Informal balance, 55-57
Inner pillow, 100-101
Inserts, 107-9
Interlock Mono canvas, 11

Key chain, 125-26
Kits, 5-6

Leaf stitches, 49, 71, 357
Left-handed needlepoint, 51-52
Letters, stitching, 69
Lines in design, 60-62
Lithographer, 64

Mending, 37-38
Mesh count, 11-13
Metallic yarn, 20
Mixing stitches, 68-69
Mono canvas, 10
  appliqué, 40
  edge finishing, 113-15
  interlock, 11
  mesh count, 13
  piecing, 20
Monochromatic colors, 63
Mottos, 70

Needlebook, 24, 118
Needlepoint bag, 23
Needles, 16-18
  book for, 24, 118
  size, 16
  threading, 17-18
Novelty yarns, 19
Numbers, stitching, 69

Opaque projector, 65
Original designs, 6-7, 64-80
  choosing stitches for, 68-70
  distortion of canvas, 70-71
  projects, 71-73
  sample drawings, 74-80
  size of, 64-65
  transferring, 65-68
  See also Finishing

Painting designs, 66-67
Paints, acrylic, 66-67
Pearls, 36
Pencil holder, 120
Penelope canvas, 9-10
  edge finishing, 113-15
  mesh count, 11-13

Penelope canvas (cont.):
  piecing, 20
  for samplers, 48
  for upholstered items, 124
Persian yarn, 19
Picture framing, *see* Framing pictures
Piecing canvas, 38-39
Pillows, 99-109
  backing, 101-2
  final sewing, 105-7
  inner pillow, 100-101
  inserts, 107-9
  trimming, 102-5
Pincushions, 109-10, 122, 124
Plastic canvas, 15, 124-26
Poking vs. continuous motion, 29-30
Prefinished articles, 5
Preshrinking pillow fabric, 100-101
Primary colors, 62
Procedures, basic:
  cleaning needlepoint, 50-51
  equipment, 9-24
    canvas, *see* Canvas
    frames, 22-23
    needlepoint bag, 23
    needles, 16-18
    ruler, 21
    scissors, 21, 37
    tape, 21
    tweezers, 21
    waterproof marker, 21-22, 66, 82
    yarn, *see* Yarn
  general techniques, 24-35
    backing, 34-35
    beginning and ending threads, 28-29
    canvas preparation, 24-25
    continuous motion vs. poking, 29-30
    direction of work, 30-31
    handling yarns, 26-27
    stitch tension, 31-32
    stitching a design, 33-34
    thickening and thinning yarns, 32-33
  left-handed needlepoint, 51-52
  projects, choosing:
    designs on charts, 5
    hand-painted designs, 4-5
    kits, 5-6
    list of projects, 7-8
    original designs, 6-7
    prefinished articles, 5
    ready-center pieces, 3-4
    stamped designs, 4
  samplers, making, 48-50
  special techniques, 35-48
    appliqué, 40-43
    compensating stitches, 36-37

Procedures, basic (cont.):
    special techniques (cont.):
        covering the canvas, 35-36
        detached-canvas technique, 34-35
        piecing canvas, 38-39
        ripping and mending, 37-38
        shading, 45-47
        shadows, 47-48
Projects, choosing:
    designs on charts, 5
    hand-painted designs, 4-5
    kits, 5-6
    list of projects, 7-8
    original designs, 6-7
    prefinished articles, 5
    ready-center pieces, 3-4
    stamped designs, 4
Proportion, 58

Ready-center pieces, 3-4
Repetition in design, 58-59
Rhythm in design, 58-59
Ripping, 37-38
Ruler, 21

Sampler, making, 48-50
Sayings, 70
Scissors, 21, 37
Scissors case, 117
Scrapbook cover, 111-13
Secondary colors, 62
Shading, 45-47
Shadows, 47-48
Stains, removing, 87-88
Straight stitches, 71, 352, 353
Stamped designs, 4
Stitch tension, 31-32
Stretcher frame, 93-99
Surface embroidery, 70

Table-top wastebasket, 120
Tape, 21
Tapestry yarns, 19, 26, 27
Tassels, 104-5
Techniques:
    general, 24-35
        backing, 34-35
        beginning and ending threads, 28-29
        canvas preparation, 24-25
        continuous motion vs. poking, 29-30
        direction of work, 30-31
        handling yarns, 26-27
        stitch tension, 31-32
        stitching a design, 33-34
        thickening and thinning yarns, 32-33
    special, 35-48
        appliqué, 40-43
        compensating stitches, 36-37

Techniques (cont.):
    special (cont.):
        covering the canvas, 35-36
        detached-canvas technique, 43-45
        piecing canvas, 38-39
        ripping and mending, 37-38
        shading, 45-47
        shadows, 47-48
Tension, stitch, 31-32
Tertiary colors, 62
Texture, 59-60
Thickening and thinning yarn, 32-33
Threading needles, 17-18
Tied stitches, 71
Tracing designs, 53
Transferring designs, 65-68
Tweezers, 21
Twisted cord, 102-4
Two-step edge finishing, 113-16
    belt, 115-16
    book cover, 118
    brick doorstop, 119
    eyeglass case, 116-17
    needlebook, 118
    scissors case, 117

Ultra Suede, 102
Unity in design, 54-55
Upholstered items, 124

Variety in design, 58-59
Velcro, 125
Vertical lines, 60, 61

Waste canvas, 16
Wastebasket, table-top, 120
Waterproof markers, 21-22, 66, 82
Wooden pincushion, 122, 124
Wool rug yarn, 19

Yarn, 18-21
    acrylic, 6, 20
    Angora, 20
    backing, 34-35
    beginning and ending threads, 28-29
    characteristics of, 18
    cleaning, 50-51
    embroidery flosses, 20
    handling, 26-27
    knotting for storage, 23-24
    mending, 37-38
    metallic, 20
    nap, 27
    novelty, 19
    Persian, 19
    quantities, 20-21
    ripping, 37-38
    tapestry, 19, 26, 27
    thickening and thinning, 32-33
    wool rug, 19